Nature beyond Solitude

Nature beyond Solitude

Notes from the Field

John Seibert Farnsworth

Foreword by Thomas Lowe Fleischner

Comstock Publishing Associates
an imprint of
Cornell University Press
Ithaca and London

First published 2020 by Cornell University Press

Library of Congress Cataloging-in-Publication Data

Names: Farnsworth, John Seibert, author.
Title: Nature beyond solitude : notes from the field / John S. Farnsworth.
Description: Ithaca [New York] : Comstock Publishing Associates, an imprint of Cornell University Press, 2020. | Includes bibliographical references.
Identifiers: LCCN 2019020924 (print) | LCCN 2019980215 (ebook) | ISBN 9781501747281 (paperback) | ISBN 9781501747304 (epub) | ISBN 9781501747298 (pdf)
Subjects: LCSH: Farnsworth, John Seibert—Travel—California. | Farnsworth, John Seibert—Travel—Oregon. | Farnsworth, John Seibert—Travel— Washington (State) | Natural history—Fieldwork—California. | Natural history—Fieldwork—Oregon. | Natural history—Fieldwork—Washington (State) | Ecological reserves—California. | Ecological reserves— Oregon. | Ecological reserves—Washington (State) | Ecology—Research— Calfornia. | Ecology—Research—Oregon. | Ecology—Research— Washington (State)
Classification: LCC QH318.5 .F37 2020 (print) | LCC QH318.5 (ebook) | DDC 508.79—dc23
LC record available at https://lccn.loc.gov/2019020924
LC ebook record available at https://lccn.loc.gov/2019980215

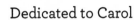

Dedicated to Carol

The question is not what you look at, but what you see.

Henry David Thoreau, journal, August 5, 1851

Contents

Foreword

Welcome to the New Golden Age

Several days of rain have saturated the hills a few miles above the sand terrace where I squat. The river is swollen over its banks, brown with sediment, carrying debris, spilling out of the granite gorge. Clouds stream past in an atmospheric river that promises to deliver snow to the mountains tonight. Even here, in the high desert, this afternoon's wind has some bite.

I sit, paying attention to these simplest sights—clouds, sand grains, the color of water, direction of the wind. All this, part of the practice of attention we call "natural history."

Natural history represents a practice of compassion, of "feeling with." Too often, people—even those predisposed toward conservation—lump all of non-human life into one amorphous bundle and label it "Nature." This is good as far as it goes, but "Nature" hides at least as much as it illuminates. We tend to have our deepest compassion for *individual* beings, not for general categories. Mother Teresa took on mass hunger by looking each person in the eye as she lifted a ladle to their lips. Look into enough eyes and some sense of caring for humanity as a whole can emerge. The same goes for "Nature"—we need to watch an individual bird struggle to stay warm as it fluffs up against swirls of snow, or contemplate the purple gentian flower blooming an inch above the grassland of the high Andes, tenaciously clinging to the ground as a fierce wind knocks human observers to their knees. Watching a particular bird sing—*this* redwing, from this fence post—or a particular flower blossoming—this lavender jewel we call *Penstemon*—helps us transcend the vague notion of "Nature," or worse yet, "the environment," and replaces it with texture, depth, and a realm of specificities. And in the process, *awe* suffuses our beings—from the simple recognition that something like a paradise tanager *actually exists*. If this expansion of consciousness is not a spiritual practice, I don't know what is.

Natural history, too, is ultimately political in that its practice shifts relationships of value and power. We fall in love; we change the way we relate to the world. We foster this falling-in-love in ourselves first. Then, love by love, friend by friend, story by story, we engage hundreds, thousands, millions of others—and we just might make a brand-new world.

The great jazz musicians Wayne Shorter and Herbie Hancock, in an open letter to the next generation of artists, concluded, "Lastly, we hope that you live in a state of constant wonder." Natural history, more than anything I've ever experienced, yields recurring states of wonder—wonder in the familiar and the exotic, in the near and the far.

The author of the volume in your hands herein declares "a new golden age of natural history." A message that I approve, and applaud. John Seibert Farnsworth has contributed to this golden moment by his own ongoing practice of attention—in this book he recounts his practice of encountering, and befriending, new landscapes. His temporary encampments at field sites along the west coast of North America provide glimpses into the world as it really is, uncluttered by media masks, and liberated from preconceptions.

Yet what is the value of these brief relationships with landscapes and the field stations that concentrate their essences? Why does it matter, one might ask, for a grown man to, basically, just wander around and look at things? Well, for starters, it makes you, the reader, laugh, and it makes you wonder. And humor, insight, and curiosity are all too rare in our world today.

There is no match, of course, for years-long, deep connection with a place. Where one comes to know the scent of specific shadows, the sequence and timing—what an ecologist refers to as *phenology*—of flowers: which colors blaze forth with which others, which autumn leaf transformations precede which others.

But there's another type of value, too. Like the medieval minstrels who roamed from site to site, carrying the news from one village to the next, collating and curating stories from each—John Farnsworth's travels between field stations serve this ancient function. His observations become tales that enliven campfires, stimulate conversations, prompt listeners to lose themselves, to ponder, and to wonder. He has taken up residency—temporarily, but long enough to peel away stories—and then moved on, building a bank of stories to share with us all.

Listen to these songs. Let the music lift you into your own stories, remind you of your own special places. Sit back and bask in these words. Let the narrator, this big bear of a man, show you five ways to befriend a new place. This is the work of the world, and he's a fine guide.

THOMAS LOWE FLEISCHNER

Sundowner

Books on nature seldom mention wind; they are written behind stoves.

ALDO LEOPOLD, *A Sand County Almanac*, 1949

There's just enough left of the sundowner breeze to keep the bugs away.

I sit here tonight, alone at a picnic table near the vacant dorms of a remote field station in the Channel Islands, watching something I've never observed before. A female acorn woodpecker is taking a dust bath in a shallow depression where the soil seems especially powdery, a place where birds have apparently done this before. She hunkers down low, dips her head first, shaking her bill side to side to stir up the dust, then arches her back, flinging dust toward her tail while she flops to her belly and begins flapping her wings as if drowning. I've seen quail do this, and house sparrows, and I've heard that this is how many birds deal with ectoparasites, but it's the first time I've watched a woodpecker bathe.

I am tempted to view this scene as comical. Field guides tend to describe the acorn woodpecker's face as "clownish" or "clown-like," and when birds thus perceived lie on their bellies and flap in the dirt, it's hard to ascribe them dignity. But this woodpecker seems quite earnest about her bath, so I observe the ritual with appropriate solemnity.

Finally bursting from the dust, the woodpecker seems heavy, as if gaining altitude is a struggle. Straight up she flies, landing vertically on the broad trunk of a eucalyptus tree immediately above the bathing site. Her white belly is still the color of the dust. Briefly she seems to rest, propped up by stiff tail feathers, and then she flies over to an adjacent tree, another stately eucalyptus, still climbing steeply. The woodpecker stops momentarily at a cavity entrance, and then disappears inside. I imagine that she tracked a great deal of dust in with her.

I enjoy writing *in situ*,[1] on site. This way I'm not only writing *about* nature, I'm writing *from* nature. Right now I'm writing at dusk, *from* dusk, during a drought, from just beyond the canopy drip line of a dry, dusky eucalyptus that shelters a dusty bird that has just bathed.

It was not my intent, when I first sat down at this picnic table, to describe a woodpecker's bath. I'm not even certain I intended to write. It's more accurate to say that I was prepared to write, with notebook and pen at the ready, should anything seem remarkable. There are also binoculars on hand, and a glass of wine.

The breeze tails off for the night, and a mosquito buzzes my ear. I realize that I'm having to deal with my own little ectoparasite at the moment. While this realization connects me to the woodpecker now bedded down in its cavity, I assuredly won't be indulging in a dust bath anytime soon. My better options seem to be to slather myself with repellant, or to go inside.

I go inside.

Although I've skipped the dust bath, I'm doing the same thing the woodpecker just did, retiring for the night to an interior domicile. But I'm not nearly as connected to the bird now as I was a few minutes ago. Here, indoors, I'm no longer employing skills of observation, which are some of my most well-developed skills. Now I'm merely remembering, reflecting, and sipping wine.

The living room in the house I grew up in had a marble fireplace that was rarely lit, and the books in the bookcase to the right of the mantel were dusted more often than read. Although I was a precocious reader as a child, I perused few of them: *Profiles in Courage, David Copperfield, The Lives of Saints, The Collected Poems of William Wordsworth*. Reading four books from the living room bookshelves was plenty, and I suspect that none of my siblings read more from that particular library than I.

---

1. *Situ* is the ablative case of the fourth declension Latin noun *situs*, which is most simply translated "site." The ablative case is tricky, because nouns in that case tend to function like adverbs. Therefore, when I say that I plan "to write *in situ*," I'm describing as much *how* I'm planning to write as where. Unfortunately, the ablative case doesn't translate well into English.

Our family room had a brick fireplace that was inevitably fired up prior to Halloween and rarely went out before Easter. On cold Colorado nights Dad would put a chunk of coal the size of a cantaloupe in the back of the firebox before going to bed, and the embers would be ready for a fresh log the next morning, no kindling needed. That fireplace had a built-in knotty pine bookcase to its left, and those books were dog-eared and edge-worn. When I close my eyes I can see *Walden* sitting on the same shelf as *A Sand County Almanac* and *Silent Spring*, all three in paperback.

Our copy of *Walden* included the essay "On the Duty of Civil Disobedience," because *Walden* itself didn't fill out the book. Were you to send a book manuscript the size of *Walden* to a publisher today, it would probably come back with gentle advice that there were too few words.

Walden has plenty of words, the best of which is the adverb "deliberately." The author wrote, famously, "*I went to the woods because I wished to live deliberately, to front only the essential facts of life, and see if I could not learn what it had to teach, and not, when I came to die, discover that I had not lived.*"

Walden was more than a book to me. It was a manifesto. To an impressionable adolescent still called "Johnny," this manifesto suggested that the best way to experience nature was alone. Indeed, solitude was the only way to experience nature deeply. Truly. Transcendentally.

I write this book to interrogate that mentality, seeking my own conversion.

Yes, my experience of the woodpecker's bath this evening was solitary, and had I been distracted by companionship I might have missed it entirely. Solitude plays its role, especially for introverts such as myself, and it's a gracious role. But I find myself searching for other paths—focused, communal, enduring alternatives—to augment the experience of the natural world. Such paths need not take the place of solitude, but would go beyond it, completing the experience of nature beyond solitude.

When I was an undergraduate, the three nature writers who had the strongest hold on my psyche were all men. Regrettably, I did not investigate women writers until my postgraduate studies, at least in part because I read for my bachelor's degree at a small, now-defunct college in Santa Fe, New Mexico, run by the Christian Brothers. I don't recall having read any female authors during those years, regardless of subject matter.

Until I discovered Annie Dillard, shortly after graduating, my three favorite authors were Henry David Thoreau (*Walden; or, Life in the Woods*), John Muir (*My First Summer in the Sierras*), and Edward Abbey (*Desert Solitaire: A Season in the Wilderness*). Aside from their maleness, what these three had in common was that they turned to solitude as a remedy for the disruption of living in a modern world. Their writing is highly reflective, at least in part because of the composition process each employed, writing from field notes after considerable time had passed.

John Muir's first summer in the Sierra took place in 1869, when he was thirty-one years old. He didn't write about that summer until 1911, at the age of seventy-three. We must be amazed that, even with the aid of field notes and sketches, he could remember his experiences so vividly, describing them forty-two years after the fact.

By his own admission, Edward Abbey wrote parts of *Desert Solitaire* in a bar in Hoboken, New Jersey. The book was published more than a decade after the experiences it describes, but in the book's preface Abbey claims to have taken most of his writing "direct and unchanged" from his field notes. I've read his handwritten field notes from the two summers he spent at Arches, and the greater part of the book's material didn't come from them.[2]

Ironically, much of the time Thoreau spent writing in his cabin on Walden Pond during the years 1845–47 went into the composition of the book *A Week on the Concord and Merrimack Rivers*, a tribute to his brother John, who had died in 1842. The book was about a boat trip the two brothers had taken in 1839.

Thoreau's biographer, Joseph Wood Krutch, himself an important nature writer, wrote of the process of composing *Walden* that

> there is ... abundant material to illustrate the fact that [*Walden*] was put together out of materials previously written, some of which were composed during Thoreau's actual residence by the pond site, some of which were already in existence before he went there, and some of which were not put on paper until long after he had left.[3]

None of this is to take away from the genius that went into Muir's, Abbey's, or Thoreau's writing, or to negate the profound effects that their books have had on readers like me. (Indeed, I must confess to having written the thesis for one of my master's degrees about *Desert Solitaire*.) I am, however, proposing a more distinctly immediate process for the book you are about to read. Please note that I am not undertaking this project as a critique of the trope of the solitary nature sojourner, or to suggest that I've found a better way to go about nature writing. Instead, this is a personal quest to unlearn some of what I've learned before and try a different way to go about my business.

---

2. I have written about this at length in "What Does the Desert Say? A Rhetorical Analysis of *Desert Solitaire*," published in the journal *Interdisciplinary Literary Studies*.
3. Krutch 1948, 100.

My method in the pages that follow, writing *in situ*, will not only entail writing from the place I'm writing about, but as nearly as possible from the moment as well. My commitment to the reader is to describe today's events today, never putting the writing off till tomorrow. While there are certainly times when I will need to close the notebook, slip it into my pocket, and trudge up the damned hill, I'm hoping that hiking can become part of composing, especially if I don't take too long after arriving at the summit to attend to my notes.

One of my mentors, a former editor, worries about this approach, but I've assured her that there will still be room for redaction once I'm back in town. Where my notes need tightening up, especially in terms of deleting the unremarkable, I will do so. But these are field notes, not a collection of essays. Let the genre be what it is.[4]

For me, the commitment to writing *in situ*, where description is almost contemporaneous with observation, is about hoping to engage in a more intense level of experiencing and evoking. My writing activity will need to become a process of deeper immersion than anything I've written in or about nature before, and I will have to find ways to eclipse the logistics of fieldwork itself in order to facilitate the writing. The bottom line here is that I go into the woods to write deliberately, writing in the present, from the place. In the parlance of Dr. Elliot Coues, who wrote about keeping ornithological field notes in 1874, I must let the paper on which I write "smell of the woods."

The appreciation of nature takes so many forms—it should not come as a surprise how well it lends itself to collaborative endeavors. My plan here is to seek out a specific sort of communal experience of nature where teams of researchers have committed to gathering data for over long periods of times: decades, at the very least, and, in one instance, centuries. During this exercise, I will spend six months in the field, dividing time among five field stations following, generally, a south-to-north trajectory. My timing may seem strange, at first, since I will end up in the northernmost, highest-altitude station right before the winter solstice, but this is intentional. I have chosen these stations with an eye toward long-term ecological research projects, and my field time in the earlier stations corresponds with nesting/denning periods, peak migration, et cetera, of the ongoing studies I most want to write about.

---

4. The first draft of this manuscript, submitted for formal peer review, contained without apology the original spellings I'd made in the handwritten versions of my field notes. That did not go over well, so you'll find corrected spelling and grammar in the notes that follow. Those wanting to read some wonderful field notes with the original misspellings preserved should consult the journals of the Lewis and Clark expedition. I recommend Bernard De Voto's edition, which is faithful to the originals.

I could not be more excited about the diverse palette of field stations I will visit during this project. The first is the eldest, run by a flagship research university in partnership with a venerable natural history museum. The second is run by another public research university, this one renowned for environmental science, in partnership with the world's largest nature conservancy. The third is a citizen science project run through a national park conservancy, a project where I've been a volunteer for some time. The fourth is an experimental forest, part of the Long Term Ecological Research Network, run through a three-way partnership between the US Forest Service, the National Science Foundation, and a land-grant research university. The fifth is an educational field campus run as a partnership between a national park, the forest service, local tribes, the nation's first dedicated college of environmental studies and sciences, a major metropolitan city, and an institute devoted to environmental education.

At each of these stations I will have the opportunity to hang out with people who have immersed themselves in these sites longer than Thoreau did at Walden or Abbey did at Arches. Significantly longer. Among the things I want to investigate in this book are how long-term ecological projects foster unique ways of experiencing the natural world. My hypothesis here is that numerous researchers at numerous field stations are experiencing nature in profound ways that rival or even surpass the transformational/transcendental experiences of Thoreau, Muir, and Abbey. Ultimately, evoking their experience is what most fascinates me about this project, and I am guided by Thoreau's observation that one can never get enough of nature. This manuscript is not intended to become a field guide to field stations; rather, these are field notes from a search for vigorous, long-term ways of experiencing the natural world.

Let this be both my discipline and my pledge—an honest chronology, written *in situ*, that takes its depth from the immediacy of the writer's experience.

Nature beyond Solitude

1

Notes from the Hastings Natural History Reservation

Don't trust your memory; it will trip you up; what is clear now
will grow obscure; what is found will be lost. Write down everything
while it is fresh in your mind; write it out in full—time spent now will be
time saved in the end, when you offer your researches to the discriminating
public. Don't be satisfied with a dry-as-dust item; clothe a skeleton fact,
and breathe life into it with thoughts that glow; let the paper smell of the
woods. There's a pulse in a new fact; catch the rhythm before it dies.

ELLIOTT COUES, *Field Ornithology*, 1874

June 19
Last full day of spring

I'm five minutes early, but the deep voice on the other end of the speaker tells
me that I'm right on time. It's the kind of voice that sells pickups on TV. Full-
sized pickups. I punch in the code, the electric gate swings open noiselessly,
and I drive into the reservation, pulling over just inside to await Vince, the reserve director. A University of California, Berkeley, official-business-only pickup arrives in no time. The Cal pickup dwarfs Little Dog,[1] and Vince is covered
in sawdust. When he shakes my hand he warns me that I've arrived on the cusp
of a heat wave. But I already know that. A nationwide "heat bubble" has been
forecast stretching from here through the desert southwest, and extending

---

1. Through no fault of my own, my compact truck has a name. The sobriquet "Little Dog" was
bestowed on it years ago by my beloved nephews during a sea-kayaking trip to Mulegé in Baja.
Their father's superduty truck, as you can probably imagine, was referred to as "Big Dog."

through much of the Midwest, lasting most of the week. The forecasters have prophesied all-time records being set in places like Phoenix and Death Valley. But it's only in the 90s here, right now, in this rolling oak savannah. We won't hit 100 until tomorrow.

I am ready. I've brought along a broad-brimmed "soaker hat" that my mother sent out for my sixty-second birthday, back on the first of this month. Polyester. I looked it up on the Internet and was informed that it's tan, and that its braided trim adds a rugged accent. In the mirror, it looks like a cowboy hat trying desperately to pass as something else. When I'm finally unpacked and able to stroll the reserve, I'm happy to discover a faucet at the side of the road halfway between my study and the labs, as if someone put it there specifically so that I could keep my hat wet during the commute. I stop, remove the hat to wet it for the first time ever, and learn a quick lesson when an earwig washes out with the first gush. Before I can protest, it scrambles up under the internal sweatband. Pincher bug! From now on, I'll let the water run for a moment before inserting my hat into this faucet's stream.

I know the earwig is harmless. All the same, I flush it out rather that capture it by hand.

When I get up to the labs, conversations focus on the impending heat wave. They are worried about the birds, of course. Acorn woodpeckers are cavity nesters, and it's expected to get hot enough inside some of the trees to kill nestlings. It's anyone's guess how many birds will be lost over the course of the next week.

I'm immediately snatched up by Natasha, a fourth-year PhD candidate who wants to climb to a few nest cavities tomorrow. Protocols require a safety assistant whenever technical climbing is involved, and so it is that I'm pressed to service. We'll weigh chicks and we'll get to do some banding, she promises. It will be fun. I find her smile convincing.

Natasha's face clouds slightly with what appears to be her singular concern: whether I'm a morning person. I assure her that I can be up at first light, but she waves off such silliness. "I usually start work at 7:00," she explains. But tonight the grad students are planning to camp out on the top of a hill. They've borrowed a nine-person tent from the reserve director, but some are now thinking that it will be too hot for a tent. Regardless, we won't be starting until 9:00 tomorrow. She hopes we'll be in the shade most of the morning, so I'm not to worry about the late start.

I poke around the lab a bit. It's narrow and cluttered. Along one countertop sits an array of clear, plastic boxes—Tupperware?—peppered with tiny air holes and occupied by black widow spiders, females, one spider per box. At the moment four teams of researchers are present at the reservation, studying acorn woodpeckers, western scrub-jays,[2] black widow spiders, and western bluebirds. There's history here, decades' worth. Part of that history is narrated by a bumper sticker affixed to an office door that proclaims, "Bluebirds rule. Woodpeckers drool." I tell Natasha that I look forward to working with her tomorrow and then I wander away, my hat almost dry in the afternoon sun. I wonder, rhetorically, what it would be like to be Natasha's age again, looking forward to a hilltop campout during the almost-full moon on a hot evening one night prior to the summer solstice.

This year, for the first time in my life, the full moon will sync with the summer solstice.

The breeze comes up at 5:30 p.m., and transforms the reservation. Birds suddenly remember their songs, and my ears are drawn back outside. I've been assigned a studio in the schoolhouse, which was built in the 1920s to serve as a boarding school, back when this was still the Hastings Ranch. The original curriculum featured lessons in the morning and horseback riding in the afternoon for those who had finished their lessons. Current events were discussed at lunch, and French was spoken at dinner. In modern times the official language here is birdsong, and cell-phone service has never made it out this far. But we have electricity here in the schoolhouse, and I was smart enough to pack a small electric desk fan in one of my duffels. For the rest of the week, that fan will be my prized possession.

I'm here for two weeks, actually, which is a good thing. They charge researchers twenty dollars a night for stays up to a week, but for longer stays the room rate is discounted to fifteen per night. With a research budget like mine, this is a very good thing. It's probably an even better thing for the crew here studying the cooperative breeding behaviors of acorn woodpeckers. They've been conducting this study, here at Hastings, for forty-five years.

A quick word about the birds. Acorn woodpeckers fascinate scientists because they live in groups, often with multiple breeding males and females, and nonbreeding helpers. The breeders share mates readily, and females lay eggs in a common nest, which is always a cavity nest. They hoard acorns in communal granary trees, which hold thousands of acorns in holes drilled by the group over a period of years. They have brilliant black and white faces, and the adults have a glowing yellow eye. Red crowns. They are quite vocal, even for woodpeckers. Some would call them "articulate."

---

2. The American Ornithological Union split this species three weeks after I wrote these field notes; these particular birds are now considered California scrub-jays.

June 20
Summer solstice

Regardless of the prospect of a late start, I awaken at daybreak. The dawn chorus here at the schoolhouse is particularly raucous; the Steller's jays and the western scrub-jays compete to outshout each other, while the California quail scream about Chicago. I hear the wakka-wakka-wakka of nearby acorn woodpeckers. Far off, I hear the squeeze-toy screams of a red-shouldered hawk. Crows in the background further contribute to the chorus' discordant timbre. As an aficionado of the universal dawn chorus, I rate the one at this field station a courtesy grade of B minus. Fine effort, but too many corvids. Otherwise, the morning is delightfully chill, and I slip into a lightweight fleece sweater before switching on the teakettle. I can barely wait for the tea to steep before heading outside with spotting scope and binoculars. My impatience causes me to spook the wild turkeys that congregated over by Little Dog. Tomorrow morning I'll know to pause on the porch, opening the screen door slowly.

The birds I'm seeing are all fairly common hereabouts, but no less enjoyable for their familiarity. Old friends: the blue-gray gnatcatchers, an industrious black phoebe, frantic Anna's hummingbirds, bumbling California towhees, an ash-throated flycatcher, an orange-crowned warbler, and plain-old warbling vireos. Acorn woodpeckers and western bluebirds, everywhere. Cavity nesters seem to define the avian community in these parts—this community is distinctly oakish.

The solitary part of the morning passes all too quickly, and I forgo the morning shower knowing that I'll probably need it worse by midafternoon. I fill all three water bottles—two with water, one with ice tea—and then in a testament to my own absentmindedness leave them sitting by the sink. Unencumbered, I make my way to Natasha's lab, eager for whatever awaits.

Consistent with my customary punctuality, I walk into the lab at 8:55. Natasha announces that plans have changed because her major professor, Eric, spotted two woodpeckers flying to a sycamore tree last evening, and heard the chicks greet them. Our first job this morning is to find the nest cavity.

There are no trails here, once we leave the road, except for the one Natasha breaks through the waist-high grass. I follow, and quickly realize that it had been a mistake not to bring my above-the-ankle leather boots on this trip. I'd considered it, but had decided that they would be too hot. So later this afternoon it will take me half an hour to remove the grass-seed spears from my socks.

Natasha seems impervious to poison oak, almost carelessly brushing up against it, and I find it difficult to keep up with her as I choose careful paths around toxic shrubbery. At a few points I suspect that my boots have gotten into it—the oily, glossy leaves are almost impossible to avoid in these woods. I'd been warned about this by a biology professor back home; when she heard that I was heading for Hastings, she mentioned two concerns: poison oak and ticks. At least she didn't mention the rattlesnakes.

We stop at the first sycamore we come to, and immediately begin searching for woodpecker-sized holes. After a few moments we hear a voice calmly asking, "Where are you?"

"We're at the sycamore on the cabin side of the creek."

"That's the wrong tree."

"Are you sure?"

"I'd be able to see you if you were at the right tree."

Pause. Then, "So where is it?"

"Come toward my voice."

We find the right tree in due time. Eric is uphill from it, but we can barely see him through the thick understory. This sycamore is twice the size of the first, and when we arrive at its base, we are greeted by dozens of mosquitoes. They are tiny, and I'm wearing a long-sleeved shirt, as is Eric. Natasha's arms are bare, and the mosquitoes find her attractive. She comments on them, but doesn't waste energy slapping them away. We have birds to find, and she raises her binoculars toward the canopy, as do I.

We can't get a good view from where we are. Eric thinks the nest cavity will be on the uphill side of the tree because adult woodpeckers have been approaching the tree from that direction. However, the poison oak is especially thick on that side of the tree, and there's no way to get a view without wading through it.

Natasha wades through it.

I can't believe what I'm seeing. Since my move to California in 1984, the avoidance of poison oak has been a major preoccupation. I'll hike at night, I'll hike in the rain, I'll hike uphill on a sweltering day, but I won't willingly cross through poison oak. In her next thirty-two steps, Natasha will entangle in more poison oak than I've touched in the past thirty-two years. But not without protest.

"I'm swimming through poison for you, Eric."

"I can see that."

I've never supervised a PhD student—my college doesn't offer doctorates. But I've been one, and I'm certain that the relationship between PhD students and their supervisors[3] is one of the least understood of all human

---

3. I earned my PhD in Great Britain, where the operative term is "supervisor" rather than "adviser," the word commonly used in the United States.

relationships. No metaphor really works: not adviser/advisee, not employer/employee, not preacher/choir, not master/slave, not even teacher/student. Colleagues? Sort of, but not really. You don't wade through a thick thatch of poison oak for a colleague.

We ultimately identify two cavities that might contain nests, but the only way to know for certain, short of observing woodpeckers using them, is to peer inside. The decision is made to use a camera scope, so Natasha and I hike back to the woodpecker shed to pick up a remote camera and a huge telescoping pole. It would probably be more productive for me to hang out here with Eric in case woodpeckers happen by, but I'm hoping to pick up a water bottle when we get back to the lab. I end up borrowing one of Natasha's.

We return. I do not follow when Natasha wades back into the thicket of poison oak with the camera. After all, I've already earned my PhD.

I realize, somewhat gradually, that somewhere during the course of that last round trip back to the lab my hiking boots have failed miserably. Well, they're not "boots" really, not in the sense that they cover my ankles. They are the sort of hiking shoes a fellow like me uses when trekking through arid regions like Baja, where I've done a great deal of my trekking this past decade. But Baja doesn't have grass spears like they have here in the oak savannah, and at this point my ankles are thoroughly pricked. I look down at my footwear and am shocked to see dozens and dozens of grass spears entrapped in the mesh. And it's a good thing I can't see my socks from here.

I realize, belatedly, how wrong this is. I train my binoculars on Natasha's legs and, through the poison oak, I can tell that she's wearing all-leather boots, calf-high, the kind without the cooling mesh. Now I scope out Eric's feet. Yes, all-leather boots. The warm kind. The kind that protect your ankles from grass spears.

I don't remove the spears. No. I've tramped through enough poison oak at this point that I'd only be aggravating my problems. It's better just to bleed in silence.

"This one's empty," Natasha reports.

Oh yeah. Woodpeckers.

Natasha emerges from the thicket, and moves to another possible nest cavity on my side of the tree. The camera transmits its live image to Natasha's cell phone, and she squints to see deeply into the cavity. It, too, turns out to be empty. We regroup, and Eric suggests that one of the field assistants be reassigned to sit in this grove until the woodpeckers return so that the location of the nest cavity can be discovered. This could entail sitting here alone for hours, just a forlorn field assistant hanging out with the mosquitoes. He asks which assistants are doing the least critical work today, and Natasha runs through the day's assignments. She is ultimately in charge of scheduling the workflow, although she tells me later that the field assistants usually get to choose their own daily assignments according to interests and specialties. Usually.

Eric vanishes into the forest; Natasha and I return to the lab. She quickly downs a pint of water, and then we head for the shed where the climbing equipment is stored. We're back to plan A, which involves us hiking through a lot more waist-high grass. She leads the way, encumbered with a stout climbing rope and an impressive assortment of technical gear, no doubt paid for by the National Science Foundation. She has forgotten her field notebook, a formal document using the Grinnell method, but once we arrive at the tree she is relieved to discover that I'm carrying two notebooks,[4] either of which we can use to record the information and then transcribe it later into her notes. I finally feel that I'm making a contribution.

This tree is an enormous valley oak, the girth of its trunk as voluminous as any oak I've ever seen. I estimate that it would take six undergraduates, hands outstretched, to encircle this tree. I girdle it with the anchor sling, careful to reverse the gates of the twin carabiners when connecting it. This is a common safety precaution among climbers, and Natasha is encouraged to see me set up a proper anchor without needing to be instructed in how to do so. She belongs to a tribe where field craft such as this is crucial, and now, as far as she's concerned, so do I. I don't mention that I learned how to set a proper climbing anchor before she was born.

She climbs athletically, obviously an old hand at the ascenders, and yet I can hear her labored breathing once she's eight or nine meters up. I make a mental note that at least she's human. When she finally arrives at the branch, she snugs herself up, withdraws a hammer from her tool satchel, and, using the claw end, begins to open up the nest cavity. Years ago the Hastings researchers developed a system of adding a "bottom door" to the cavity entrances. It's held shut with a couple nails driven halfway in, and in theory can be removed easily to give the researcher access.

She calls down that this is an "ant tree," which I duly note. I will later learn that this means she'll have ants biting her arms as she works. Acorn woodpeckers prefer to nest in ant trees whenever possible; the ants protect their eggs against predators, especially snakes. The strategy seems to be less effective with PhD candidates.

---

4. I carry an unruled pocket notebook for what I consider "jottings," and a larger ruled notebook for more detailed sketches and narrative description. The Farnsworth system works thus: the more time I anticipate having to write, the larger the notebook I write within. Later that day it all gets transcribed into the same computer, and it's these transcriptions that I consider my working field notes.

Once the cavity is opened up, Natasha reaches in and counts, by feel, that there are five eggs and zero chicks. I make the appropriate notation in my field book, 5E, ØC. I'm barely noticing, at this point, the pain inflicted by the spear grass on my ankles and feet. She withdraws one of the eggs and holds it up to sunlight, finally pronouncing it to be "fresh." The lack of a reddish tinge has told her that it's been laid in the last three days. I make the appropriate notation, which will help the team decide when next to visit this nest. It's important to their protocols to be able to predict a hatch date.

Natasha closes the nest, and then rappels down smoothly. I notice that she is not using gloves during this operation, and wonder whether this is something that has changed since my era of technical climbing, or whether Natasha is as impervious to rope burns as she seems to be to poison oak. And mosquitoes. And ants. She steps away from the rope, and we coil the gear without talking, her tending to the rope while I daisy-chain the anchor.

Getting to the next tree—what will end up being our final tree of the morning—involves another long hike through waist-high grass. On the way we come across a patch of invasive star thistles; Natasha uproots the closest one. When she moves toward her second victim, I wrestle with another, but find myself wishing I were wearing gloves to defend from the prickly stems. Clearly, my professorial hands are softer than those of this PhD candidate. And my ankles are absolutely agonized. I suffer in silence, refusing to notice that she is uprooting three thistles for every one of mine.

We come to a barbed-wire fence, and Natasha hops up on a log and then bounds over the fence, gear and all, as if gravity were momentarily suspended. I'm tall enough to straddle the highest wire if I select the perfect spot for doing so, happy at my age to risk the crotch in order to save the knees.

The oak to which we're hiking is just on the other side of the fence.

This tree is at least four centuries younger than the one Natasha climbed previously, its trunk no more than a third as large in circumference. As soon as we arrive at its base we can hear the begging calls of the nestlings. Natasha can distinguish hatchlings from nestlings and nestlings from fledglings by voice alone, and she estimates that these chicks would turn out to be no more than ten days old. Healthy chicks grow at a consistent rate, and their weights would help us determine a hatch date accurate to within a day.

This nest cavity is significantly lower than the first, and Natasha free-climbs the tree, observing proper safety precautions, of course. She once again opens the bottom door of the cavity hole, at which point the chicks began squealing much louder. They want to be fed. Groping around, once again by touch, Natasha dictates, "No eggs, two chicks." She withdraws both chicks with one hand. From my perch below they clearly seem to be in the first stage of development: featherless, with eyes still unopened. Natasha, however, notices "visible feather tracks," and asks me to make a note of this. She weighs each chick gently, calling down "thirty-three point four" for chick number 1, and "twenty-five point five," for chick number 2. I watch as the chicks peck at Natasha's hand, beaks wide open, hoping for an afternoon treat.

Back in the lab, we consult the charts and discover the chicks to be eight days old. We list their hatch date as June 12, my wife's birthday, which gives them a band date of July 2, once they are three weeks old. To maintain accurate records, it is important to band these chicks before they take flight for the first time.

I watch as Natasha enters the data from my notebook into the computer. The chicks now have a history, and are officially part of one of the longest ecological studies currently in progress. But the time has come for me to call it a day. There being no more climbing in store, I excuse myself under the pretense that I want to tend to my field notes, which is only partially true. What I really want to do is to get the hell out of my socks. I return to the schoolhouse, shower with a special soap that cuts the oil of poison oak, throw every stitch of clothing into the laundry, and then take the long drive down canyon to Monterey, where I will tell the friendly salesclerk of an outdoor sports shop that I want to purchase the cheapest full-leather, above-the-ankle hiking boots that they've got in a size 11.

I wear them all the way back to the reservation. These boots need to be broken in by 7:00 tomorrow morning.

June 21
First full day of summer

I arrive for work early, and watch from a picnic table outside the lab as the various field assistants show up. I know only a few of their names at this point. One is wearing a helmet. She will be driving a 4WD Kawasaki Mule to a site where she'll watch a nest, noting her observations every minute. Another shows up carrying a portable blind, set for a day observing in solitude. One has been assigned to continue to watch for a nest location in the sycamore glen we visited yesterday. She will spend her day tolerating mosquitoes. Finally, I see one who must have gotten an earlier start trudging up the hill carrying yet another portable blind. I'm guessing he drew the short straw this morning. I will soon learn that these kids[5] spend a lot of time in portable blinds.

I'm to be partnered up with Natasha once again. I notice things today that escaped me yesterday—details like how she wears glasses but not sunglasses while in the field. When I ask why, she explains that her eyes are fairly bad and she doesn't own prescription sunglasses. Duh. We joke about grad-student poverty, but I secretly resolve that if I'm ever elected president of these United States there will be funding for proper eyewear for all postgraduate field researchers.

Natasha is not looking forward to climbing the first tree. It was last climbed by another fourth-year PhD student, Mickey, and he reports not being able to access the cavity because the rope has slipped away from it, becoming entangled in a cluster of twigs. Natasha will have to pull herself up atop the limb, which is twelve meters off the ground, tether herself to it with climbing slings, and then reposition the rope. And this will all happen on an ant tree.

We understand the problem when we arrive on site. The rope gets jammed at the point where it attaches the messenger, and won't pull through a cluster of twigs. After half a dozen unsuccessful attempts, we decide to reverse the process and try to pull it around the other side of the limb. As I pull down the quarter-inch nylon messenger, I feel a bite, and notice five ants attacking my right arm. I find it hard to believe they've descended twelve meters of messenger line to attack me, but Natasha assures me, "That's nothin'."

Nothin'. I brush off ants as she reties the messenger. In my world, every bite counts.

The reversal was successful, and Natasha quickly ascends. Minutes later, when she finally reaches the branch, her discomfort becomes apparent. When I ask what's wrong, she replies, "I really don't mind the ants until they start getting on my face."

(She explains later, when we return to our Mule, that the soldier ants, which are larger, were not biting her but instead were spreading pheromones that would instruct worker ants where to attack. She explains that the pheromone smells like lemon furniture polish, and adds that the locals call these critters "lemon ants.")

She doesn't surrender to the attack. Once her ascenders have jammed against the limb, and once she has rigged tethers to keep her attached to the tree after she climbs above her rope, she climbs the steps of her *étrier* rope

---

5. No disrespect intended. I note that many educators shy away from referring to students as "kids," but after living for a decade in a dorm with more than four hundred twentysomethings, the usage becomes inexorable, even in field notes.

ladder while hugging the thick limb tightly to her chest. The scary part is when she finally swings a leg over the limb, rolling atop it like a sailor straddling a yardarm. I watch this maneuver through my binoculars, barely able to breathe. She is covered in ants.

She sits up, brushes ants off her arms and face, and then quickly inserts a camera scope into the cavity. She reports that the nest is empty, and I record this in her notebook while she resets the climbing rope, swings down to it, and rappels down.

Natasha coils the rope while I once again daisy-chain the anchor. We watch as a field technician comes across from the opposite hill. As she approaches, I ask quietly to make certain I remember her name. "Is it Amanda?" Natasha nods yes, and whispers, "She's a bluebirder."

Amanda is following a route of nest boxes to note which are being used, and by whom. She averages seven miles a day running her various routes.[6] When we greet her she asks whether we'd like to see some ash-throated flycatcher eggs, and of course we would. We follow her, traversing sidehill through the tall grass, and at this point I'm in love with my new boots.

The nest box is nailed to a tree about five feet high, just low enough for Amanda to peer in through its hinged top. In turn, we are invited to take a peek. There are five eggs, marble sized, streaked longitudinally, and half buried in a nest made of coyote dung. Amanda announces that they were laid thirteen days ago, but she doesn't know how long it takes flycatcher eggs to hatch. (We look this up once back at the lab, and learn that these eggs should hatch in a couple more days.)

The second and third climbs of the morning are uneventful, at least in comparison to the rigors of the first. We return to the lab at 10:00 and enjoy two hours of down time in which to catch up on our respective field notes. But we head back out a little after noon, this time accompanied by Kaija, the Mule-driving field assistant I'd seen wearing a helmet earlier this morning. We gather at the woodpecker shed to grab the banding gear, and I ask Kaija whether she's a student. She answers "kinda," and then explains that she's taking a gap year but that she'll be attending Yale in the fall. She drives, I ride shotgun, and Natasha jumps into the back to ride in the metal bed with the gear. She reports that the metal is hot, and Kaija grabs her a blanket out of the Mule's bonnet.

Kaija drives like a madwoman, clearly flirting with the Mule's top speed. I look over to check the speedometer, but the Mule doesn't have one. At this

---

6. I discover later that she also jogs down to the reservation gate and back every day, in order to stay in shape.

point I wonder whether I should be wearing a helmet as well. On the upside, the Mule doesn't have a windshield, and the windchill from the breeze is welcome at this speed.

Natasha free-climbs to the artificial cavity, carrying a cloth bag in her teeth. Once properly situated, she pops open the top and tenderly removes four twenty-one-day-old chicks.[7] The chicks are gently bagged while Kaija spreads a blanket as if for a picnic, arranging the necessary banding tools and supplies. I notice that there's a certain amount of ritual involved in this process. Here at Hastings, things are done a certain way.

The first chick to undergo the process is the only one who shows any sign of distress, which it communicates by sticking out its tongue. It attempts to bite Natasha's hand at first, which causes her to giggle. She takes quick measurements, then weighs the chick, speaking only in numerals while Kaija makes notations in Natasha's notebook. A blood sample is taken for genetic analysis. At this point I am asked whether I'd like to choose the color bands. I decline, explaining that I'm too color-blind to make sense of this. Kaija explains that they use a "haphazard banding system" at Hastings, choosing the color bands randomly and only rejecting those choices that might be confused with other members of the particular group. She demonstrates how it's done, closing her eyes and then rooting her fingers through the bag of bands to find the right one. Natasha rejects her first choice because one of the colors is already used by one of the parent birds, but the second choice is deemed perfect.

I ask Kaija whether she closes her eyes for luck or because she was trained to do so. She indicates that this is a function of her training, and then adds that it's good she can't look because she would always try to select pretty combinations for the birds. This, apparently, would not be good for the science.

I ask Natasha what would happen if a bird got loose. She decides to show me. Once banded, the bird is set "free" on her leg. The chick wants nothing of freedom at this point, however, and seeks security by hopping down between Natasha's legs.

Natasha moves the chick to Kaija's upturned baseball cap, and withdraws a second chick from the bag. In short order we have a "hatful of babies," as Kaija puts it, and they are cute beyond words. I am granted thirty seconds to photograph the group before they're returned to the bag and then to their nest. But there is ritual here as well. Each time Natasha places one of the chicks into the nest, she repeats the invocation "Live long and prosper."

---

7. Whenever possible, acorn woodpeckers are banded twenty-one days after hatching at Hastings because they're old enough at this point to have full plumage but not yet old enough to fledge.

Kaija divulges a bit of field station folklore, that when Natasha was a new PhD student four years ago, after she'd returned banded birds to a nest, her adviser, Eric made her climb back up, remove the birds, and then replace them properly because she hadn't uttered the invocation the first time.

Live long and prosper indeed.

We return to the lab, and plans are laid out for tomorrow. Natasha and a field assistant plan to leave at 4:00 a.m. and hike a mile to a nest where they'll set up what is called an "ambush trap." This device traps a bird inside the nest cavity, but needs to be tripped by someone who is watching the nest opening. This needs to be done while it's still dark and the birds are still asleep. I'm asked whether I want to assist with this project, but I demur. While all this activity has been enlightening, it's time to get more directly in touch with my writing.

I kindly volunteer, instead, to return to the ant tree that Natasha climbed first thing this morning, and to watch from the shadows to discover where the birds in question were nesting. This sort of job is usually reserved for the field assistant with the lowest seniority, at least the lowest academic seniority, but I can't imagine anything I'd rather do after the frenetic pace of my first couple days at the reservation. I'm ready for a bit of solitude.

June 22
Second full day of summer

At Hastings, ornithologists annotate their field notes in "bird time" rather than "people time." This, believe it or not, is because birds do not transition to daylight saving time the way people do. So we don't expect the woodpeckers to become active until 6:00 this morning, people time, because it's only 5:00 their time. We should be grateful that sunlight governs avian life, not Congress. Local wisdom here on the reservation observes that the early bird doesn't get the worm if the worms are still in bed.[8]

I get to my field station a bit early anyway, eager to find a perfect spot for my observations. The perfect spot doesn't exist, however, especially if I want a flat spot, because the only relatively flat ground is west of the granary tree, where I'd originally planned to set up. Once on site, I immediately realize that as the sun rises it will shine through the branches and pretty much blind anyone silly enough to be peering east through a spotting scope.

---

8. A whiteboard outside Eric's office tracks all the daily projects, assignments, and modes of transportation. It's also used by the field assistants to communicate extracurriculars. In a few days, I will see a note saying, "Swimming meet here at 1330 (people time)."

I elect to let the still-unseen sun be my guide, and climb a steep hill east-northeast of the granary tree. It's not easy in this tall grass, which can make a steep slope slippery no matter what sort of boots you're wearing. I'm carrying a camera with a heavy telephoto lens in my daypack, two liters of water, a spotting scope on a tripod over my shoulder, and a camp chair. A pair of binoculars are around my neck, of course. I'm guessing the slope to be around 30 percent, which means for every one hundred meters I travel horizontally, I climb thirty meters vertically. I get to a point where I'm level with the granary tree's canopy, at least 150 meters away from it. There's a lovely, stout oak here to provide shade, and I circumnavigate the tree looking for its ID tag. Every proper oak on the reservation has been numbered, tagged, measured for girth at breast height, and located topographically. A few also have names. This tree is no. 5067. Unfortunately, there is no flat ground anywhere near it. I find a rock on which I can prop up the front legs of my camp chair, and dig in the rear legs as far as I can without creating environmental havoc. When I finally take a seat, sitting feels like a tentative activity.

I make a note of the time: it's 6:45. That's people time. The birds still think it's early. I have plenty of time to set up my spotting scope, meter the light for my camera, draw a not-to-scale map in my field notes, and munch on a granola bar while waiting for the first woodpecker to visit the granary tree. It's a wonderful morning.

A flock of four female black-headed grosbeaks flits up the hill and takes a position on a young oak just below me. Each one claims a top branch, to each her own, and their buffy breast feathers practically glow in the morning sunlight. It's as if they are posing for me, but the camera is on the ground and I worry that I'll frighten the birds away if I stoop to pick it up. The grosbeaks don't rest in the treetop for more than ten seconds, and then they're off, rushing away in unison as if synchronized by the gods themselves. I ask myself how they all decided to fly in the same instant. Moments later, a breeding-plumage male alights on one of the branches that has just been vacated. I can't resist a bit of interspecies communication, and whisper, "You're late." He looks at me as if to say, "Tell me what I don't know." Then he, too, is off.

The first acorn woodpecker won't show up for an hour, but it's a good hour. There are no hawks around this morning, or falcons or anything else that might prey on perching birds, and species by species they make their presence known. I hear, in the distance, the sweet fluting of a hermit thrush, a hermit who seems to be enjoying his solitude as much as I am this morning. I hear the bouncing ping-pong warble of an orange-crowned warbler, and the similar song of a wrentit, almost as if the two species are harmonizing. Unseen from my perch, I hear an oak titmouse[9] defining his territory—*tuwi tuwi tuwi*. So far this week I've heard a dozen titmice for every one I've seen. I'm confident that this will change soon: once you start seeing titmice in oak woodlands this thick, you see them everywhere you look. My eyes just have to get oaky.

I hear the woodpeckers before I see them. The first one to fly up to the granary tree comes from the other side of the hill to my right. I hope that this won't become a pattern, because if it is I've chosen the worst possible location to figure out where they're nesting. And for the next two hours, every woodpecker sighted comes from that direction, and every time they leave the granary tree they fly off in that direction as well.

I stick to my post somewhat stubbornly, perhaps because of the effort that went into climbing this hill. The birds finally cooperate, and I'm able to observe three woodpeckers on the tree at one time, none of which is the adult female associated with this group. This is interesting, because the group that owns this granary is relatively small, two males and a female. I notice the molt pattern of one that may be a juvenile—it seems that this one has joined the group recently. I can see that all three woodpeckers have been banded, but I can't come close to deciphering the colors of the bands. I attempt to discern the colors photographically, adding a teleconverter to my long lens that in essence gives me the equivalent of a 900mm lens. But I'm ultimately too far away to resolve the bands. Frustrating.

Shortly after 9:00, at a moment when there are no woodpeckers visiting the granary, I move to a different location, crossing over to the ravine from which I'm assuming the woodpeckers are coming and going. It's cooler over here, which is welcome, but I have to choose between a good view of the ravine and an unobstructed view of the granary tree. I elect to go with the former, setting up under tree no. 5410. It's the only way I'll discover a nest if it's in these parts. I don't bother setting up the scope this time—this will be a job for ears and binoculars. I sit, and scan, and scan for a full forty-five minutes without a single woodpecker flying by.

Time for a new strategy. The heat has grown to the point where the woodpeckers will soon be taking their siesta. I move downhill to tree no. 5648, setting up directly underneath it, due west of the granary. This is where I'd originally planned to start the observations, but now the sun is high enough to permit eastward viewing.

---

9. I can't help feeling a certain tenderness for the oak titmouse, *Baeolophus inornatus*, if for no other reason than its species name, *inornatus*. That can be translated "unadorned," which was probably the intended meaning for this plain brown bird, but a Latin scholar might also take it as an idiom for "uncelebrated."

Nothing. At one point I see an acorn woodpecker departing the granary tree—I hadn't seen it arrive—and it flies up the far hill toward the tree under which I'd originally stationed myself. Perhaps I should have remained there.

I head back to the schoolhouse to take my morning shower. A belated shower, one that will have to be rushed because I want to attend a seminar being offered at 12:01 people time. I understand that these seminars are a weekly event, and that attendance is required for student field assistants. This sort of mandatory fun is practiced at many biological field stations. Today's topic is "My Friend the Black Widow."

Two of the researchers here are arachnologists—they study spiders. They are part of a Canadian group that has been studying black widows here at Hastings for the past five years, discovering all sorts of things that we never knew about *Latrodectus hesperus*. The team will be leaving the station next Monday, and are using this opportunity to hint about their preliminary findings.

Everyone here at the field station attends. Today there are eleven student researchers, all clustered in those wonderful years between twenty and thirty, and three of us crusty old guys. Generational change in life science is evident here: all three of the old guys are male, but only two of the student scientists are not female. As far as I'm concerned, this is good for science.

I can't help thinking, as I listen to the fascinating seminar, that this is probably the only passive entertainment any of us will partake in this week. There's no television out here, and we're not allowed to stream music or videos on the Internet because of limited station bandwidth. The first Canadian researcher lectures us on spider morphology, and the second Canadian researcher delves into spider behavior. It's the best show in town, and I find it absolutely riveting. Spooky, as well.

Tonight there will be a potluck, and it's supposed to have a Canadian theme. I'm bringing a watermelon, Canadian or not.

June 23
Well into summer

The potluck party last night made for some interesting ethnography.[10] I was one of the first to arrive, after having lugged a well-refrigerated watermelon up the hill. I handed it off to Mickey, the fourth-year PhD student from Cornell

---

10. With apologies, I write these next six paragraphs in the past tense from the perspective of the morning after, having fallen asleep shortly after the party's conclusion. Yesterday turned out to be a longer day than those to which I'm accustomed.

who I'm scheduled to start working with in a few days, and he asked, "Is this for dessert?"

I answered in the affirmative, and could immediately see that this was the wrong answer. Mickey explained that the tradition among the group was to eat a watermelon prior to dinner, since everyone would arrive at the party hot and parched. When I agreed that this made sense, Mickey began to carve the watermelon, as if historical precedent had ordained that faculty are exempt from any task as tedious as carving a watermelon.

I had noticed elements of a faculty-student caste system prior to this. For example, at the black widow seminar the students, without exception, sat in the hard chairs lined up in rows in front of the podium. Faculty, other than me, sprawled in more comfy chairs to the side of the room. When, after the seminar, I was introduced to a student I had not yet met, she was surprised to learn that I was a professor. What sort of professor, after all, sits in the hard chairs?

It's not all bad. I also noticed that the faculty, without exception, ate last at the potluck, as is right and proper. The fare was mostly student food, after all, with two types of mac and cheese, two types of meatloaf, and some sort of potato thing that was gone by the time I got to it. It would be ugly for faculty to come between students and such a feast.

One last ethnographic observation: a number of the female students dressed up, and by "dressed up" I mean dresses, while the males, whether faculty or student, were pretty much attired in shorts and a T-shirt. It was the first time I'd seen any of these researchers wearing anything but long trousers. Regardless, there were a lot of ant bites, mosquito bites, scrapes, cuts, and poison-oak rashes on display. As a group, regardless of gender, it was readily apparent that the student researchers had been putting in their field time.

The absolute star of the party was an acorn woodpecker named Almost. He showed up one day with a broken wing, and can no longer fly. During the day, when the student researchers are out in the field, Almost lives in an aviary just thirty meters from my study. At night, however, he spends his time with the gang, sleeping around with typical woodpecker promiscuity. Throughout the party he migrated from shoulder to shoulder, begging a grain of rice or a sip of beer.[11] Almost vocalizes whenever he's not the center of attention, and his various calls became a source of concern for the resident male who rules this particular parcel, which for purposes of science is designated "RE17." The resident male, better known as "4314,"[12] vocalized angrily, and then repeatedly

11. Almost is only allowed two sips per party.
12. 4314 is one of the older birds currently in the study, coming up on eleven years old. He has had serial mates recently: a new female every year for the past three years.

swooped the deck where we were enjoying watermelon and stuffed mush-rooms. When that didn't work, he flew to a nearby utility pole and drummed loudly—the ultimate warning in the language of woodpeckers. Almost almost ignored him, perhaps because he'd already had his first sip of beer.

I have been asked to look for a nest cavity in a meadow called "Horsetail," which is flanked by two creeks. There is a population of six woodpeckers here, and although Natasha has stationed field assistants in blinds here several times during the current breeding season, no one has been able to find a nest cavity.

The lower half of the meadow is full of horsetail rushes, which explains how this nesting site got its name. The upper half is studded with a couple dozen pink marking flags, each one demarcating a black widow nest.

I startle two does and a fawn as I enter the meadow, and then in turn sur-prise the two Canadian researchers who had presented yesterday's lecture. They're conducting a quick transect of the meadow, looking for new webs while walking shoulder to shoulder, up and down the meadow crosswise, moving a few feet laterally between each pass. It's the same pattern you'd use if you were mowing a lawn.

They tell me that there haven't been any woodpeckers around, but I've al-ready spotted one and I see a couple more within the next minute. It's prob-ably easy to miss woodpeckers when you're searching for black widow nests.

The arachnologists leave a few minutes after I set up my observation post, off to their next transect.

A kind breeze strikes up, strong enough to generate wind chill but gentle enough not to interfere with the birding. I get up to inspect the granary tree and to check out the two artificial cavities I'm told have been installed. They are there. Empty. When I return to my chair it's covered with leaves. I've sta-tioned myself beneath a California buckeye, a summer-deciduous plant that is absolutely lush when in bloom in the spring, but which sheds its leaves during the dry days that follow. With buckeye foliage, it's everything or nothing.

Hermit thrushes call back and forth across the meadow, the one claiming, "This is my side," the other claiming, "This is my side." Far up the hill I hear the wakka-wakka call of an acorn woodpecker. I wish I knew how to converse with the bird. Even here in a meadow alone, I'm a bit too dignified to attempt the wakka-wakka. A few of the students at the party last night could mimic it perfectly after an ale or two. Oh, to be young.

The beauty of this meadow distracts me, and I catch myself hoping I don't find the nest cavity today so that I can return tomorrow to finish the job. My level of distraction intensifies when I move my spotting scope away from the horsetails, past the monkey flowers, and into a patch of leafy sage. Not only do I get a better view of a perched woodpecker from here, but I get better smells as well. Over on this side, the meadow smells like nature is supposed to smell, at least to someone who grew up in Colorado.

Butterflies become a distraction as well, not only because of their number, but for their diversity. As the day warms, butterfly activity increases proportionally to how bird activity decreases, a perfect relationship for naturalists. The most abundant species in this meadow is the western tiger swallowtail, but I'm also seeing painted ladies, California hairstreaks, a callippe fritillary, what I'm almost certain was a Mylitta crescent, common buckeyes, and a few California sisters. As if determined not to be upstaged by the order Lepidoptera, a tarantula hawk lands on the deerweed, *Acmispon glaber*, to my left. In this setting, the huge, red-winged wasp seems far less ferocious than it actually is.

The day finally heats up to the point where the woodpeckers stop flying, and my thoughts turn to lunch. While I pack up my gear I notice the parallel sapsucking lines encircling the live oak behind me. It appears that this tree's entire trunk has been tattooed. When I mention this to Natasha back at the lab, she confirms not only that acorn woodpeckers are sapsuckers, but that they tend to prefer live oaks for this purpose. It's apparently a major source of nutrition for the Horsetail Group.

This news makes me want to find a nest all the more. I ask Natasha whether acorn woodpeckers ever excavate nest cavities in live oaks, and she says that it's uncommon, but that she's opened up four live-oak nest cavities belonging to the Horsetail Group over the years.

With this information, tomorrow's search expands dramatically.

June 24

It has cooled down so much that I'm actually wearing layers this morning: a light sweater over my shirt, and a field vest over that. By 6:30 I have my station set up just uphill from the deerweed where I ended up yesterday. I've splurged today, bringing along not only a tripod and a chair, but a portable writing table as well. It's a bit of a load to transport, but I'm feeling like the ultimate nature writer once I'm set up and ready not only to make observations, but to record them as well. It's a trade-off, however—I've left my heavy camera back at the schoolhouse to make room for the lightweight table. I'm certain to miss a great photo at some point this morning.

I don't see my first acorn woodpecker for fifteen minutes. It perches at the very top of the granary tree's crown, probably to maximize the sunlight hitting it. I'm wanting it to fly, and I'm wanting it to fly off in my direction so that I know I've set up in the right spot. When it finally takes off, the bird flies right past me and up to the top of the next ridge, perching on a leafless oak that appears to have recently died—the leaves are gone but the smallest twigs are still intact. The woodpecker alights on the highest point of the tree, once again maximizing its exposure to the sunlight.

Fifteen minutes later, two woodpeckers appear on the granary tree. It will be the only time I see multiple woodpeckers visit that granary today.

I keep hearing acorn woodpeckers, but they're back over my shoulder, and too far away to be part of this group. Or are they? After thirty minutes listening to their chatter, I decide to investigate. I move to a spot where the meadow doglegs to the right, and at that point I see a large but not ancient sycamore with at least four woodpeckers on it at any given moment. Wondering whether this is a known nest, I leave my spotting scope behind and hike toward the sycamore, hoping that I've finally discovered the nest for the Horsetail Group. I stop at a distance of about fifty meters, however, and when I scan it through my binoculars I can see messenger lines running from the trunk to upper branches. The tree appears to have been climbed this season. I watch the woodpeckers go about their business for a few minutes before returning to my spot up in the meadow. This same location that teemed with life when I discovered it yesterday now seems a bit lonely.

The next couple of hours pass slowly. I try to make a note every five minutes of what I'm seeing and hearing, even if it's only a monarch butterfly or a blue-gray gnatcatcher. Once again a woodpecker flies from the granary tree to the dead oak on the ridge, and then afterward seems to descend to the sycamore. This seems too unusual, as if that bird were breaking the rules of *Melanerpes formicivorus* sociality. I make an earnest note.

Twice during the morning I make small excursions to investigate woodpeckers I'm hearing but not seeing. One of these involves a climb up a ridiculously steep hill, richly vegetated in poison oak, where it takes a good five minutes to gain thirty meters in elevation. By the time I get where I wanted to be, there are no woodpeckers in the vicinity.

I remind myself, once I've returned to my observation post, that one must never consider mornings like this a waste of time. I'm here because the nest, if it exists at all, has been difficult to find. Had it been easy to find, like the one in the sycamore that any greenhorn could have located, populations would be far more vulnerable.

Just then, I hear a *karrit-cut* call coming from the granary tree. It's a soft call, the sort of voice you'd use at tender moments with members of your family. I scan the tree, trying to find its source without success. This goes on for more than a minute, and then, suddenly, the woodpecker appears through the leaves about three-fourths the way up the tree, and is flying straight toward me. I lower my binoculars slowly, so as not to frighten it. It glides directly over my head, down the meadow. At this point I break into a run, instinctively, so that I can see where the bird goes once it passes the dogleg. I get there just in time to see it alight on the sycamore.

I'm fairly certain that this is a violation of the woodpecker code of conduct, and I return to my field notes to document the incident. Natasha will hear about this!

It occurs to me that maybe the researchers don't actually know what's going on out here. What if . . .

I decide I'll need to get the tag number of the sycamore in order to make a full report. Leaving my gear behind, I plan to circle back to the road and come up behind the tree so as not to scare the birds away. If I can get close enough to the tree to read the tag with my binoculars . . .

A minivan comes along soon after I hit the road. New York plates, and a Cornell University license-plate frame. The vehicle stops, and I recognize one of the most famous ornithologists in the universe, Dr. Walter Koenig, a man some have called the father of behavioral ornithology.

The window is rolled down. The man is wearing a nondescript University of California, Berkeley T-shirt. Gray. I ask, "Are you Walt?"

"Are you John?"

We shake hands. Walt apologizes for not showing up until now. He had originally planned to be here on the nineteenth, the same day I arrived, but he was moving back into a house that had burned down in the Tassajara fire last year, and the contractor was late, and an occupancy permit had not yet been granted, and the moving van was . . .

We digress.

I describe the location of the sycamore and ask whether that could be an outpost of the Horsetail Group.

"No, they're back this way," he gestures with his hand.

I explain the situation, a strange thing to be doing with someone you've just met who knows a lot more about situations like this. But I know that Walt has probably been up every one of these trees. Multiple times. When he figures out what I'm trying to determine, he tells me that the group in the sycamore is different. They're called "the Lower Long-Field Group."

Could birds be flying back and forth between both trees?

"They shouldn't be."

Remembering my manners, I pass along greetings from several ornithologist friends who, when they heard I'd be joining Walt at Hastings, insisted on being remembered. Walt chuckles at hearing one name, and nods appreciatively hearing the other two.

We part, agreeing to connect soon. I tell him not to rush, assuring him that I'm being kept busy. He drives off, and I'm left with the feeling that I've just met a rock star. A humble rock star, if that's possible. But still, I've just met the Eric Clapton[13] of academic ornithology.

I return to my observation post, and notice two birds perched atop the dead oak on the ridgeline. Sighting them with my scope, I zoom all the way in. There, perching on adjacent twigs, both facing the direction of the sun, is an acorn woodpecker side by side with a western scrub-jay.

DAMN!!! That was the fabulous picture I knew I was going to miss. All because I wanted to write on a table this morning.

I pack everything up, slog it back to my pickup truck, and drive slowly[14] to the lab.

Back at the lab, when I relate my observations to Natasha, she says exactly what I expected her to say.

"That's unusual."

That's it. In summary, I interpret her viewpoint to be:

1. The birds are not following the rules.
2. Birds don't always follow the rules.

This is why I'd never make a good scientist. That and my inability to discern the color bands.

Natasha attempts to cheer me up by announcing that she'll be leaving the lab at 2:00 to set up an ambush. Would I like to assist?

I ask whether I get to be "ground crew." She smiles and nods. "Of course."

An "ambush" is a capture technique developed at Hastings. During the day, when birds are not occupying a cavity, a small plastic ball just large enough to block the entrance hole is rigged[15] on monofilament line so that, in the wee

---

13. This analogy may be a bit loose. For one thing, Walt Koenig looks a lot more like Kris Kristofferson, with a bit of Willy Nelson thrown in.

14. Although the speed limit on the reservation is fifteen miles per hour, if Vince catches you exceeding twenty, he makes you park your vehicle outside the gate. Permanently.

15. The rigging setup is a bit more sophisticated than I'm describing here. I'm purposely omitting a key detail of how the system is rigged in order not to encourage amateurs without permits to attempt captures on their own. Please understand that to do so would be a violation of the Migratory Bird Treaty, which protects all woodpeckers even though many woodpeckers are not migratory.

hours of the morning, while the woodpeckers are sleeping in their cavities, they can be trapped safely (and without stressing the birds) for banding purposes. This particular group, known affectionately as the "Road 1 Group due to its proximity to a road, currently comprises four individuals, one of whom is not banded. Banding the unbanded bird is the objective of this exercise.

Setting up this ambush is labor-intensive because Natasha has to recut the bottom door, which has grown shut since the last time this cavity was opened. She tells me that recutting a door is always more difficult than opening the hole initially. This tree has two active cavity holes, so she's having to rig an ambush device on both.

While she works we chat about the sort of community that is formed at a place like Hastings. Having lived here almost full time for the past four years—she returns home for two months in August and September—she confesses that "sometimes the social situation is trying." Part of it is that new research assistants tend to come along every six months, and every new batch changes the personality of the community. Although Natasha is only twenty-seven, she ends up being the "old lady" of the group, which contains a mix of grad students and undergraduates, a few of whom are still in their teens.

Natasha is keenly aware that her time at Hastings, at least for now, will soon come to an end. The moment has come for her to write up her dissertation, a project for which she already has more than enough data. She will be replaced next year by a postdoc, and that position has already been advertised. While she has her eye on a couple of interesting postdoctoral fellowships, she is mindful that academia has its dark side, and she isn't certain that she wants to spend the better part of the coming decade trying to earn tenure in a cutthroat environment. Part of me wants to assure her what a privilege it is to teach about your passion as part of a community of scholars, but I refrain. She needs to talk, and I need to listen.

Academia is a great system, but it's also a broken system, and nowhere is it more broken than in figuring out how to deal with a fourth-year PhD student. Natasha is a brilliant, hard-working, articulate, competent, highly educated, well-published individual who has absolutely no idea what's in store for her a year from now.[16]

Once the ambush mechanism is set up and functioning properly, Natasha ties the monofilament to a long spool of parachute cord, and then drops the spool straight down into the poison oak. It is now the ground crew's job to retrieve the spool and walk the line out to a clearing, tying it off to a tree on

16. Let me be clear that I don't consider this Natasha's fault, or Eric's fault, or even the fault of their university. The system, here, is at fault. And I'm part of that system.

the other side. I recall, suddenly, my first day on the job when Natasha told her major professor, "I'm swimming through poison for you, Eric." I also recall reflecting on that incident, writing, "You don't wade through a thick thatch of poison oak for a colleague."

Perhaps I was wrong. I grab the spool, wade through a thicket of poison oak, and then come back for the other spool.

My part in this ambush is finished as soon as I write it up in my field notes. Not so for Natasha. Tomorrow morning at 4:30, she will get up, dress hurriedly, return to the Road One site with her major professor serving as ground crew. They will trap two woodpeckers, one unbanded, and then she will climb the tree in the dark. She will sort through the sleeping woodpeckers to find one without bands, and band it. Then she'll rappel back down into the poison oak and call it a day as the sun rises. Even though it will be Saturday, it will be her third straight morning pulling off an ambush.

For me, however, tomorrow morning's ambush is already history. The moment I get back to the schoolhouse, I throw my clothes into the washing machine with some Dawn[17] dishwashing detergent, and then immediately jump into the shower, where I scrub down with the same detergent. Although it makes me unusually slippery, the Dawn was Natasha's suggestion, and I trust it explicitly.

June 26

No entry yesterday due to a conjugal visit. My wife came down from the Bay Area. We went into town—up to Jack's Peak, actually—to help an old friend celebrate his birthday, and had almost[18] nothing to do with birds for the greater part of the day. It was glorious.

We leave the schoolhouse early this morning to hike up Poison Oak Hill, hoping to complete the climb before things heat up too much. My wife, Carol,

17. For the record, let me state that I have not accepted a promotional fee from the makers of Dawn dishwashing soap. But those who live around toxic shrubbery should know that the local wisdom here at the Hastings Natural History Reservation is that Dawn works better than any other detergent at cutting urushiol, the oil found in poison oak. Similarly, those who rescue birds from oil spills swear that Dawn is far more effective than any other detergent. None other than NPR's "Morning Edition" has reported on this: "Why Dawn Is the Bird Cleaner of Choice in Oil Spills," June 22, 2010, http://www.npr.org/templates/story/story.php?storyId=127999735.

18. Actually, prior to the party we made a quick detour to Point Lobos State Park to observe the nesting Brandt's cormorants. So cute. While hiking out to Bird Rock we saw a pair of amorous peregrine falcons, perched on a nearby rock, with an agitated seascape in their nuptial background, and once again I didn't have my camera along.

brought along the amazing new binoculars I'd given her for her sixtieth birthday a couple weeks ago, and we plan to break them in magnificently, adding to the list of birds I've seen at Hastings this first week.[19]

Vince asked that we keep an eye out for a spring along the trail, and report back to him whether it's still flowing. We find it easily; although it's just a seep at this point, it's covered with dozens of California sisters, *Adelpha californica*. Puddling. They are not here because of thirst, but are rather using their tongues to extract minerals—salts and amino acids—from the damp soil. Carol puts up with me while I explain this as if she were one of my students. At least I don't charge tuition.

Other than being buggy and hot, the hike is magnificent. And deceptive. When we emerge into the higher-up zone where black oaks increasingly take the place of white oaks, I tell Carol that I think we are topping out. But it takes at least another mile of climbing to get where we are going, all the while anticipating that the summit of Poison Oak Hill will be just around the next bend. But the effort is worth the 360-degree view at the end—so many oaks in the valleys below! A dusty green, down there, that even a color-blind fellow can tell is a totally different green than if all those trees had been conifers. It's the dusty, windless, heat-distorted green of oak woodlands in California in June. And views like this are all the more spectacular when you've earned them by putting one foot in front of the other, regardless of the forecast.

The best part, considering that this is summer in California, is that we hike for more than three hours without ever encountering another human being. The downside of this is that I've had to break through dozens of spider webs that crisscrossed a trail that no one has ascended recently. A few times I see the webs in advance, and we can find a stick to take the web out. Or duck under it. But most of the time I didn't know the web is there until I've already walked through it. It's a good husband who takes the lead on a hike such as this.

We don't make it back to my pickup at the trailhead until 10:30. I'd left a spare liter of water in the bed in an insulated bottle. It's cooler than the water we'd carried with us, the greater part of which we'd finished during the hike. We both take a long chug out of the thermos, and then I pour what remains into the soaker hat and over my head. Glorious.

When we get back to the schoolhouse I check the online Hastings weather station, which reads 97 degrees Fahrenheit and 10 degrees relative humidity. Not exactly perfect hiking weather. We shower vigorously, scrubbing and scrubbing, as befits a couple who in June have summited a hill named after

---

19. We had been hoping to see mountain quail once we got high enough up the hill, but didn't luck out in that regard.

its most distinguishing ecological feature, poison oak. After an early lunch, as Carol drives off, her car's digital thermometer proclaims that it's now 101 degrees. Watching our little VW disappear around the bend, I am reminded of Edward Abbey's blessing, "May your trails be crooked, winding, dangerous, leading to the most amazing view."

Amen. Especially the part about the amazing view.

June 27
Monday of my second week on the reservation

I'm sitting in a blind as I write this, listening to a persistent drone coming from insects in the field behind me.

The greater part of my birding avocation has been structured around the avoidance of blinds. For example, there are two types of citizen scientists who make up the bulk of the Golden Gate Raptor Observatory.[20] Half are "band-ers," indoor birders, people who sit long hours in a cramped, uncomfortable, plywood blind on a predetermined schedule, regardless of forecast, hoping to capture raptors by dubious means so that they can attach a cheap piece of jewelry to their ankles. The birds' ankles. The other half, noble hawkwatchers, stand tall atop Hawk Hill while braving the elements, scanning the skies and the glorious horizon in order to commune with the avian gods themselves.

I, of course, belong to the latter group.

This morning I'm sitting in a blind. As I understand the protocol I'm not supposed to talk, stretch, listen to music, smoke cigars, or pleasure myself in any way. All in the name of science. When I signed up for this duty, the only question asked of me was "Did you bring a chair?"

Yes, I brought a chair.

I'm sitting in that chair now, waiting for a specific bird to come to a specific tree and vocalize. Yes. I'm not even supposed to take a pee until bird X, a breeding female, perches in tree Y, a granary tree. And I'm a tea drinker.

There are three blinds in this field. They only really need two blinds to conduct this experiment, but I'm along and they need to hide me for the sake of science.

We are determining how well acorn woodpeckers identify members of their own group by sound, and whether they can distinguish members of other groups by their vocalizations. We've set up a speaker forty meters from the granary tree, and have marked ten-meter increments with beribboned sticks.

20. We'll get there in chapter 3.

When the focal female perches in the granary tree, we'll play a recording of a wakka call from birds with whom she doesn't have a cooperative breeding relationship.

My blind reeks of insect repellent, someone else's insect repellent, but the mosquitoes are feeding on me nonetheless. I squirt on some of my own, a few dashes of pure DEET. It keeps them from landing, at least for now.

This particular woodpecker group, called the "Plaque Group," has been particularly uncooperative with our experiment. Emily, the research assistant who has spent more time in a blind this year than any of her peers, tells me they once went four days with the Plaque Group without being able to make the playback call. Emily is stationed on the other side of the field from us, and communicates quietly with Mickey via walkie-talkie. She controls the big microphone pointed at the granary; Mickey controls the playback speaker, and videotapes the entire experiment. Spotting scopes point upward out of both of their blinds, and from mine as well.

Presently, a purple finch perches where we want our subject to be. The focal female is perched in a neighboring tree, happy to let *Haemorhous purpureus* keep us locked up all day in these blinds. The finch is lovely, I suppose, although I've never seen the color after which it's named.[21]

My blind is close enough to Mickey's that I can eavesdrop on the walkie-talkie conversations. I'm not supposed to chat, but if I see the focal female alight in the granary, I'm free to volunteer that information in a whisper. This happens numerous times, and each time Mickey instructs Emily to begin recording, and then he initializes the playback. It plays background noise for thirty seconds before getting to the first wakka call, and if the focal female has already left the granary at that point, he aborts the playback. This happens at least a dozen times.

I've been warned that Emily and Mickey sat here for four hours yesterday morning without running a successful trial. This is the part of science that the general public rarely sees, the hours of tedium and monotony that one must endure to make valid observations.

The sunlight finally hits the top of the granary tree, and I check my watch. It's 7:00, straight up. People time. A covey of California quail scurries by— single file, full speed, each bird separated from the bird ahead by at least two meters—on the far side of the ravine below us. Their sharp calls back and forth tell a story about how close they are as a community. Pwitt, pwitt, pwitt.

---

21. The National Geographic Field Guide, incidentally, states that the purple finch is not really purple, but rather is rose-colored. Other field guides describe this color as "raspberry." If you think that's confusing, try being color-blind for a couple weeks.

28 *Nature beyond Solitude*

They regroup noisily in a willow, looking not unlike Christmas ornaments. Once everyone has been assured that everyone else is settled in, the pwitting subsides. Success!

7:30. A woodpecker flies to a lower branch, and by the time I can ID it as a male, Mickey has already read the color bands, identifying it as male no. 5153. I comment, sotto voce, on how fast he is, and he replies, quietly, that he spends so much time with these birds that he knows their band patterns by memory. He adds, as if amused by his ornithological excesses, that this is true for at least half the birds involved in his experiment. I suspect that this is a low estimate, instinctually realizing that I won't see him consulting a bird chart in the near future. I'm an academic; I know this sort of person.

Mickey becomes relatively talkative around 8:00, relating the saga of the two brothers we're currently watching, 5152 and 5153, both of whom are perched on a dead, upturned branch on the right side of the granary. For a year the former had been exiled from the group by the latter, consigned to languish alone on a utility pole. As the story unfolds, when the Plaque Group was abandoned by its helpers, who wanted to become breeders in a neighboring group, 5152 was permitted by his brother to return, and immediately took up duty feeding the nestlings for whom he was already an uncle.

This is the type of story that can only be told by long-term ecological research projects. These are the stories for which I've come to Hastings.

Finally, a little before 8:30, I spot the focal female lower in the granary than her usual perch. She is foraging for insects, and I have a difficult time directing Mickey to her spot in this giant oak. He finds her just as she begins swallowing— to me she almost seems to be choking. Mickey begins the playback immediately, almost forgetting to instruct Emily to start recording.

The focal female reacts visibly to the first wakka call coming from the hidden speaker. She is clearly on alert, clearly acting the sentinel. When the playback vocalizes a second strange wakka, a male appears at her side, and then she immediately flies toward the speaker tree to investigate.

Success!

The protocol of this experiment prohibits us from making a second playback at this site for forty-eight hours so as not to habituate the birds to the process. So we pack up the blinds, load all the gear into Little Dog, and head for a location known as the "Y Group." Even though the windows are open, when we crowd together in the pickup's tiny cab I am nearly overwhelmed by our collective toxicity. It's as if all three of us bathed in DEET this morning. Let the bugs beware.

For purposes of the study, the next granary tree is a stately, leaned-over sycamore that is actively defying gravity, and has successfully been doing so for centuries. The lower branches are all covered with long, flowing lace lichens, *Ramalina menziesii*, which, effective this year, has been designated the official lichen of California. The upper branches of the sycamore are adorned with the sky itself, which today is cloudless. California does not yet have an official sky, but if we did, this would be it.

We begin the second experiment at 9:15.

The soundscape is different here, no insect drone to speak of. My attention is drawn to a group of eight dark-eyed juncos foraging on the footpath just to the left of my blind. A male western bluebird lands, seemingly curious as to what sort of nourishment the juncos are finding. The bluebird hops along, almost comically, and I notice that there are colored bands on each leg. Fashionable Hastings jewelry.

In less than an hour—at 10:05—Mickey spots the focal female and initiates the playback procedure. Like the first time, the female perks up and begins actively scanning the surrounding trees. When the second wakka call is broadcast, a male alights just behind the focal female, just as had happened in the Plaque Group earlier. The entire group, even the fledglings, are in their alert sentry modes, and then several males leave the granary, searching for the intruder. The focal female stays put, for now.

We observe for the requisite ten minutes, and then for a while longer because the Y Group seems fairly upset by the prospect of intruders having come so close to their granary. Things are completely settled down within twenty minutes, however, and we once again pack up our gear.

While we pack, I mention to Mickey that during both the playbacks I observed a male come nearby the focal female, both times landing on the same branch. I ask whether this is mate-guarding behavior. Mickey is intrigued by the question because, while he has observed this phenomenon himself, he has never classified it as such. Now he wants to go back through the videos and determine the extent to which this happens. He thanks me for the insight.

When I trundle my gear down the hill to Little Dog, Emily comments that I've joined them on a good day. I tell her that I subscribe to an alternate narrative—that I've brought them luck. She doesn't know me well enough to realize that I'm joking. One should be careful about joking like this when one holds a teaching appointment.

We get an unscheduled one-hour break before heading to the third site because the video camera had shut itself down during the playback, and Mickey wants to rectify the problem before we proceed with another experiment. This is fine with both me and Emily—she needs to catch up with her data entry, and I need to transcribe these field notes.

12:30. We are back in the blinds a half hour into the afternoon, and my only shade is that which the blind itself provides. It stands to reason that during the morning experiments I was able to set up my blind in oak shade, but now that it's truly hot there's no shade that will provide me an adequate view of the granary tree, which in this case is another sycamore. We have a breeze, which is welcome, but the air being blown around by this breeze is somewhere in the upper 90s. It is becoming apparent that acorn woodpeckers do not choose their granaries with researcher comfort in mind.

1:00. I don't really see any birds flying around—at this point I'd settle for a phoebe. I'm told that it's unusual for acorn woodpeckers to stay away from a granary tree for more than fifteen minutes, but we've just gone a half hour, a hot half hour, without a single sighting. We hear them, over in a tree to the west, but apparently that doesn't count.

1:30. An hour has gone by now without a single ACWO sighting. And the breeze died. Somewhere out in the world, on this Monday, the British pound sterling is probably continuing its collapse as a result of the Brexit vote, the Trump campaign is probably continuing its tailspin,[22] and the Supreme Court is expected to announce its decision on the Texas abortion law. Meanwhile, Dr. Farnsworth continues to sit patiently watching a sycamore that has been abandoned by its woodpeckers.

At 1:50, finally, the focal female alights atop the granary tree; Mickey and I sight her simultaneously. Incredibly, the first woodpecker to visit the tree this afternoon is the one we're looking for! The playback is initiated immediately, and the results were equally immediate when the first intruder call is broadcast thirty seconds into the playback. The focal female, after a quick scan in the direction of the speaker tree, flew off in the direction where her group has been roosting. Immediately thereafter, two males and the focal female fly directly to the speaker tree, loudly making their own wakka calls. At the same moment, another female, who happens to be the focal female's mother, alights atop the granary tree in the precise spot where the focal female was perched at the start of our experiment. She spreads her wings out wide and makes her own wakka call: Mother is now in charge!

I'm no scientist, and it is not for me to make conclusions regarding Mickey's project. You'll never convince me, however, that acorn woodpeckers can't differentiate between their own calls and those of another group. While I will never be able to distinguish one woodpecker voice from another, it's just another day at the office for these birds.

---

22. Funny to read this in January, when I finally get around to editing, and realize how wrong I'd been about the prospect of a Trump presidency during the summer months.

By the time I get back to the schoolhouse it's all I can do to pour myself a glass of ice tea. It's only 2:30, but I count on my fingers to discover that I've just put in a nine-hour day. And I still have to transcribe my field notes. I shower first, not only to counteract poison oak but also to rid myself of all the DEET I'm wearing, and then transcribe away until 5:30. I don't need my fingers at that point to realize that I've just put in twelve hours.

Enough of this. I pour a cleansing ale into a frosty mug, and decide to work on my own tomorrow.

June 28
Farnsworth goes rogue

I've started my own project, of sorts. There has been some interest in determining whether there's enough difference in the facial topography of various birds to be able to distinguish them visually from each other. Someone had set up some nest cameras to take a series of photos of each bird emerging from that cavity, but the results had not produced useful photographs.

A few days ago, one of the research assistants noticed that I had a sophisticated camera outfit with a superzoom lens, and asked whether I could take profile shots of the woodpeckers where the leg bands would be identifiable. I told them I'd take a stab at it once I had some free time. So this morning, once the light was good, I spent an hour stalking the Plaque Group, which is the group most habituated to human presence since it's right here by the old barn. But after an hour, perhaps longer, I had no usable results. Indeed, my best shot turned out to be of an unbanded bird.

Part of the problem was that the birds spend the great majority of their time in the top third of the tree. This creates a photographic challenge; I was going to have to find a way to get up to their level, or a way to bring them down to mine.

Walt drives up just as I am pondering this quandary, and I ask him whether anyone has ever had luck enticing woodpeckers to a feeder. He replies that the results have been mixed. When researchers put out something such as dog food, the scrub-jays had always beat the woodpeckers to it. He suggests I try using acorns, and takes me into a building labeled "museum," which seems to function as Walt's storage shed. He uncovers two crates of acorns—one from valley oaks, the other from live oaks—and invites me to help myself.

Now I need a base for my acorn feeder, and after a bit of poking around the old barn I happen on an unsplit log about forty centimeters in diameter and about forty-five centimeters high. It would have made a great chopping block, but has the necessary characteristics for a serviceable bird feeder, especially since it is free.

I set up between two granary trees, level the feeder so that the acorns can't roll off, and then pace off twenty meters to the nearest shade, where I set up my camera on a tripod and unfold my camp chair. I forego the blind, hoping that the woodpeckers will habituate quickly to my presence, especially with so many delicious acorns sitting there.

Come and get it!

That was at least two hours ago, but I've had a pleasant morning—writing, reflecting, and waiting here in the shade. The woodpeckers seem to be waiting as well, and I'm hoping that they are not more patient than me. The certainly seem to be less hungry.

Meanwhile the work of the field station goes on around me. The director's son, who will be off to college in the fall, pressure washes the windows of the library to prepare them for painting. Kaija scoots off in a Mule, behelmeted. The bird-watching here behind the barn is spectacular; the bird-listening is even better. And the woodpeckers migrating back and forth between the two granary trees are quite entertaining, especially when a red-shouldered hawk flies near and is chased away by a squadron of them.

I move my chair back so that I'm now thirty meters away, figuring that it's worth the sacrifice of photographic resolution to actually get some photos. I don't give this new position ample time, however, because my stomach begins to rumble and this is the first time in days that I'm free to deal with the rumbles the moment they want to be dealt with.

The interlude back in the schoolhouse is a heavy one. I check in on my email while making a sandwich, and am informed that a member of the residential learning community I direct has just died in an automobile accident while in England.

I take the portable writing table out with me when I return to my post—the need to write is more acute than the desire to photograph woodpeckers. And perhaps I can do both.

The shade has moved in the interim, so I move with it, camp chair, tripod, camp table, and the rest of my kit. When I attempt to refocus my camera, the tripod needs to be lowered, as if I've grown shorter in the last hour. Perhaps I have. One of the trials of being a teacher is to survive some of your students. When twenty-one-year-olds don't get to become twenty-two-year-olds, the educational enterprise loses some of its meaning.

My time sitting in the meadow's gloom is cut short, mercifully, by Walt's current postdoc, Mario, who wants to meet me. He had just returned from a conference of conservation biologists that was keynoted by my colleague, Dr. Michelle Marvier, and when he discovers that I'm from SCU he wants to know whether I know her. My status elevates when I report that our offices are adjacent to each other, and that we've team taught together in Baja.[23]

My new friend studies scrub-jays and acorn dispersal, and spends a great deal of time on Santa Cruz Island, where I'm heading in a couple of weeks. He wants to hear all about my work while telling me everything about his work, but he's heading to Europe first thing tomorrow and there's simply no time. We exchange cards and I promise to read the paper he's about to publish. He makes a generous offer—that I can use his desk in the air-conditioned office he shares with Eric. I express my gratitude as I turn the offer down, explaining that my writing process is to write *in situ* whenever possible. And with that, he's gone. Such is the nature of field stations.

I return to my tasks with greater energy, and yet I feel that the outer world has somehow encroached on my sojourn here in the oaks. Although I've left an away-on-sabbatical auto reply on my e-mail, the outside world still seems to know that it can reach me with all its bustle and its cruel news. I can filter out the spam, but I'm stuck with the reality that there's an ecosystem beyond this reservation.

Every half hour or so I wander over to the minuscule library to soak my hat in its outside spigot. While moseying back this time I discover a short section of branch, no more than a foot long, riddled with acorn storage holes, all of which are empty. A mini granary. I pick it up, carry it over to my feeder, and install it on the side away from the camera. Perhaps this will plant a suggestion inside the heads of my woodpecker friends. It can't hurt at this point. And even if it doesn't promote the consumption of acorns, I enjoy the aesthetic when I peer through my viewfinder back at my post.

Five minutes later a woodpecker dives down from the uphill granary tree and swoops the feeder, no more than a meter above the acorns. It doesn't land. Was this a test? Have these poor critters been tricked so often by Hastings researchers that they've grown wary of handouts?

I hear nestlings above and behind me, and break out the binoculars for the first time today. Before I can remove the rainguards or objective covers, however, I hear a loud crack, and a stout branch crashes down. I can feel the thud through my boots, the way you can when you fell a large tree.

Eric heard it too, and we arrive at the crash site at the same time. He explains that valley oaks tend to drop branches when it's hot, and when we locate the spot where the crack originated, he points to a cavity tag inches away. Indeed, we are able to find the top half of a woodpecker cavity on the end of the fallen branch. Our feathered friends, it would seem, are complicit in this incident.

---

23. Indeed, Dr. Marvier is one of the real-life professors on whom I modeled Dr. Awesome in my previous book, *Coves of Departure: Field Notes from the Sea of Cortez.*

Although neither of them heard the crash, the station manager and the steward show up within minutes. They both take the incident in stride—a day in the lives of those who dwell in the shade of valley oaks.

"Oh well," says the station manager, "more firewood."

"I'm thinking that it's more suitable as campfire wood."

"Yup. That's the size to cut it up."

Before heading up the hill to fetch a Mule and a chainsaw, the steward, Jaime, apologizes to me for the noise he's about to make. He seems to understand writers.

As we disperse, Eric suggests I add some water to my feeder. We root around in the barn for a tray that belonged to some long-ago experiment. I wash it off in the library spigot, and my feeder now has a birdbath. How can they resist?

I return to my writing post and notice, for the first time today, the enormous branch directly above me, too large for me to encircle it with my arms. I consider my situation—this is a live oak after all—and then decide that the shade is worth the continued risk.

Once situated and recomposed, I wonder whether this loss of limb has in any way traumatized the Plaque woodpeckers. Do they contemplate their mortality in the wake of such events? Do they wonder what would have happened had anyone been inside that cavity?

Natasha shows up soon after the firewood has been hauled away. At first she is excited to hear the news, hoping that a branch she hates to climb is the one that fell. We walk up to the tree, but the despised branch is still there, looking deadly indeed. I point out the cavity where the branch broke off, and Natasha has a name for it: Sloth Face. She waxes poetic, or at least Shakespearean, and says, "Alas, poor Sloth Face, I knew it well."

On that note, I decide to call it a day, but I leave my feeder stocked with eight acorns, four from a valley oak, and four from a live oak. If any are missing tomorrow morning I won't know whether squirrels, jays, or woodpeckers made off with them, but my money is on the woodpeckers.

I bump into Mickey and Emily on my way "home," as I'm beginning to consider the schoolhouse. They spent the day up with the Haystack Group, far from the beaten path, and were unable to conduct a playback. They look hot. Mickey says, "We needed your luck."

June 29
Beyond solitude

I am reflective today, perhaps feeling the impending finality of my stay. Only three more nights—how do weeks pass so quickly?

I hardly seem connected to that world I so recently left. The day before I departed for the sabbatical I marched—yes, marched—in a velvet-trimmed doctoral robe at commencement. I had just posted my grades, and had cleaned up my desk to make space for my sabbatical replacement. I granted him access to my files—lecture notes, PowerPoints, group worksheets, exams—somewhat magnanimously. Although one should never appear to be too easy to replace, neither should one appear too difficult.

I couldn't wait to be done with the classroom, at least for the time being, because I anticipated this moment, this reflective interlude where time shifts gears and I'm once again feeling deeply connected with the world around me.

When I arrived at the Plaque Group's territory this morning, seven of the acorns were gone. The other had rolled off the stump. And the face flies were back.

I'm sure there is a more taxonomically appropriate name for these insipid members of the order Diptera. But the researchers here all call them "face flies" because that's where they always want to be—in your face. Sometimes they'll land high on your cheek and then crawl slowly toward your eye. Natasha says they want a drink of your tears.

I'm hatching a theory about acorn woodpeckers identifying each other visually that has nothing to do with their faces. I've noticed that almost every time a woodpecker flies from one tree to another within its territory, it announces its arrival with a short wakka call while spreading its wings wide. The wing is boldly patterned on each side, white and black. There's a moon-shaped white wing patch on the dorsal side. The ventral side is more complex, however. The primary feathers are black at the tip and white at the base, resulting in a somewhat square carpal patch, which of course is white. The white parts of the secondary feathers, however, extend almost to the end, and the tertials end with a white dot, looking like exclamation points. The underwing coverts have more of a mottled gray look, almost streaked, and the wing linings are patterned in black, looking as if the bird is wearing brocade. And the alulae are spotted, a row of white pearls on black.

Now it seems to me that if you're an acorn woodpecker and someone just landed on your tree, you're going to learn a lot more, a lot more quickly, by recognizing distinguishing markings in that dorsal underwing pattern than by looking at the incoming bird's face. Which is why, according to my almost-hatched theory, the newly arrived spread their wings while making the wakka call after landing in a tree where other birds are present. The wide-winged display may be an acorn woodpecker's way of announcing, "Hey guys, it's me."

Which means this whole project with the feeder, where I'm trying to determine photographically whether facial patterns are distinguishable, may be for naught.

Emily and Mickey walk by up the driveway on the other side of the Plaque Group's upper granary tree. They don't notice me, and I don't call out to them. While I'm eager to find out what Mickey thinks of this new theory, I haven't thought it through enough yet for a road test.

A bee hovers around my camera, searching for nectar. It takes the bee about ten seconds to figure out that digital cameras are not flowers, and then it buzzes off, still in pursuit of its original objective. We could learn a lot from the bees.

I've noticed a great deal of commerce centered on the stump of the granary tree branch that fell off yesterday—not only acorn woodpeckers, but oak titmice as well. I'm guessing that they are sapsucking, but it's possible that they're also interested in the tree's changed topography. Or maybe insects have gathered there?

I climb the hill on the far side of the granary, binoculars in hand, but looking back I can't discern insects or a flow of sap. A shame I didn't bring my spotting scope to work today, but the camera is borrowing the scope's tripod because I didn't bring a second tripod to Hastings. While I watch, a Nuttall's woodpecker lands on what's left of the Sloth Face cavity. She seems to be searching for insects, and doesn't seem to be finding anything of interest. I watch as she hops to another branch and then enters into a tagged cavity as if she owned the place. She pokes around for a bit, emerges, and continues to forage down the limb.

At least now we know that it wasn't insects. I can't help thinking that it might just be curiosity that brings all these birds to the Sloth Face break this morning. A very old, well-known tree has changed, and the bird community is familiarizing itself with its new landscape. Treescape.

It's already hot up here on the hill, but I am unperturbed by face flies. Carol and I noticed this during our hike up Poison Oak Hill—the face flies only bothered us in the shade, abandoning us whenever we stepped out into the heat of a meadow.

I retreat to the shade and the face flies. And my solitude.

I had been warned, both by Eric and Walt, that it could take weeks for the birds to warm up to my feeder. Despite its lack of early success, I'm enjoying the morning enormously. It's not just that the woodpeckers are good company—there's something primitive about what I'm doing, something that resonates with my ancestral past. I sit here as if waiting in ambush, mind clear and senses alert, an exercise in patience. This is how my forbearers made a living; the Farnsworth clan honed its hunting prowess back in the Pleistocene. Connecting with my paleo-history connects me with my humanity, especially in a world where our ability to pay attention is more and more disordered. As

I sit here under a live oak in a natural history reservation, I can't help thinking about the increasing number of ADD students I teach, a higher percentage of them every year. Their doctors write us notes that say they need to be given extra time on tests. What those kids really need to do is spend extra time in a duck blind. Without their iPhones. Those who don't want to shoot ducks, bless their souls, will be issued cameras with a cumbersome telephoto lens.

June 30
Oriole!

When I woke up this morning there were still a couple birds I wanted to see before leaving Hastings in a few days: the Bullock's oriole and the yellow-billed magpie. I was able to scratch the oriole off my list soon after breakfast, when a first-year male showed up in the granary tree I've been watching.

I would not object to coming back as an oriole in my next life. Eat lots of fruit, hang out in riparian areas in the summer, head down to Mexico in the winter. A good life. And all that yellow! I imagine that it would be hard to feel depressed when you're decked out in yellow feathers.

Walt stops by, and I ask him how abundant orioles are here. He nods his head and says, "I've had two PhD students do dissertations on them." I take this to mean that they're fairly abundant. Walt adds, "We used to lay out red yarn. The orioles love that stuff, and would weave it into their nests. It helped us locate the nests."

Walt and I arrange to get together later in the day for our long-overdue chat.

But not this morning. The reserve director, Vince, has been threatening to give me the grand tour ever since I arrived, and today is finally the day. We fill our water bottles, check to make certain the Mule has plenty of gas, and then we're off, with Vince saying, "I hope you're ready to be out for a few hours."

I am. I've even brought water.

First he takes me up a grassy hill topped with a weather station tower. This panorama is the tour preview. From here we can see where the huge adjacent ranches begin, and what properties have been added to the original Hastings ranch. Vince details how the physical plant developed, from the original homestead cabin—still standing and now known as the "Woodpecker Shed"—to the various research facilities. He tells me about the original research, which was all conducted by Stanford faculty, but how when the reservation was ultimately offered to Stanford, they didn't want it. Instead, Mr. Hastings spoke with Joseph Grinnell, founding director of the Museum of Vertebrate Zoology at UC Berkeley. Grinnell's vision was to take a large tract of land that had been heavily impacted by humans, remove the sources of impact such as cattle grazing or timber harvesting, and then monitor the land closely as it recovers. That, in essence, has been the reservation's story ever since.

As we travel the back roads, Vince narrates the rich history of this place, and the Mule bounces us as much through time as through the landscape. We stop at an ancient, abandoned tin-roofed cabin built near springs that stopped running after the Loma Prieta earthquake. We traverse a thickly wooded hillside that has not burned in recorded history. We transect research sites scattered here and there—as we blast past one of them, Vince says, "The mouse people work down in that ravine." The mouse people!

Maintaining so many historical buildings stresses the reservation's budget. Vince complains about the far-away university administration being more of a hindrance then a help in this regard, and that the folks up in Berkeley no longer seem to understand this project. He worries about what will happen in the future, especially if the founding Hastings and Arnolds families are no longer able to assist as benefactors. The problem, it seems, is that too few people appreciate this sort of large, long-term ecological laboratory. The other problem, it goes without saying, is that this sort of research doesn't come cheap.

The tour ends all too soon.

According to the weather station I visited earlier, it's only 90 degrees when Walt and I enter his office. He flicks on the air conditioner, and is momentarily distracted by a large package that someone has left on his desk. It's his new boots, calf high, and he opens them to show me what a proper pair of Hastings boots looks like. "They're good for climbing too." He doesn't have to specify that he's referencing tree climbing rather than mountain climbing. Although Walt will officially retire a few days from now, his tree-climbing days are not over.

He asks how the chapter is coming, and I tell him that I have seventeen thousand words of transcribed field notes. The word count doesn't seem to make an impression, so I add, "That's just short of sixty pages," and he nods appreciatively. Walt has authored or coauthored four books, 206 technical articles, twenty-eight general articles, nineteen book reviews, and four obituaries. He appreciates productivity.

Moving us from small talk to whatever's next, I tell Walt that what got me interested in writing about his work was a paper he and Eric published a few years ago, "What We Don't Know, and What Needs to Be Known, about the Cooperatively Breeding Acorn Woodpecker *Melanerpes formicivorus.*"[24]

I ask what he most valued about long-term ecological studies, and without batting an eye he says, "Long-term studies give you a chance to change your mind." He spins his chair around to the computer behind him, and begins searching for a particular set of photographs, saying, "Let me show you two photographs from the schoolhouse." It takes him a while to find the photos. The first is black and white, a photo taken during the 1930s after the schoolhouse had stopped functioning as a boarding school and was instead functioning as the local public school. The photo is taken from the perspective of a plowed field, and the schoolhouse looks somehow lonely, but I can't figure out why.

"Now let me show you a recent photo taken from the same spot."

He pulls up a recent photo, in full color, of a thick grove of oak trees. The grove is so thick that it completely hides the schoolhouse. Only by lining up the hills in the background can you tell that the photo was taken from the same vantage point.

Walt explains that even though he lived in the schoolhouse from 1982 to 2008, he never noticed the oaks filling in the neighborhood. From one day to the next, there wasn't a sufficient amount of change to register in his consciousness. "Things happen gradually, and humans aren't geared to see that way."

Walt tells me that when he first started conducting research with the local population of acorn woodpeckers, there were only six groups in this valley. He rattles off their names as if it were yesterday. Of course, many of these groups, such as the Plaque Group I've befriended, are still in business.

"Now there are so many groups that I could never name them all without my field notes." Without opening his notes, he recites a dozen names of new groups that have established themselves during his time studying them here, and then asks me to guess why there are all those new groups.

"More oaks?"

"Not only that—the trees are older."

---

24. If you enjoy reading scientific papers, I recommend this one highly. The authors came up with a list of twelve questions that still puzzled them after all those years of studying acorn woodpeckers, starting with why the dark eyes of fledglings gradually fade to the white eye color of adults, and ending with why breeding females nest jointly. The one question I found particularly interesting was why acorn woodpeckers seem to be hiding their mating activities. In forty-five years of close observation at the Hastings Reservation, no researcher has ever witnessed acorn woodpeckers copulating. Koenig and Walters want answers about this.

Of course.

There's a short lull in the conversation, and so I tell him about my new theory, mentioning how the woodpeckers display their wings, stretching them wide while making a wakka call, when they land after coming from another tree. I ask whether he thinks the woodpeckers can identify themselves by the ventral view of their wings.

He laughs. "Heck if I know! Somebody ought to study those birds."

I laugh too. And then I ask how long he'll continue to study them.

He frowns at this point, and insists that woodpeckers are "too much trouble." He tells me that he's happy to leave the woodpecker studies in Eric's hands, but then goes on to say that he's still got funding for his oak studies, and that "I'll keep counting acorns until I can't remember how to do it."[25]

I ask whether it's hard to walk away from the woodpecker studies. He looks up at the ceiling and replies, "We used to have hundred-bird parties. In other words, every time we'd banded another hundred birds, we'd throw ourselves a party. After that, we started having thousand-bird parties." He predicts that the next thousand-bird party, which will mean that there are six thousand birds in their database, won't take place for a couple more years.[26]

His response doesn't really answer my question, and I decide not to press it. Of course it must be hard to walk away from decades of work. Why ask?

We chat a bit about the Hastings Reservation, and I ask whether he shares the same concerns that Vince brought up during our tour this morning. He does, but he's also concerned about other things, such as whether Eric will be able to continue to receive funding from the National Science Foundation to continue the woodpecker studies. If that doesn't happen, it could put the reservation in a grim fix, financially. He concludes by telling me that he loves Hastings, something that doesn't really need to be said.

I change the subject, telling him that I haven't yet seen a yellow-billed magpie.[27]

Walt tells me that they used to study the magpies here, which I knew. He says that he banded all the magpies on the reservation when he first started working here, which I didn't know. He insists that the magpies always seemed

25. The day prior to this interview, Walt had affixed decals to the front doors of his minivan that say, "California Acorn Survey Official Vehicle."

26. He is wrong on this point. The current count is at 5,975. While there may not be twenty-five more woodpeckers banded this season, the goal will easily be achieved next spring. I've asked to be invited to the party.

27. A drawing of the yellow-billed magpie, *Pica nuttalli*, serves as the Hastings Reserve icon, and can be seen on the doors of all the pickup trucks. The bird itself, however, no longer breeds on the reservation. A creature of the oak savannah, this magpie is endemic to California.

to be in decline, here at Hastings, but that the local population suffered two major hits from which they haven't recovered. First, Walt says with a frown, "the rancher next door ten-eightied his ranch." He refers here to the rodenticide called "1080,"[28] which was applied by cattle ranchers to control ground squirrels. The second hit, according to Walt, was when West Nile Virus came to California in 2004. It killed as many as ninety thousand yellow-billed magpies, which was estimated to be half the population at that time. According to the North American Breeding Bird Survey, there has been a cumulative decline in the yellow-billed magpie population of 73 percent since 1966.

"The West Nile Virus hit crows pretty hard too," Walk explains, "but they came back. We don't really know why the magpies aren't rebounding as well."

July 1
Mourning, once again, the end of my favorite month

A friend in the political science department back home forwards an article of environmental interest about once a week. I'm one of forty-nine colleagues on his list, most of them dear friends. This morning's e-mail brings us a *New York Times* article by Michael Shellenberger, "How Not to Deal with Climate Change." I peruse the article. In a nutshell, Shellenberger is against the recent decision to close the Diablo Canyon Nuclear Power Plant here in California.

I try to convince myself that I don't really have a horse in this race, but the world seems to be tugging me back, and I can feel myself resisting as I sit here enjoying the morning coolness of a country schoolhouse built before my parents were born.

I find a house spider in the bowl I'm planning to fill with cereal. It sits there placidly, seemingly unconcerned about nuclear power plants. Still clad in my skivvies, I carry the bowl outside and introduce the spider to the great outdoors. There are no wild turkeys out here this morning, nor is the resident phoebe anywhere to be seen. If there was a dawn chorus, I've missed it. A chipmunk scurries away as I return indoors.

Today is my last full day here at Hastings. There's nothing really on my schedule other than a birthday party this evening for one of Eric's two boys, who turns eight today. They've come here as a family, and I think it's absolutely

---

28. Sodium fluoroacetate, commonly known by its catalog number, was banned it 1972 by executive order of President Nixon. During the Reagan years, however, the ban was lifted, and the results were often catastrophic for scavengers that might feed on the dead or dying squirrels, including coyotes, eagles, and yellow-billed magpies.

marvelous to have kids around. Their mother teaches a college course back in Virginia every fall, and then homeschools the boys here at Hastings every spring.

More than a decade ago, Shellenberger coauthored a provocative polemic on the death of environmentalism. The basic thesis was that modern environmentalism is no longer capable of dealing with the ecological crisis. Part of their critique is that environmentalists tend to consider the environment as a "thing." Something we need to protect. In other words, the environment is something "out there" that needs to be fixed.

This is the message the house spider wanted to send me this morning. The environment is not just the oak grove on the other side of my windows. It's also the inside of my cereal bowl. It's everything that goes into my cereal bowl: oat flakes, raisins, nonfat milk, house spiders. It's not just the energy that went into manufacturing and transporting my bowl; it's the resources I'll consume in order to wash it in a little while, and what happens to the soapy water after I rinse it.

While Dr. Farnsworth wants everyone to consider the marvelous oak groves here at the Hastings Natural History Reservation, and the habitat they create for so many wonderful critters, Ms. Spider wants everyone to contemplate the cereal bowl, which a moment ago served as her habitat.

A California towhee flies up against the window directly behind my computer. It pecks at something, twice, wings flapping all the time, and then turns, landing on the clothesline three meters away from the window. There's something buggy in its beak, but I can't tell whether it is an insect or a spider, just that it has legs. Had legs. The towhee gulps, and the legs disappear.

For a moment, I consider ending the chapter right here and driving home a day early, but skipping tonight's party would keep me from saying proper goodbyes to the community. That wouldn't feel right, so I decide to shift gears from writer to photographer and spend the day decompressing with woodpeckers.

I began to stroll, one foot after another, without any real destination in mind. No binoculars, scope, chair, et cetera. No daypack. Just me, the camera, and my soaker hat. After two intense weeks of writing, it feels good not to be in writing mode—nice to have an afternoon to waste.

The hat dries out all too soon, but I am near the new barn and there is a spigot I know of there. At this point I suspect that I know the whereabouts of every freestanding outdoor spigot on this ranch. As I approach, I notice several woodpeckers sitting atop fence posts, apparently lazing away the afternoon, just like me. I decide to pursue them photographically, with freshly wetted hat, and I end up spending a few hours with them. It's fun just to click the shutter release without having to record field notes.

I get some great shots of two birds sharing a fencepost, but the point comes when the members of this woodpecker family need to get back to work. I watch as the three birds I'd been spending time with congregate on a black locust, and then one disappears through a cavity opening.

A nest? Have I just discovered an active nest that the researchers did not know about?

The woodpecker pokes its head out of the hole. I take a dozen shots, bracketing the exposures, and then head back to the schoolhouse to start packing.

A couple hours later, I take my camera to the birthday party, having switched to a shorter lens that might work with humans. I show the photos to Natasha, and she agrees that the cavity is worth exploring—at least scoping.

July 2
Postscript

I departed the reservation early this morning after having given my studio a good scrubbing. I stopped by the lab on my way out, but Natasha had not yet gotten down to the locust tree. When I arrived home a few hours later, an e-mail awaited. It turned out that the cavity I'd photographed was indeed an active nest, and the woodpeckers turned out to be pretty feisty, actually attacking the scope. I would like to have seen that.

The group, by the way, is called "Knoll." To me, however, they'll always be "Fencepost."

Hastings bird list, June

Red-shouldered hawk
Red-tailed hawk
Cooper's hawk
Turkey vulture
American crow
Steller's jay
Western scrub-jay
Acorn woodpecker
Downy woodpecker
Nuttall's woodpecker
Northern flicker

White-breasted nuthatch
Oak titmouse
Wrentit
Bushtit
Blue-gray gnatcatcher
Ash-throated flycatcher
Black phoebe
Western bluebird
Bullock's oriole
Lesser goldfinch
Purple finch
Hermit thrush
American robin
Lazuli bunting
Spotted towhee
California towhee
Chipping sparrow
Dark-eyed junco
Warbling vireo
Wild turkey
California quail
Mourning dove
Anna's hummingbird
Chestnut-backed chickadee
Bewick's wren
Black-headed grosbeak
Orange-crowned warbler
Black-throated gray warbler
Warbling vireo

2

Notes from the Santa Cruz Island Reserve

You could spend a lifetime studying a hedgerow, or a pond.

ROGER DEAKIN, *Notes from Walnut Tree Pond,* 2009

July 6

I get to the dock early, but prior to my arrival eighty-five Ventura Junior Life-guards have already queued up along the main pier. Three encaged harbor seal pups are waiting dockside as well; the young pinnipeds exhibit more sang-froid than their escorts, a team from the Fort McArthur Marine Mammal Care Center, who seem concerned that junior lifeguards might take interest if they notice the seals. The lifeguards and the escorts are only going out to the island for the day; the seals and I have other plans.

I have been careful to follow the rules. I'm limited to sixty pounds[1] of per-sonal and/or research gear, plus ten pounds per day food allowance. That gives me 170 pounds, not counting a corpulent daypack that carries camera, com-puter, binoculars, a just-published hardback, and my journal. But no piece of luggage can weigh more than forty-five pounds. And no cardboard is allowed

1. Sincere apologies here for jumping back and forth between the metric and imperial systems, but this seems to be the story of my life. In the original field notes I went with sixty pounds, which is a bit more than twenty-seven kilos, because the weight limit was thus imposed, imperially.

on the island. I've got four pieces of "luggage" in the form of a cooler and three plastic tubs, each weighing forty-two pounds. Exactly. And if I've forgotten anything, I'll have to do without it until July 16.

I'm wearing my new boots, which were far too heavy to pack. I've brushed them out carefully, per instructions, so that I'm not transporting any seeds from Hastings.

I stack the tubs atop the cooler on a hand dolly, and roll toward the dock, ready to be weighed. Two scraggly backpackers, weighed down with water containers, have formed a line. When the attendant sees that I'm obviously a researcher going to the field station, he waives me along to the far catamaran—no need for college professors to stop at the scales. I realize, to the dismay of my persistent thirst, that it had not been necessary to limit myself to a one-pint-per-day ration of beer.

A thick marine layer blankets the southern California coast, and we run into a medium swell. Although Independence Day has already come and gone, the infamous June gloom is still here. One of the junior lifeguards sitting near me on the upper deck announces loudly to his companions that they should go downstairs to the bow and "get splashed." They hustle away, thee brave boys on a mission, only to return, five minutes later, drenched. Two of the three change into dry sweatshirts. I'm guessing that their mothers must have anticipated this scenario. What a shame the third fellow was born into a family where a single hoodie was considered sufficient to get a lifeguard through the day!

I watch as hundreds of low-flying sooty shearwaters pass us by—stern to bow, off the port side—all within half a meter of the water's blue-gray surface. They blend in as if a permanent feature of the seascape, their stiff, narrow wings outstretched in a posture unique to the procellariid family of the tubenose order, which includes the fulmars and the petrels as well. A fellow in a windbreaker that identifies him as a member of the Channel Island Naturalist Corps joins me at the upper deck rail, and tells me that there are more sooty shearwaters on this earth than any other bird. Bar none. It has recently been estimated, he adds, that there are 20 million of these birds worldwide.[2]

When I tell him that I did not know that, he mentions that their annual migration is "forty thousand miles." I knew this, of course, but I keep my casual familiarity with shearwater natural history a secret just in case our voyage ends up taking longer than it's supposed to.

---

2. While I've been able to corroborate this estimate of the worldwide population of sooty shearwaters, 20 million would not qualify as the greatest number of birds of any species worldwide. For example, the North American population of dark-eyed juncos is estimated at 630 million birds.

Sure enough, the boat slows, and the captain urges everyone to the bow to view a herd of common dolphins. The junior lifeguards stampede forward, squealing with delight at the spectacle ahead even before they've witnessed it. It turns out to be spectacular, nevertheless. I estimate the herd size to be around 750 animals, while the first mate estimates it at six hundred. There are several humpback whales around as well, apparently feeding on whatever prey the dolphins and shearwaters are enjoying. I count three whales, the mate counts four.

The dolphins streak in two by two to play briefly in our bow wave before it's someone else's turn. I've spent dozens of hours watching this performance from the bows of dozens of boats, and still have not discerned precisely what the rules of the game are. It's good to hear the joy of the junior lifeguards, many of whom are watching the play of dolphins for the first time. Their joy reminds me of what my joy should resemble. I recall the first time I encountered a large herd of common dolphins off the entrance to Monterey Bay. What bliss! We'd been whale watching, Carol and I, in a new boat, but when the dolphins showed up we decided that dolphin watching was a superior activity, at least for the time being.

We circle around for a good ten minutes before the engines finally rev and our voyage continues. Chagrin is expressed by the junior lifeguards as with a single voice, "Awwwwwwwww." The mate, on the intercom, reminds us all that this is a transit, not a whale-watching charter.

The reserve director, Dr. Lyndal Laughrin, had arranged to pick me up at the Prisoner's Harbor dock, but the steward from The Nature Conservancy is there instead. Lyndal, who has a cold, has to be somewhere else this afternoon, but will try to catch up with me this evening if he's feeling better. In the meantime, I've been assigned Room 4, one of the private rooms, and I'm free to move in.

We pass through a massive gate, well marked to keep out trespassers, that demarcates the lower third of the island, which is part of Channel Islands National Park, from the upper two-thirds that are controlled by The Nature Conservancy. To open this gate one has to be TNC staff, or one of the many ecologists working on restoration projects here, or someone such as myself with a permit to conduct research through the UC Santa Barbara field station, or faculty of one of the classes being taught at the field station. The restricted part of the island is nicely underpopulated: free of backpackers, lifeguards, and ne'er-do-wells.

It's a long, rocky, but riparian road to the field station, long enough that it's easy to forget we're on an island. We pass thrice through axle-high running water. Great swaths of the valley floor are covered with invasive fennel, a yellow-topped member of the carrot family that grows thick in clusters taller than me. The steward tells me that it has taken over almost all of the land that was previously tilled for agriculture.

We emerge from the riparian zone into the island's main valley, and drive past the original ranch buildings, many of which are exquisitely built of bricks that were molded and fired on site. The brick winery, a brick chapel, and a brick stallion barn, together with freshly painted wood-framed houses, shearing sheds, barns, and outbuildings, create the impression that time has been suspended on this ranch. After this, the field station comes as an architectural disappointment. Plywood, mostly, thrown together by work crews with orders to build expeditiously.

On arrival, the first call I hear is the wakka-wakka of an acorn woodpecker, almost as if a spokesbird for the species wants me to know that although I've departed the mainland, I haven't been abandoned by *Melanerpes formicivorus*. Feeling strangely at home in this anomalous place, I locate Room 4, which is much smaller than my previous studio and lacks the historical gravitas to which I grew accustomed during my days in the Hastings schoolhouse. While I will enjoy being in a queen-sized bed this time rather than a lower bunk, I will not enjoy having my own kitchen and bathroom such as I had previously. I check for a cell-phone signal—I've been warned that a local system has been installed but that it only works within a hundred meters of the main office. Room 4 is close enough, it would seem. I text my wife the news of my arrival.

Two researchers show up in a white pickup truck. They are female, they are energetic, and they are quite dusty. They are here to shower and to resupply, in that order. We introduce ourselves, not by university affiliation by rather by our respective projects: they investigate intertidal invertebrate colonization as part of a study that goes back to the 1990s. They are returning from a site they visited at 5:00 this morning, and are eager to be off to the showers. By the time I unpack my food supplies and make lunch of ham and cheese rolled up in a flour tortilla, they return, hair still wet. They grab a frying pan and some cutlery, toss some food into a cooler, toss the cooler into the truck bed, and are off, intending to camp out at their next site tonight so they don't have to leave at 3:00 in the morning to get there in time. The tide waits for no woman. They tell me they'll return this time tomorrow, and they warn me not to leave sandals outside my room, or anything else, because the foxes will steal them.

As they depart I see my first island fox, which trots along smartly around the corner, one building over. It sees that I see it, and lies flat, its ears back. I've seen bobcats do this in the wild, with mixed success, as if they really believe they can become invisible. I wonder whether this tiny fox realizes that I'm new to the station.

I have been reading up on these island foxes, and I know that the Santa Cruz Island subspecies, *Urocyon littoralis santacruzae*, is the most diminutive of the six extant subspecies. Still, I had not expected this degree of insular dwarfism. The fox across from me is smaller than a house cat.[3] They say that adult island foxes will weigh four pounds, but I cannot imagine this one tipping the scales much beyond three.

It actually seems to shrink, lying there, as I watch. Has it flattened itself more over time? After I've stared at it for a full minute, I make a single sharp kissing noise, at which point its ears perk up. Gotcha. Even though the fox realizes that its invisibility scheme has not worked this time, it holds its position. It seems to want to learn about me as much as I want to learn about it. But what I really want at this moment is to take its portrait. I head to Room 4 to get my camera, but when I return the fox has vanished—this time successfully.

My new friend belongs to the same genus as the gray fox over on the mainland, but through the process of adapting to the limited food resources on an island, it has evolved to be a much smaller critter. The theory is that smaller animals can make do with smaller territories, especially during periods of food scarcity. Island foxes stand no more than five inches at the shoulder, and their tails are two vertebrae shorter than those of their gray fox ancestors. It is easy to see how golden eagles could have preyed on them, back in the days when *Aquila chrysaetos* terrorized this island. A golden eagle would easily be four times the size of a Santa Cruz Island fox.

Island foxes are among the cutest mammals on the planet. I'm told that they have gray fur on their heads—it seems bluish to me—and that their sides are a ruddy red. The belly is white. Lacking natural predators, they tend not to find humans intimidating, indeed appearing tame even though they are technically wild. I have been told that they will approach to within three or four meters if I sit quietly outside the field station at dusk. I plan to spend a lot of time sitting quietly outside at dusk.

The island fox is currently on the rebound from endangered status. There were two thousand foxes on Santa Cruz Island in 1994, but canine distemper and golden eagle predation reduced the numbers to under 135 by 2000. A stable population of one hundred animals was left in the field while a captive breeding program was initiated with twenty-five foxes. The population hit a low of fifty-five, and as recently as 2004 it was estimated that there was a 50 percent chance that the island fox would go extinct within a decade. That didn't happen, of course, and the current population on this island is estimated at 2,100. In short, the fox I just saw is one of conservation's biggest success stories even though the population is still reliant on conservation efforts. A month ago, at a meeting of the Island Fox Working Group, we'd all reminded

---

3. My previous cat, Scupper, may he rest in peace, tipped the scales at twelve pounds.

each other of the need to remain vigilant. On an island like this, things can go horribly wrong in a heartbeat.

Or horribly right. This field station changes its complexion in a heartbeat. I go from feeling I have the whole place to myself to, quite suddenly, sharing it with two faculty, three grad students, and twenty-two undergraduates from the University of California system. They are engaged in a course on California ecology known as the Natural Reserve System Field Course. The course is open to students from all the UC campuses, and has been characterized as "fifty days of nonstop nature." They've returned to the field station just long enough to shatter my midafternoon solitude—I had just taken a writing break to observe a trio of ash-throated flycatchers. The young naturalists expeditiously use the restrooms, refill water bottles, and demolish a two-pound bag of tortilla chips. Then the whole assemblage blasts off in three pickup trucks, students in the back, to go tide-pooling. Low tide has been scheduled for 5:00 this afternoon.[4]

How I wish there had been something like that when I was in college! A shame to have gone through school in an era when people thought of education as a thing that took place while students sat in rows of desks. Straight rows.

I spend the afternoon writing, unpacking, poking around the library, and attempting to fit my literary aspirations into the space that has been provided. During the hottest part of the afternoon I conduct a quick survey of butterflies in the field below the field station office, but the closest thing I see to a butterfly is a variegated meadowhawk, a dragonfly. This dearth of Lepidoptera seems strange, and yet I have much to learn about this ecosystem.

As afternoon turns to evening the temperature drops and the class returns. One of the faculty who runs this class "meets" me, or maybe not. We both have a strong impression that we've met previously, recently, but neither of us can figure out where, because it wasn't at the island fox meeting in early June. We run through the possibilities: we were both in the UK about a year ago, but I was in Scotland while he was in London. Was it Mexico? Were you at an AASHE conference in Minneapolis? A Christmas bird count in Point Reyes? What did you do last summer? Finally, his fiancée joins the conversation, and I recognize her the moment she recognizes me. Last December, I had run a two-day workshop for the University of California system at the Sedgwick Reserve in the Santa Ynes Valley, where she made one of the presentations. He had accompanied her to Sedgwick, just as Carol had accompanied me, but neither significant other had participated in the workshop other than for the dinner

4. We have mixed semidiurnal tides along the Pacific coast of California, with two highs and two lows of different heights every lunar day.

and social the first night, at which time the four of us had enjoyed each others' company.

The more time I spend in these reserves, the smaller my world gets. And that's a good thing, because it speaks of a growing ecological community. We might not all know each other, but we all know people we all know.

July 7

The dawn chorus here on the island surprises me. I was expecting a concerto dominated by song sparrows, which I've seen in abundance here at the field station. Instead what I hear are ash-throated flycatchers, at least a dozen of them, and little else. The bird checklist I got from the National Park Service lists them as rare summer residents on Santa Cruz Island, but they are certainly abundant in this valley.

I step out of Room 4 at sunrise, eager to get my topographic bearings. I keep having to remind myself that I'm on an island, since the steep hills lining the valley block out ocean views entirely. I soon become convinced that, other than me, the only things up at sunrise hereabouts are island scrub-jays, acorn woodpeckers, ash-throated flycatchers, and a solitary island fox that seems to want to keep its distance. I'm not getting full-throated biodiversity here, not on this walk. This, perhaps, is the strongest indicator that I'm on an island. I caution myself not to be disappointed. And I remind myself of how hard these Channel Islands have been hit by the current drought. It's much worse down here than what I experienced in Carmel Valley a week ago.

I have breakfast with Dr. Kathryn McEachern, a botanist with the United States Geological Survey who lives in Ventura. She speaks softly with the remnants of a Tennessee accent. She is here surveying an endangered plant, Hoffmann's rock cress, *Boechera hoffmannii*, endemic to at least two of these Channel Islands and listed as an endangered species.[5] It's a short-lived perennial that is partial to rock outcroppings in the shade of oaks but will also live in chaparral. Today there are fewer than two thousand of these plants alive, anywhere, and half of those are part of outplanting experiments conducted by Kathryn. She's here at the field station, with family and friends who are functioning as additional research assistants, to resurvey the outplantings and determine how many are surviving, although she points out that the plants they're looking at this week are the "great-grandchildren" of the vegetation she actually planted.

---

5. In 2005, it was estimated that there were only 244 individual plants worldwide.

I ask her how the restored plants are doing as a general rule, and she answers almost plaintively that the drought is taking its toll. As the oak canopy thins out, leaf litter and dropped branches are making it difficult for the rock cress seeds to germinate. Kathryn tells me that the seeds are too small and the leaf litter is too thick. The good news, however, is that the specimens in her outplantings are doing as well as plants in their native locations. *Boechera hoffmannii* is a bit less endangered now than it was a few years ago.

As far as the world of plants is concerned, Kathryn is hopeful when it comes to the future of Santa Cruz Island. She has been here long enough to witness the changes to the vegetation since the removal of grazing animals, and she asserts that the speed with which the ecosystem recovers blows her mind. Given half a chance, nature is once again proving that it can do the heavy lifting of ecosystem restoration once domesticated animals stop functioning as keystone species.

It's not all good news, of course. The fennel went wild after the removal of the grazing animals. Ungulates kept it in check, relatively speaking, and now it flourishes, even in drought conditions. Kathryn tells me that it seems to be able to self-irrigate by drawing moisture from the fog, using its fine filaments to help droplets condense.

I hear song sparrows singing, finally. The time has come for a midmorning stroll. Since I've just been writing about fennel, I decide to spend some time with it. The field below me was mowed, probably at the end of the rainy season. The fennel is rebounding stealthily in the mowed area, unlike most of the grasses, and when I come to the edges of the mowed sections it springs up well over my head, perhaps ten feet tall. Each stalk is topped by spreading umbral of dull yellow flowers, an inflorescence typical of the carrot family, apiaceae. Its leaves are similarly carrot-like, almost feathery in texture. I look for pollinators and see nothing more than yellow jackets and hoverflies. I realize, once I've walked through fifty meters of flowering fennel, that I've not seen a single butterfly.

Nor have I seen a single raptor yet during my time on the island.

I continue my walk, my eyes to the ridgelines at this point. Yesterday evening, when I finally caught up with the reserve director, I mentioned that I wasn't seeing any raptors. He insisted that they should be around, especially red-tails. The unasked question was whether I was missing them, but the author of these field notes doesn't miss hawks.

This late in the morning I should be seeing raptor activity in a valley this big. From my present vantage point I can see a mile of ridge in every direction on each side of the valley, but I'm not seeing a single red-tail. I make a mental note of this before returning my focus to butterflies, and once I get back to

Room 4 I look up the red-tailed hawk on the checklist for this island, where it's listed as an uncommon permanent resident—basically the same rating that has been given the bald eagle. This particular checklist defines "uncommon" in the typical way: while it's present in small numbers in suitable habitat, it is not certain to be seen on any particular day.

Strange, to go a couple days without sighting North America's most common hawk.

There is an extensive insect collection in one of the labs near Room 4, and I visit it to find out what sort of butterflies I should be seeing hereabouts. The specimen drawers are enclosed in two side-by-side vaults, and I search the first vault in its entirety before discovering that Lepidoptera are located in the second. For some reason, the second vault smells much more strongly of mothballs than the first did, but I push on regardless, wondering how long it's been since someone investigated this collection. When I finally pull out the main drawer of butterflies, I discover that I should be seeing many of the same species I was seeing at the Hastings reserve: anise swallowtails, monarchs, California sisters, common buckeyes, painted ladies, red admirals, variable checkerspots, et cetera.

I resolve to keep my eyes peeled in this matter, especially for the anise swallowtail, for whom fennel should serve as a larval host plant.

Shortly after lunch, the field station becomes a cloud of dust. The students have returned from their final outing, and all are in the process of packing, scouring, sweeping, mopping, and rolling up tents. They have it down to a science at this point; this is the penultimate stop in their fifty-day learning adventure. All that's left, at the next field station, is to execute a research project and write it up for a grade. I pity my colleagues who, after having lived with their students 24-7 for the better part of two months, will have to conclude the experience by grading a stack of science papers twenty-two deep.

Eager to leave the dust and the noise behind for a while, I familiarize myself with the five instars of the anise butterfly's caterpillar, as well as the appearance of its egg and its chrysalis. The first two instars appear black to me, although the field guide calls them a dark brown, with an irregular white band around the middle. The third and fourth instars become more green after each molt, maintaining the white band, and the fifth instar is predominantly green, but striped, looking like something that fell off a tiger. The egg looks like a tiny pearl, and the chrysalis appears leaf-like, with a distinctive shape that I'm certain to remember.

I head out into the afternoon heat. The sea breeze is at least an hour away, which makes this a perfect moment to hunt butterflies and caterpillars. I start on a hillside, examining the close fennel stalks with naked eye while scanning the ones farther back with my binoculars. I look at young plants, old plants, plants thick and thin. I check down toward the base, and back up at the top, careful to investigate the undersides of leaves and umbels. I do this for at least five hundred plants, at the somewhat hasty rate of about six per minute. In the time this survey takes, I don't see a single swallowtail, a single egg, a single caterpillar. Worst of it all, there is not a single chrysalis. Even if the species was in diapause, I should be able to find these.

Nor do I see or hear a hawk of any sort. There are ravens here, a family with three fledglings, gathered on a single eucalyptus branch, the fledglings trying unsuccessfully to sound as ominous as their sire. They are cute, in their own way, but not in the same league as an island fox.

The sea breeze finally kicks in, and I return to the field station, ready to pour a tall ice tea.

On the way to what has now become my private refrigerator, I bump into the intertidal researchers, who have just returned from their overnight. They report having slept poorly because a mother fox and two kits investigated their sleeping bags repeatedly throughout the night. I mention that a retired colleague had warned me not to camp out on this island without a tent. Back in his research days he'd had a fox piddle on the feet of his sleeping bag. The fox was apparently scent-marking turf.

The intertidal researchers once again scurry off to the showers.

I decide to investigate the online literature regarding the local anise swallowtail population. I find a 1984 article from the *Journal of Research on the Lepidoptera*, by Scott E. Miller, called "Butterflies of the California Channel Islands." It indeed lists *Papilio zelicaon* as residing on this island. In talking about the long history of the island's "weedy hostplants," Miller endorses the theory of another entomologist, J. A. Powell, that Channel Island insects are undersaturated, and that they periodically go extinct in times of stress and then recolonize later. Now all I have to do is figure out when was the last time someone observed anise swallowtails around here.

Next, I scan a recent (2014) paper, "Contributions to an Arthropod Inventory of Santa Cruz Island, California,"[6] and find that *Papilio zelicaon* is not listed in their survey results.

Hoping that citizen science might shine some light on this mystery, I check with iNaturalist, searching within the parameter of the entire island, not just the reserve. Recent observations are listed for acmon blue, American lady, California sister, gray hairstreak, red admiral, California skipper, marine blue, western pigmy blue, mournful duskywing, common buckeye, echo azure,

6. Naughton et al., 2014.

hedgerow hairstreak, northern checkerspot, checkered white, common checkered-skipper, monarch, and the pale swallowtail, *Papilio eurymedon*. However, there are no recent observations on iNaturalist of anise swallowtails. Zip.

Neither is there an observation of a red-tailed hawk. Indeed, the only raptor observations listed in iNaturalist are the American kestrel, burrowing owl, and osprey. I should point out that there's nothing conclusive about the lack of an iNaturalist observation. On the other hand, it's less of a mystery at this point why I wasn't finding caterpillars on the fennel this afternoon. I'm becoming concerned that the only anise swallowtail left on this island might be the one pinned to the specimen drawer in the lab behind me.

A shame there aren't any caterpillars munching back all this fennel.

I've been at the desk too long. I get up to take one last look for raptors, and I resolve that on my return I'll switch from writing to reading. I've brought Terry Tempest Williams's new book along this trip, *The Hour of Land*, and I'm hoping that chapter 2, written about Theodore Roosevelt National Park in North Dakota, won't be quite as reverential as last night's chapter turned out to be.

The ravens are right outside my door as I emerge. They're perched in a live oak this time, still working on the voice of the next generation. They fly off as I pass, and reconvene atop the barbecue pit, a cast-iron affair made from the bottom half of an ancient mooring ball. Perched there, black tricksters on a black grill, they seem to be lecturing me in their telepathic way that I've spent too much time indoors today. Why am I at a field station if I intend to spend half the day indoors?

The problem with tricksters is that they occasionally hit the mark.

July 8

I wake up at first light, hearing the dawn song of a nearby passerine that I'm having difficulty placing. High-pitched, somewhat mechanical, highly repetitive. Almost annoying at this hour. I wonder whether it's a Pacific-slope flycatcher, which makes me think that bugs aren't going to have much chance around here, especially with the overabundance of . . .

That's it! Perhaps. I sit up in bed, listening for the dawn chorus of the ash-throated flycatchers. They have not roused yet, and will not do so for at least another hour. Meanwhile, I have stumbled on a possible solution to the butterfly problem that so intrigued me yesterday. With an unusual density of flycatchers in the area, a large butterfly like the anise swallowtail wouldn't stand much of a chance. If the ash-throated flycatchers don't get it, there are black phoebes and Pacific-slope flycatchers to contend with, all three of which are common in this valley.

I throw on a hoodie and slide into some socks—it's too early to bother with trousers. I'm up, I'm on the Internet, and trying to confirm the diet of the ash-throated flycatcher. BirdWeb tells me that "insects are the most common food." Not helpful. The Cornell Lab of Ornithology website says, "Captures insects off vegetation and on ground. Flycatches somewhat less often, usually using different perches in between sallies." Slightly more helpful. And then I notice, on the same page, that the ash-throated flycatcher "nests in cavities, such as woodpecker holes."

Of course! That explains the unusual density of flycatchers in this neighborhood, where the other most common bird is the acorn woodpecker.

I switch to Google Scholar, entering the scientific name, *Myiarchus cinerascens*, and the word "diet." Not much there, except for an article that mentions that, in addition to flycatching, flycatchers feed on caterpillars.

Uh-huh.

Before closing the computer and heading up to breakfast, I attempt to satisfy my curiosities one step further. Last night, shortly after I'd fallen asleep, I heard a strange animal noise that sounded almost cartoonish. Screechy, barklike, high-pitched, multitonal, insistent. The sort of noise you'd expect a squirrel to make if a squirrel weighed four pounds. Or maybe how a poodle with acute tonsillitis would bark. On a hunch, I switch over to YouTube and search on the keywords "island fox bark."

Sure enough, that was my mystery noise.

I've accepted an invitation to accompany Kathryn McEachern in the field this morning as she finishes up her annual survey of the endangered Hoffmann's rock cress. Also accompanying Kathryn will be her son, Carson, who is about to begin his sophomore year at Western Washington University, and an intern, Morgan, who recently finished her undergraduate studies at Berkeley.

Kathryn shows up in an extra-dirty pair of white jeans with the knees worn through. Although she will spend the greater part of the morning on her knees, measuring and evaluating plants, she doesn't bother wearing kneepads. I hearken back to the only botany class I ever took, where a hand loupe, dissecting kit, and kneepads were all required equipment, and ask why she doesn't wear them. She shrugs her shoulders, and says, "I suppose I should . . . but I never do."

We'll be using an unmarked National Park Service pickup—4WD Super Duty—to shuttle us this morning, but before we begin Kathryn takes pictures of the passenger-side door, pointing out that she'd "wrapped it around a tree yesterday," as she put it.

The truck is as huge as it is powerful, but Kathryn doesn't like it. As we pull out she complains, "It's too big for these roads. You'll see."

Even though we will never exceed the ten-mile-per-hour speed limit on this island, I fasten my seat belt, just in case my door springs open. Meanwhile, Kathryn explains that they don't have access to all-terrain vehicles because all federal vehicles are purchased by the General Services Administration, and are required to meet certain requirements such as being "made in America." No Kawasaki Mules like we had up at Hastings.

We park at the base of a hill where the road up is too steep for this particular truck. The question comes to mind whether any road too steep for a Ford Super Duty 4WD pickup might be a bit too steep for me, but I remove my field vest and saddle up my pack anyway. At least the ravens won't be scolding me for sitting indoors this morning. And at least we're climbing a north-facing slope.

The road quickly inclines to the point where my heels won't reach the back-slope, and every step is a matter of toes and the balls of my feet. My calves are screaming before I get even close to the point of wheezing, but I push on, because one never wants to be left in the dust by a botanist.

Kathryn turns around at one point and, in her just-above-a-mumble Tennessee lilt, says, "It's kinda steep."

I huff agreement.

It's at that point that I hear, for the first time on this island, the distant-sounding screech of a red-tailed hawk. I pause, snatch up my binoculars, and scan the far ridge, less to confirm the identification, more to catch my breath. Kathryn continues walking; perhaps she's seen hawks enough for a lifetime. But the hawk is nowhere to be seen; it must be over the next ridge.

The higher we climb into the chaparral, the more serious this drought appears. We have entered a biome that evolved to flourish in arid conditions, but the flora here is clearly struggling. There are dead manzanitas everywhere, and half the ones that still have vegetation already have a few dead limbs. Kathryn reports that even though it's been no drier than the previous year, "this year the drought seems more profound—it seems very suddenly to have gotten worse." She searches for words, and only comes up with a sentence fragment, "A new state of nothingness."

She points out a native patch of rock cress that I can barely see under the chaparral. It's smaller than I anticipated, but exquisite. I kneel down on all fours, and when I squint from its own level I can imagine the plant as a fire-works display, with a rosette burst at the base and a slender stream of flowers shooting higher. Gently, Kathryn encourages me forward, explaining that her patch is just up the road.

We get to the field site just as I hear the redtail again—this time I see her as well. She is huge, and from her molt pattern I surmise that she's a first-summer subadult, just getting the first couple red feathers in a tail that's mostly still showing brown, banded juvenile plumage. I watch her soar until she again crosses over the ridge. When I lower my binoculars I notice that Kathryn has been waiting for me to finish my observation. "There used to be birds here," she says. She points to a dead manzanita just uphill from us, saying that a scrub-jay used to perch here and scold the researchers when they were first planting seedlings.

She invites me to walk around the plot and look for new shoots, but in-structs me to be careful where I step. One doesn't want to tread on endangered seedlings. I take out my camera and begin photographing the plot while Kath-ryn begins setting up her survey. She talks while she works, and I ask questions about the recovery plan, which was adopted in 2002. The plan lays out specific criteria for removing this plant from the endangered species list, commonly referred to as "delisting." It specifies that there need to be more than two thou-sand viable plants spread over at least ten populations on this island. These populations need to be either stable or increasing, and there needs to be evi-dence of natural recruitment for a period of at least fifteen years that includes the normal precipitation cycle.

Kathryn asks, rhetorically, what it means for a population to be viable and self-sustaining in an era of climate change. She continues by asking, "How do we even know what the normal precipitation cycle is?"

I don't have an answer—she knew I wouldn't—but I assure her that it's a worthy question.

When the survey begins I move uphill, camera in hand. I stop at an island bush poppy in full bloom,[7] and snap off what would have been a full roll back in the days of film. This poppy is an endemic evergreen shrub, and these indi-viduals reach almost twice my height. The leaves are a bluish green that even I can see, the four-petaled flowers bloom a slightly more mellow yellow than a buttercup, and it seems to be the only plant within a couple hundred meters in any direction that is not doing poorly. The island bush poppy is an example

---

7. I learn later that the island bush poppy, *Dendromecon rigida harfordii*, blooms most of the year.

of an island gigantism,[8] which is to say that it grows to twice the size of the mainland species from which it descended.

My hopes are somewhat elevated when I return to Kathryn's site. There's nothing like large yellow flowers to take your mind off a drought. I photograph her from a distance, at least whenever her head pokes up above the level of the chaparral. Most of the time she is on hands and knees, calling over to Morgan a plant's measurements, and describing whether the plant is vegetated, reproductive, et cetera. Morgan, sitting nearby on mineral soil devoid of vegetation, records everything on preprinted charts. It is obvious that the team has spent many, many hours doing this, their conversation animated only by the flow of data from researcher to recorder.

I sit uphill in silence, enjoying the competence in Kathryn's voice. It occurs to me that this is how to save a species from extinction, not so much by making speeches as by making observations. If *Boechera hoffmannii* is around a century from now, it will be because a botanist got down on her knees to collect seeds, and then again to plant seedlings that she'd grown from those seeds, and then numerous times again to figure out why some of them thrived while others did not. No speech required, just a bunch of stoop work, no doubt followed up by a fair amount of paperwork. However, although grant applications need to be written and reports filed, the most important part is to check with the plants themselves to see how they're doing.

The survey moves downhill, slowly—what Kathryn calls "botany speed"—for ninety minutes. They measure and describe every subject plant they can find, marking them for next time with numbered toothpicks. We gather together, finally, at the bottom of the plot, searching to make certain that there are no more seedlings, and then together hike back up to the starting point to retrieve our gear. I depart first to give my old knees the time they'll need to negotiate such a steep descent. Within a few minutes Carson catches up, but he slows to my pace to accompany me, telling me that the best part is yet to come—there are cookies waiting for us in the cooler in the pickup's bed.

Fig Newtons. Glorious.

We do not return directly to the field station. This will be Kathryn's last day at the reserve, and she wants to fill the pickup with diesel so that it's full for whoever uses it next. This involves climbing a steep, somewhat technical jeep track to a US Navy outpost atop a hill at the eastern edge of the island, a road better suited to burros than Fords. The navy defines this mountaintop base

---

8. In essence, the "island rule" says that when mainland species colonize islands, large species tend to become smaller—this would be the dwarfism of which the island fox is a prime example—and smaller species, such as the bush poppy, tend to become larger (gigantism).

as an "instrumentation complex," but the hellish nature of its long driveway makes the installation seem sinister. Near the top we pull up to the huge, aboveground diesel tank, but it runs dry after we pump a couple gallons. There's no one around with whom to discuss this.

Kathryn leaves me a half gallon of 2 percent milk that's only a week old. Soon after her party leaves, the intertidal researchers leave as well. They'll be departing on the same boat, since there's only one boat a day. If you want to leave the island, I was originally told, you will do so at 4:00 p.m. Or swim.

I feel suddenly alone at the station. When I arrived, there were two groups of researchers plus a class of twenty-two. Now it's just me. But within half an hour I hear trucks coming up the valley floor, and a biology class from UC Santa Barbara arrives, fresh off the boat. They look clean. They're only stopping here briefly to coordinate supplies before moving on to a remote site, but I'm assured that they'll be back tomorrow evening.

I return to my study to write, but when they zoom off I start thinking that it might be happy hour. Yes, I can distinctly hear today's ration of beer, my meager pint of refreshment, calling my name. I respond obediently, and am surprised when I walk into the main field station to discover another class inside, this one from Western Washington University. A smaller class, significantly less clean—they've been backpacking for a few days. Some of them have made it to the showers, others are setting up their tents in a grassy spot east of the main building. I look around for their leader, Adam Dillon, who I'd met a month ago at a meeting of the Island Fox Working Group that was held at the Santa Barbara Zoo.

We shake hands, renew our acquaintance, and I ask, "Why the tents?"

"This is a field course," he replies. "Even though it costs us the same to camp here as to bunk the kids, I feel better with them sleeping outdoors."

Yes. I would have expected Adam to say this. He's the real deal. Tall, slender, hair prematurely gray, the wings of Mercury tattooed to his calf. Still working on his PhD dissertation at Colorado State. For the past four years Adam has been trapping foxes here in the Channel Islands. I had been invited to assist with one of his operations, but couldn't make the date work. And now I'm sharing a field station with his class of twelve undergraduates.

This course is called Wildlife Recovery and Reintroduction: The California Channel Islands Project. I ask whether there's a lecture tonight, hoping that I might attend, but the course has moved beyond the point of lectures. The students will spend this evening prepping for an exam to be given in two days. Tonight they create the flash cards, tomorrow night they memorize them.

July 9

Deeply committed, now, not to spend any part of another morning indoors, I decide that the time has come to attend to island scrub-jays. At breakfast[9] I ask Adam whether he can recommend a good site, preferably within walking distance, to observe scrub-jays, and of course he can. Hike west along up the valley until I pass through the next eucalyptus grove, and then through a large wash until I get up to a grassy knoll. "Great spot," he assures me, "although there are plenty of scrub-jays around the field station as well."

Yes, I've seen them here, but I'm thinking that I'd like to get away from the station again this morning. It's starting to feel a bit downtownish, and I'm hankering for a less civilized landscape.

I decide to travel light, with just binoculars and a spotting scope, treating this as something of a scouting expedition since my destination, the grassy knoll, shouldn't be more than a mile away. It's a pleasant walk, almost entirely flat, and the section through the eucalyptus grove is heavily shaded by tall, creaky angiosperms[10] that must be more than a hundred years old and are well over thirty meters tall. The wash, which comes next, is entirely dry, but relatively birdy, with a few species I haven't yet seen on the island, including the chipping sparrow and the horned lark.

The wash also contains a few butterflies, I'm happy to report, including umber skippers, an American lady, and a California sister.

The grass knoll, on the far side of the broad wash, turns out to be a wonderful place from which to observe jays, the drawback being that the profusion of color here steals one's attention from corvids. My first distraction is a hooded oriole, a male in vibrant yellowish-orange breeding plumage. It sits atop a small oak across from a northern flicker, and makes the flicker, despite the deep red of its malar feathers, appear drab. The local color palette is rounded out by the cinnamon of black-headed grosbeaks and the rufous flanks of a spotted towhee.

It might be me, but the island scrub-jays seem bluer out here than they did back at the field station. They are certainly a much brighter blue than the scrub-jays I was seeing a week ago on the Hastings reserve. By comparison they are also larger, have a proportionately stouter bill, and a more harsh call. Even the field guides point this out.

---

9. I'm having a bowl of granola with a handful of raisins thrown in, a bit of yogurt on the side, topped generously with Kathryn's 2% milk. Adam is frying up a massive skillet of bacon. Thick bacon. It's hard to ignore.

10. The eucalyptus is the world's tallest angiosperm, which is to say that it's our tallest flowering plant.

Not only is the island scrub-jay endemic, occurring only on this island, but it is also the only insular land bird in either the United States or Canada. The explanation for this is that scrub-jays seem incapable of crossing significant amounts of water. This makes sense given the fact that they never migrate, but we don't really know why they never cross a large body of water in the first place. As I stand here on the grassy knoll, watching them, I never see one fly more than fifty meters.

I remain here on the knoll more than two hours, wishing throughout the second hour that I'd at least brought a camp chair and a writing table. And some water. I resolve to come back tomorrow, properly equipped, and make a day of it.

I begin my afternoon writing session in earnest, energized by the prospect of returning to the new observation post tomorrow and spending a day hard-core with the scrub-jays. The writing is interrupted early on, however, because three ecologists, two from The Nature Conservancy and one from the Division of Wildlife, have stopped by the field station, and the director here wants them to meet me and hear about my project. They have been working on a program to exterminate invasive Argentine ants, a project that seems to be nearly complete.

I ask whether anyone in the group has recently sighted an anise swallowtail, but none of them have been paying attention to butterflies. I'm given the names of a few entomologists with whom I might consult.[11]

They leave all too soon—the boat back to the mainland doesn't wait for ecologists. I return to my field notes as well as a bit more research on island insect populations. Despite the interruptions, I finish up before I qualify for overtime pay, and I switch back to reading Terry Tempest Williams right around 5:00. It's no use, however—before I get three pages into the text, the crew from UC Santa Barbara returns, and four new faculty move into the neighborhood. Three of them are research faculty—marine biologists—and one is a professor of oceanography. At this point all six of the private rooms here at the field station are filled with faculty, and I'm the only one not encumbered with students. Or should I say "blessed"? With two classes now present at the field station, another day at my remote observation post is looking better all the time.

The two classes don't mix much. The class from WWU is "dry" in the sense that they have no alcoholic beverages. The class from UCSB is anything but. They are surprised to learn about my one-pint-per-day beer ration, and one

---

11. This later turns out to have been a dead end. Both entomologists got back to me via e-mail, but neither had sighted the species recently here on the island.

of the TAs, Sarah, presents me with a one-pint IPA, and invites me to dip into their inventory at will. They will also be barbecuing tri-tips this evening, and I'm invited to partake of that as well.

The tri-tips are enormous. There is just enough room on the monstrous grill for UCSB's steak and WWU's chicken. I note that the WWU students have moved to the picnic tables on the other side of the field station to enjoy their repast, seemingly outnumbered by a superior force. After dinner, they prepare forlornly for their final exam tomorrow morning, soberly working their way through hundreds of flash cards.

July 10

I leave the field station heavy this morning: tripod, spotting scope, camera with two lenses, binoculars, lunch, two liters of water, and a folding beach chair I've borrowed from the reserve director. I imagine that I will appear like an absolute beast of burden, in the unlikely event anyone sees me along the road.

My heart is a bit heavy as I hike. I exchanged e-mail with my wife this morning. After an early hike, she and her sisters will be cleaning out my mother-in-law's condo in an assisted living community, getting it ready to put up for sale. My mother-in-law has had to move to a basement room where she will get around-the-clock nursing care, which she now needs. She was in her midfifties when I married her daughter almost thirty-nine years ago; time has robbed her of a great deal of spunk. I resolve to visit her as soon as I get off this island.

During my first hour of observations, the longest flight I observe of any island scrub-jay is eight seconds. These are not precise seconds, just me counting off "one thousand one, one thousand two . . ." in my head. Just after the start of my second hour, however, a scrub-jay stays airborne for seventeen full seconds before it disappears from view. This will be the longest flight I observe all day.

My observations are often distracted. A fox comes trotting along, emerging from the east side of the manzanita in whose shade I'm sitting. I have my notebook on my lap at that point, pen in hand while my camera rests atop my scope case. I pick it up slowly, zoom all the way out, frame the fox precisely and then press the shutter release button only to discover that I haven't yet turned the camera on. By the time I switch it on, reframe, and refocus, all I get for my efforts is a well-framed portrait of the fox's tail. I'm getting pretty good at these tail shots.

On hearing my shutter click the fox disappears into the grass, and here I'm using the term "disappear" literally. Two scrub-jays land on its footprints, posing thoughtfully for me. After snapping off a few shots I realize that these birds stand every bit as tall as the fox did, measuring from the ground to the crown of the head. I file this away as a good thing to have learned.

The sun finally climbs high enough that the mesquite I've been sitting near no longer provides shade. A nearby evergreen shrub, a toyon, stands more than twice my height, a stature that makes an impression in a neighborhood devoid of proper shade trees. The promising toyon is far enough off the beaten path that I don the gaiters before packing up my kit, a precaution against ticks.[12] Not paying attention, I put them on so that the logos point toward each other from the inseam of my trousers. Oh, the fashion faux pas one gets away with when wearing gaiters on a Pacific island with severely restricted access.

There's a narrow, well-traveled fox trail leading through the tall grass toward the toyon. By "narrow," I mean that the trail is slightly less wide than my boot. No more than ten paces in, I come across a significant pile of dung, composed of at least twenty dark little fox turds, each the size of your pinkie finger, lying in the middle of the trail. The message here, I'm guessing, may be that this trail is going to lead to a whole bunch of ferocious foxes, and no unauthorized entry will be tolerated. Stepping over the pile, I continue to follow the trail, but before I can travel another ten paces I come upon a second dung pile, equal in size to the first. The message this time seems to be "WE TRIED TO WARN YOU!"

Within the next ten paces I come to the first tree of a small grove where no tree is itself more than ten meters high. Here the grass has all been packed down—I suppose that this must either be a sleeping area or a lovely little day lounge out of the late-afternoon sun. I do not tread through it, opting instead to go the long way around to where I can commandeer shade between the toyon and a manzanita much larger than the one I just abandoned. It is here that I set up the best observation post I've had in years.[13]

My view, looking south, slopes down through about twenty-five meters of tall grass, after which it is more heavily vegetated. Willows mix in with live oak, toyon, manzanita, mountain mahogany, and what appears, through my scope,

12. And grass spears, of course. Magnanimous readers will note that I've learned something from my Hastings experience.
13. This includes Estación Juanito, mentioned in the second interlude of my previous book, *Coves of Departure: Field Notes from the Sea of Cortez*. Until now, I'd considered Estación Juanito to be the finest observation post in this galaxy.

to be a chokecherry. I watch four scrub-jays converge on a rounded toyon a stone's throw below me, then I notice that there is nothing man-made in my entire view, not a fence post, or a transmission tower up on the ridge above, not even a jet contrail.

Even without factoring in aesthetic consideration of nature unsullied by human artifact, the spot is so beautiful that I have no need to delve into its historical ecology. It is enough just to sit here and appreciate it—not for what it used to be in bygone days, not even for what it's become since restoration efforts began. Just for what it is. Now. Imperfect. At this moment.

As midmorning settles in I focus more on listening, less on watching. The scrub-jays are mostly silent, and the greater part of the anthem emanating from below comes from ash-throated flycatchers. They seem just as dense here as they did back at the field station. Woodpeckers, quail, wrens, and grosbeaks add their voices. The bird nearest me, a spotted towhee, is the most insistent, his check-mark-shaped trills bordering on impatience. Whatever it is he wants, he wants it now.

Every now and again the entire valley falls silent. It's possible that they've all become aware of something that has escaped my attention. A falcon perhaps, flying behind me, its view obstructed by my toyon? Whenever these silent moments happen I become aware of insect noise: flies, yellow jackets, and whatever other buzzy things are out there. Leafhoppers? There are no honeybees, however. Those were one of the first of the human-introduced species to be eradicated, and it lowered the population of invasive star thistles dramatically. My memory flashes back to Natasha, back at Hastings, pulling out star thistles with her bare hands.

Midmorning becomes late morning, and my eyes are finally drawn up to the chaparral on the opposing side of the valley. An artist painting that slope would need an entirely different palette than would be employed to paint the valley floor below. Where there's green, it's a much cooler green, and it intersperses with dead-stick gray. I take a few photographs so that I can come back to this spot and make comparisons if this drought ever ends.

As we approach noon I keep having to scoot my chair back deeper under the toyon to take advantage of what shade is left. The shrub/tree functions more and more as a blind. A flycatcher lands on a branch a couple arm lengths away, in full sunlight, its crest looking like a bad haircut at this distance. It flies off when the day's first breeze pipes up, bringing with it a puff of ocean coolness. In an instant, regardless of whatever my wristwatch might have to say about the matter, Zephyrus transforms morning into afternoon. Down below the birds shift their domains, the one on this shrub moving to that, the one on that shrub moving to this.

I watch as a scrub-jay glides for three seconds from the top of a live oak and then plops down into the tall grass, disappearing completely from view.

I grab the binoculars because I've noticed this behavior several times today, never really understanding what these birds are up to. I scan the grass where it landed, and I'm fortunate to see it return to the tree with an acorn in its bill. Of course! These scrub-jays are considered scatter hoarders. They cache acorns, but they don't store them in granaries like the acorn woodpeckers. Rather, they hide them in numerous caches, and they have an amazing ability to remember precisely where they've hidden food.

I want to see a scrub-jay retrieve another acorn, but it's not to be. At the point where the sun has moved far enough west that I'm nearly bereft of shade, yellow jackets, the bullies of the meadows, begin to harass me. I'm not usually skittery about wasps, but the yellow jackets have been ganging up on people here on the island, and warnings have been posted at the ferry landing and in the field station.

I remind myself that these little yellow brutes are part of nature, the nature I'm here to write about. I search my memory for what I can remember of the natural history of the western yellow jacket. They are a thick-bodied, social, predatory wasp. They nest in soil cavities or tree hollows, and will defend the nest entrance aggressively. They prey on insect larvae, but will also feed on carrion or rotting fruit. Unlike honeybees, they are not equipped to carry pollen. Their stingers are not barbed, which means they are not left in their victims, which means that a single yellow jacket can sting repeatedly. And, I remember reading somewhere on the Channel Islands park service website, swift movements will attract more yellow jackets. Oh yes, and only the queens hibernate to survive the winter. The males all die.

That's it, *Vespula pensylvanica*. I've run through my entire trove of yellow jacket lore without coming across a single redeeming factor. I search the horizon for my old friends, the flycatchers, hoping that they might want to come eat a few of these pests, but all the useful birds seem to be on siesta break.

I slowly pack up my kit, careful to avoid swift movements, and vigilant not to leave anything behind for the fox.

I listen for hawks on the way home, thinking that if I were red-tailed, I would be riding the thermals on an afternoon such as this, ascending on warm air until I found something cool. I make it back to the field station, however, without hearing anything new.

July 11

I had met Dr. Lyndal Laughrin, who runs the field station here, in early June at the annual meeting of the Island Fox Working Group. The meeting was hosted by the Santa Barbara Zoo, and when I walked in to what was obviously a conglomeration of eighty-some field-hardened wildlife experts, two things were immediately clear:

1. Everybody in the room knew everybody else.
2. Except for me.

I had corresponded with Lyndal to set up this visit to the field station, and then had attended the Santa Barbara meeting at his suggestion. And it was Lyndal, of course, who saw a stranger walk into the room, and who figured out it had to be me, and who came up and introduced himself. We've been friends ever since.

I was tempted, at first, to write about the working group. It's almost a complete nonentity on paper, an unincorporated gathering of people concerned about an endangered animal, working without any of the usual organizational accoutrements such as officers, bylaws, a budget, a website, or staff. Although there were a few other academics in the room, most group members worked for a range of agencies, including the United States Navy; the National Park Service; various zoos, local conservancies, and natural history museums; The Nature Conservancy; the US Fish and Wildlife Service; the California Department of Fish and Wildlife; and a nonprofit environmental consulting firm, the Institute for Wildlife Studies. There were a lot of smart people in the room.

Lyndal was clearly the archdruid of this particular sect. He started working on this island in 1965, back when it was still a privately owned ranch, and did his PhD research on island foxes. He's pretty much been here ever since; the US Census Bureau lists the population of Santa Cruz Island as "2." Those two are Lyndal and his wife, Ann.

When Lyndal started working on island foxes, little was known about them beyond a basic description. He filled in many of the gaps in the fox's natural history: diet, behavior, population dynamics, and basic ecology. During that initial research, the field station director left and Lyndal became interim director. That was in 1970, and he's been running the place ever since.

He picks me up late, having cleared his deck of all work for the day. He is wearing a white, button-down oxford shirt, camouflage trousers, hiking boots, and a broad-brimmed hat. Santa Cruz Island executive attire. We load our gear into the back of his white, open-air jeep. Within a few hours all will be covered in dust—driver and passenger included.

"I hope your planning to spend the day," he says while he loads in a small cooler. I indicate that, yes, I packed a lunch.

I don't have a chance for final goodbyes to the UCSB group, who will have departed before we return to the field station. They are in session, discussing the results of an experiment conducted previously. As much as I enjoy this field station's quietude when students are not around, I will certainly miss this group's energy.

The jeep is in its 4WD low range, and hasn't been in any other range for years. It sounds like a hot rod, having had its catalytic converter removed so as not to cause grass fires. This is standard procedure for island vehicles, few of which will ever travel a paved road again. We will not exceed ten miles per hour all day, and will spend the greater amount of our journey at half that speed. Lyndal proposes a figure-eight route that will take us through numerous geological zones, and I indicate that I am disposed to follow his lead.

The tour takes on the tone of a lecture, or at least a seminar. As we drive through the eucalyptus grove that I'd hiked in the previous two days, Lyndal tells me that one of the trees in this grove is officially the tallest flowering plant in North America. I detect a note of pride in his voice as he details how the plant was measured, and by whom.

Geology emerges as this morning's theme, and I'm amazed at how knowledgeable Lyndal is on this subject for someone who trained as a vertebrate zoologist. As we climb up the valley westward, he points out evidence of the major tectonic fault that divides the island, and under his guidance I'm able to see how the far side of the valley is moving in an opposite direction relative to the near. We stop and get out anytime we pass an endemic plant, or a buckwheat varietal, or vertebrates of interest such as a gopher snake that Lyndal suspects I might want to photograph. His off-road driving philosophy is simple: always drive as if you have no breaks, and stop the jeep before you look at anything interesting. He explains that most of the off-road accidents that happen here occur when the driver is observing wildlife. Distracted driving.[14]

These old ranch roads were originally horse trails, and the jeep's tires are often perilously close to the edge, especially on the steeper sections. The steward has placed multicolored Styrofoam crab floats and net buoys, an endless supply of which wash up on the local beaches, in places where particular attention needs to be paid.

Once we top out on the rim we shift from chaparral to grassland moving toward bishop-pine woodland, and our conversation shifts from geology to

---

14. A bulletin board back at the field station contains photographs of at least a dozen jeeps and pickups that have rolled off roads or into crevices here on the island. Many bear the same caption: "Driver wasn't paying attention."

botany. I notice that Lyndal is mostly using common names, and without really thinking it through I try a little experiment to determine whether he's dumbing things down for the benefit of someone from the environmental humanities. We are driving past scattered clusters of low-lying cactus, which he had referenced as "prickly pears" a few minutes back and which botanists would usually refer to by the genus name, *Opuntia*. When I ask whether the opuntia are native to the island, Lyndal doesn't skip a beat, and narrates the ecological history of opuntia in this ecosystem, including how ranchers attempted to get rid of it by introducing a cochineal scale insect, *Dactylopius coccus*, with the help of agricultural scientists from UC Riverside in the early 1940s.

This, of course, is what one gets when one unlocks Pandora's box: entomology laced with historical ecology, served up by a vertebrate zoologist. Lyndal pulls the jeep over, and we examine the nearest patch of opuntia for cochineals while my guide explains how the opuntia population has tended to stabilize in recent years, and why this has happened, even though the stands of opuntia are nowhere near historic levels. He finds a small, silver-white mound on one of the cactus pads, explains how the insect parasitizes the opuntia, and then asks whether I was aware that the Aztecs made a scarlet dye of these very chochineals. Cochineal dye?

I confess that I was not aware of this.

The landscape transforms shortly after we continue our journey, and we are now driving through a forest of tree skeletons. The pine cones are still in place, but the needles have been dropped by most of these plants. I am taken aback at the number of bishop pines that have recently died, their leaf litter still piled below, and I observe out loud that the ravages of the drought seem more severe here than they were back in the chaparral. Lyndal doesn't respond to this, perhaps because it's so obvious that coniferous woodland would have a more difficult time adapting to drought than chaparral. I ask him to estimate the percentage of bishop pines that have died on the island as a result of this drought, and he gives me a range between 80 and 85 percent. It's truly grim.

Over the course of our first few hours together, we talk about what has changed since Lyndal started studying the foxes here as a grad student in the late 1960s. The foxes were not protected back then, and some were being sold through the pet trade. The island was still a working ranch when he started trapping foxes here, a seriously overgrazed ranch with thirty thousand sheep and eight hundred head of cattle. I find his perspective fascinating—both he and the field station he runs predate the involvement of the National Park Service and The Nature Conservancy. He tells me that he originally got his job because Dr. Sterling, the owner of the ranch, trusted him and wanted him around. Apparently, whatever Dr. Sterling wanted, Dr. Sterling got, at least as far as the University of California was concerned. The result was good, in this case, because the field station had originated strictly to conduct geological research, but once Lyndal came aboard, its mission expanded to include field biology.

We drive.

We come to a crossroad, and Lyndal asks, "How's your time looking?" When I reassure him of my flexibility in this matter, he takes a side road to where we can observe a massive bald eagle nest on the coast. There is, of course, nothing I'd rather do at this point. The all-stick nest proves worthy of our time. I can't tell how deep it is, looking down from above, but it's as large in diameter as a tractor tire. Probably every bit as thick. We have arrived a bit late for the nesting season, however, and the fledglings have already fledged by now. Undaunted, Lyndal takes out his binoculars, scans the far ridge, and says, "There's one."

This will become a pattern throughout the rest of the day: Lyndal will generally be the first to spot a bird precisely because he knows these particular birds, including where they like to roost. I accuse him of having great eyes, but it's more than that—it's history.

The bird ignores us although I have no doubt that it's aware of our presence here on the top of a neighboring ridge, two tall fellows standing next to a white jeep. We are able to determine that it's an adult even though it's silhouetted in such a way that makes it difficult at first to perceive its white head and tail. When it turns its head our way, however, I'm able to make the call. Even then, I have trouble gauging the eagle's size through my binoculars; there are no trees nearby on the ridge where it perches, and this makes it difficult to judge scale. It seems enormous as I view its magnified image, but this may be because the ridge is closer than it appears. Or maybe it's just a huge specimen. *Haliaeetus leucocephalus* can reach almost a meter in height when it perches, and this bird seems every bit that tall as it surveys the gray seascape below.

The history of these eagles has been well documented in the scientific literature. The ranch used DDT to control insect pests in the 1950s and 1960s, and the eagles were wiped out as a result. Golden eagles colonized the island subsequently, preying on human-introduced species such as sheep. When the sheep and feral pigs were finally removed as a conservation measure, the eagles did something that should have been predictable, at least in retrospect—they began preying on island foxes. At the point when the fox population crashed, it became apparent to the conservation community—and of course Lyndal was an instrumental part of this conversation—that we needed to get rid of the golden eagles and bring back the bald eagles, which tend to prey on fish, not foxes.

It wasn't as easily done as said. The eagles had their own fans, so lethal means of eradication were never permitted. Capturing golden eagles turned out to be an enormous challenge, requiring four years of intensive, creative, and expensive efforts that ran the gamut from shooting net guns from a helicopter to developing robotic eggs that could be substituted for real eggs in the nest—the counterfeit eggs were designed to inject sedatives with spring-loaded hypodermic needles, but never worked in the field. Then, once the golden eagles had been deported to the farthest corner of northeastern California, bald eagles had to be reintroduced so that the golden eagles would not recolonize the island. And now the fox population of this island is approaching historic levels. Simple.

Within an hour we're back to the fork in the road, and we turn down toward the historic Christy ranch and, more important, the beach where we'll have lunch. My luncheon tends to be a simple affair, flour tortillas with peanut butter, jelly, and cream cheese, which I've christened "the Philadelphia PBJ burrito." They taste especially good on a beach, providing you can keep the sand from becoming a condiment. I've also brought a juicy plum along, and it turns out to be a perfect complement to the burritos.

There are no shorebirds on this beach, which I find strange. Instead, ravens function as the local sandpipers, poking through the littoral zone with their enormous bills. Lyndal speculates that they're going after mole crabs.[15] As we watch the ravens chasing and then retreating from the swash, it grows suddenly chilly. The wind has shifted and an afternoon fog begins to roll in. We both put on our vests, and will soon add a windbreaker layer as well. This fog will chase us for the next few hours, always threatening and yet never quite engulfing us.

Lyndal again asks how I'm doing on time, which is his way of offering to drive me out to Point Frazer. I assure him that I'm having the time of my life, and we're off, driving now through a low-lying coastal sage biome that presents a whole new palette of plants to learn. Lyndal seems to know them all. Various hearty buckwheats, including the indigenous Santa Cruz Island buckwheat, intermixed with California sagebrush, black sage, lemonade sumac, and goldenbrush. As we roll through this scrub, on a hillside that many would describe as "barren," Lyndal describes a rich and diverse ecology.

We park the jeep again, the road having reached its westernmost terminal. Ahead there are still a couple hundred meters of pickleweed and red sand verbena before the island itself ends. The verbena, *Abronia maritima*, is in bloom, and looks more pink to me than its common name would indicate. Lyndal

---

15. The Pacific mole crab, *Emerita analoga*, more commonly called a "sand crab," lives in the swash zone of West Coast beaches.

instructs me to check out the tide pools, telling me that he'll catch up after a while. I snatch up my camera and binoculars, leaving the daypack in the jeep because I don't expect to be gone more than a brief moment. But the pools themselves are spectacular, better than any of the tide pools to which I've taken my own classes over the years. I am surprised to see Sally Lightfoot crabs, *Grapsus grapsus*, congregating on the rocks this far north. Old Baja amigos. These are pools where one could easily spend a day, especially if properly equipped to get into the water, as I am not. Still, I'm able to decipher many of the hidden secrets of these pools, sitting up on the cliff and gazing through the clear water with my binoculars.

After a half hour down in the tide pools I head up to the terrace that leads out to the point, and Lyndal soon joins me. The ankle-high plants here are salt tolerant, and we find fox trails but do not see foxes. Salt crystals encrust everything here, and I wish the sun would break through the gray marine layer just for a moment to make them sparkle. Every now and again we come across a scatter of gull feathers and bones, which Lyndal suggests are probably the result of a peregrine falcon's hunt. The kills seem recent.

Suddenly, there is an eruption of gulls, somewhere between one and two hundred, shrieking off the cliffs at the end of the point. Lyndal and I raise our binoculars simultaneously, and I ask, "Peregrine?"

Lyndal spots the marauders first. Two bald eagles have buzzed the colony of gulls, causing this feathered flare-up. The gulls scream murder as the eagles dive down out of our view, perhaps to steal a few eggs. Or nestlings? I laugh, once they're gone, and Lyndal looks at me quizzically. I indicate the heavy camera slung down by my hip, and explain, "I've just missed another once-in-a-lifetime shot."

Lyndal has a smaller camera around his neck, a device that I had not previously noted. He laughs that he missed the shot as well. We will both get a chance at lesser shots a few minutes later when the eagles head across the bay. Lyndal seems to know where they will land, and when they do so, even though they're more than a mile away, he points them out as they perch shoulder to shoulder on the far side of a cove. Such a shame I didn't bring my scope today!

We make a short hop over to an active archaeological site in a huge shell midden nearby. Lyndal points out depressions where habitations have long ago capsized. This midden is actively being studied, but the archaeologists are not currently at the field station, and they've covered their trench with plywood. Lyndal carefully opens it up at one end, and we peer down. It's full of shell, mostly abalone shell, and Lyndal points out how the shells along the side grow smaller as the midden grows higher—clear evidence of overfishing around this site.

"So much for the myth of the Native American community achieving ecological balance," Lyndal comments.

We return to the jeep, now heading back to the east. While we drive, I ask what he considers the advantage of having spent almost five decades living and working on this island. His answer comes as no surprise after our time together: he talks about the perspective of having been able to learn the island beyond the limits of his own discipline. The people who "pop in periodically" for short visits don't get to do this, he explains. But after fifty years of trailing around with other scholars, he has been able to "learn the island" through the lenses of their expertise. Archaeologists, geographers, botanists, marine biologists, entomologists, pathologists, restoration ecologists, and even fellow zoologists have all contributed to Lyndal's understanding of the ecosystem in which he lives. He assures me that although he no longer functions as a principal investigator, he is still very much learning about the Santa Cruz Island ecosystem.

Grinding along slowly, we flush a gray, big-headed bird the size of a robin. Without seeing more than tail feathers, Lyndal identifies it as an island loggerhead shrike, *Lanius ludovicianus anthonyi*, a somewhat notorious predator that feeds on lizards, grasshoppers, and even small birds. This is a subspecies I've never seen before, although I'm familiar with its near cousins both in mainland California and Baja California Sur, not to mention similar-looking relatives occupying the same genus in the British Isles, where they are commonly called "butcher birds."[16] The particular shrike that we just flushed exists on two islands, here and Santa Rosa, but according to the latest survey there are only forty-two individuals on this island. I feel privileged to have seen one of them.[17]

We enter into the final loop of our figure eight, once again climbing to a high ridge. I can see a broad panorama of seascape from here, but there's too much fog out there for us to see other islands. For the first time today it's my turn to spot a noteworthy bird, a falcon soaring on my side of the jeep. We stop and watch the largest male kestrel I've ever seen, able to follow it for several minutes as it forages at the head of a canyon that drops off to the north.

---

16. This appellation comes from the practice of male shrikes of caching their kills on either cactus spines or some other thorny plant or even barbed wire, a way of showing off to prospective mates how well they can provide. Down in Baja, I've come across mesquites that are ornamented with lizards, looking almost as if a satanic cult has been decorating the tree for the holidays.

17. The US Fish and Wildlife Service has petitioned for the island loggerhead shrike to be listed as an endangered species, and some conservation efforts have already been undertaken on this island.

The trail from here down toward the ranch is perhaps the steepest I've ever descended in a jeep. At times Lyndal has to shift down into the granny gear, causing the old engine to backfire nervously. I'm glad I'm not driving, just as I'm glad for Lyndal's modus operandi, descending this trail as if he had no brakes. This is clearly not a road that Little Dog could have handled.

We don't return to the field station until almost 7:00. When we park, Lyndal leaves the key in the ignition, telling me that I'm welcome to use the jeep on my adventure tomorrow.

I'm as dusty as I've been in years, and almost too weary to cook. The main station house, which has been swept and mopped to the point of excess, seems a lonely place without collegians in the kitchen. I see, near the sink faucets, a red gift box, the sort you might find in a confectioner's shop. Beneath it is a note written on a coffee filter that says, *"John, ENJOY the India Pale Ales in the walk-in fridge! Hope the island provides enough material for your book! Cheers! Sarah & UCSB EEMB 170!"*

I wander out to the walk-in fridge. There I find a one-pint IPA for every remaining day of my stay. These dear students—someone else's students!—have just doubled my beer ration until I return to civilization.

I return to the kitchen, still weary, still dusty, but full of cheer. I open the confectioner's box, and find that it contains one homemade truffle for each remaining day of my stay, including tonight.

Cheers, indeed.

July 12

I return to the field station early this afternoon, at least relative to yesterday's return, with unusually spotty field notes. Thanks to a helicopter, I'm even dustier today. And perhaps a bit more toxic.

A creature of habit, I check my e-mail first. A former student-advisee-TA from Montana has written to request yet another letter of recommendation. I've previously recommended this kid for a Fulbright, an internship with the White House Climate Office, and a Rhodes Scholarship, all of which he received in due time. He paid me back by getting his honors thesis published—I had served as his adviser for that as well—and presenting me with a signed copy of the literary journal in which it was published on my most recent birthday. So now that we're all square he wants me to recommend him for a seminar. He signs off his e-mail, "Hope you're enjoying them foxes!"

I write back that I'll get the recommendation out as soon as I return to campus and that "yep, them foxes is mighty fine."

During the first year of this former student's undergraduate year, he enrolled in a lower-division seminar I teach structured around wolf literature. Despite the topic, at the beginning of the quarter I lecture about how environmental scholars should, when possible, resist the allure of charismatic megafauna, or at least recognize it for what it is. We need to be just as concerned about the future of nematodes as we are about wolves or polar bears, even though it's easier to raise money to preserve predators.

That admonition in mind, I'm happy to report that I did not spend today with the foxes, although I've seen a few because they're hard to avoid around here. Rather, the highlight of my day was watching a helicopter dropping bait beads of sugar water laced with thiamethoxam, an insecticide. These beads are being dropped in areas of Argentine ant infestation. The bait stays hydrated for sixteen hours before desiccating, the hope being that the ants will forage the beads within that time frame.

I had been invited to observe this process by Ida Naughton, a second-year PhD student working out of UC San Diego. Ida has been working full seasons out here for the past three years, usually working a two-weeks-on/four-days-off schedule. She studies evolution and ecology, with a strong concentration in Hymenoptera, an order that comprises wasps, bees, and ants.

Most people would cluster hymenopterans, especially ants, on the non-charismatic side of the animal kingdom. Scholars like Ida will tell you that we need to pay attention to them anyway. When it was discovered that Argentine ants had established on the island, they were considered one of the major threats against biodiversity, third only to (1) nonnative vertebrates such as sheep and pigs, and (2) honeybees.

Argentine ants are considered such a strong threat because they take out the native ants, many of which have coevolved with plants to form mutualistic relationships. Islands are particularly vulnerable to invasive ants; Argentine ants have wrought extensive damage on islands such as Maui and Christmas Island. They form megacolonies, and once that happens they may consume bird nestlings, frogs, crabs, lizards . . .

The one good thing you can say about Argentine ants is that they don't disperse via wings. They pretty much get where they are going by attaching to human cargo. The worst thing about Argentine ants is that, so far, they've never been completely eradicated once they've established somewhere new. A few years back, scientists with The Nature Conservancy developed this new technique using the bait balls—which the manufacturer calls "Magic Beads"—and they've made major progress toward the eventual elimination of these ants from the island. The cool thing is that they don't have to worry about killing the native ants with the bait balls, because they only drop them in areas where

Argentine ants have established, and the invasive ants have already killed all the native ants in those areas.

The other cool thing about this method is that they avoid applying the bait balls until later in the day because the balls last longer at night. This meant that I could devote the morning to catching up with my field note transcriptions, which were lagging due to yesterday's long tour of the island with Lyndal.[18]

It was a nostalgic joy to drive the jeep solo. Two of the first vehicles I ever owned were jeeps, starting with a 1948 Willy's CJ2A painted battleship gray. It didn't have a heater and I lived in Colorado, so it tended not to be the most practical vehicle I ever owned, but I was in love with it anyway during my bachelor phase. The best thing I can say about it is that I never rolled it, although I had it up on two wheels for the longest three seconds of my life.

There are fox prints all over the driver's seat when I climb aboard. A private message from a charismatic friend.

I arrive at precisely 1:00, having not been out here long enough to be functioning on island time. At least I'm not five minutes early. I am intercepted by Christie Boser, who runs this island on behalf of The Nature Conservancy. There is a film crew from *Wired* magazine present, and she seems flustered to have an educator show up as well. When she asks what I am doing I reply that I will be working with Ida, and remind her that we had discussed my pending visit at the Island Fox Working Group meeting.

"Oh, nobody told me you'd be here today."

I had e-mailed her several days ago, hoping to get a moment together, but one tends not to press the point about such things when there's an incoming helicopter flying at low level, especially when a six-hundred-pound hopper bucket is slung six meters below the chopper.

The hopper bucket passes directly over us, low enough to end all conversation.

After the chopper reloads and zooms off I am instructed to park the jeep up by the orchard and wait for Ida's return. She shows up a few minutes later, accompanied by a recent college graduate named Michaela who has just started working with the ant project. Both Ida and Michaela are swaddled head to toe, including T-shirts wrapped around their heads that they've transformed into makeshift dust barriers. In terms of fashion, they remind me of something straight out of a *Mad Max* dystopian film, only petite. Ida, being a fellow

---

18. Please note that this is the final time in this volume that I was unable to keep my pledge to describe events contemporaneously, writing them up in their entirety the day they happened. I'm tempted to blame this on Lyndal.

academic, seems glad to see me, and not at all worried about me screwing up the filming.

"Just stick with me."

This turns out to be easier said than done. Ida immediately takes over the ground crew. There are sixty 2,500-liter casks lined up, square casks, plastic, and her job seems to be to direct one of the forklift operators to pick them up and dump them into the hopper loader, which in turn is ready to refill the helicopter as quickly as possible when it returns. She calls me over and pries the lid off one of the casks. Contained inside are gleaming beads, all of them clear, each the size of a large pearl. Magic Beads glistening with sugar water and poison.[19]

The helicopter returns every few minutes, hovering just above the hopper loader while forklift operator no. 2 positions the loader over the hopper. It only takes seconds for the hopper to be reloaded with Magic Beads, but in that amount of time it's able to kick up more dust than Lyndal's jeep kicked up in nine hours of running dirt roads yesterday. Absolutely phenomenal.

I, of course, have one of those multifunction head sleeves that can be fashioned as a pretty cool dust bandana, cowboy style. It's back in my duffel at the field station. I finally figure out a way to defend against the dust, but it's not nearly as elegant as Ida and Michaela's system. It involves pulling the handkerchief out of my back pocket and holding it over my mouth and nose right before the next swirling cloud of dust hits. At that point I'm certain that I look much more like an out-of-place college professor than a cowboy, but that sort of displacement is the price one pays writing in the field rather than a sterile office. And I can worry about the dust in my ears later.

The film crew seems to have suffered through all the dust and heat they can handle, but the cinematographer wants one last shot. He huddles with Christie and she calls instruction up to the helicopter on her walkie-talkie. Ida and Michaela vanish, but I stay close to the cameraman, expecting something good. Sure enough, the helicopter flies straight west up the valley, pivots tightly, and then begins a strafing run directly overhead, flicking on the hopper broadcaster moments before flying overhead. Yes. Thousands of Magic Beads are released for our cinematographic entertainment. I snap off a few shots with my still camera, and then lower my head, hoping that my Tilley hat will absorb the brunt of the abuse.

It does.

---

19. In a subhead of the *Wired* magazine article published a month later, the bait beads are referenced as a "Sugar Ball of Death."

The next time there's a lull in the action I ask Ida whether she's seen anise swallowtails on the island. She explains that she's not really an entomologist, just a hymenopterist, and that she rarely ID's butterflies past genus. This characterizes the modern world of science, of course, where being an entomologist, one who specializes in insects, is perceived as being a broad generalist in a universe where we encourage our budding scientists to specialize. I push her a bit about whether she's seen any genus-level swallowtails, and she says she saw some in the spring, in March or April. She assures me that they must be on the island, and refers me to the insect collection in the field station. I tell her that I've seen the *Papilio zelicaon* specimen, but that I can't locate a record of them being included in butterfly surveys since 1986, and that they don't appear on iNaturalist either.

She asks whether I've been inspecting inside the bracts of fennel, and I ask her to show the best way to do that. We walk over to the nearest fennel plant, and she shares her technique, pulling the bracts back gently even though this is a hearty invasive species that stands up pretty well to a machete. She looks momentarily puzzled, having expected to find aphids here, but there are none. She grows more interested in my swallowtail observations at that point, and suggests that the yellow jackets might be preying on the caterpillars.[20] In the end, she promises to keep an eye out, and to email me if, when, and where she sees *P. zelicaon.*

Feeling glad to have formed this new alliance with one of the ant people, I retreat from the field of battle. Once one watches the first dozen helicopter reloadings, there's not much more to learn unless you're a pilot. And I crave the relative peace of the jeep, which seemed so noisy and dusty only yesterday.

I return to the field station in second gear, enjoying the probability that I won't meet up with traffic on this road. I can barely see through the jeep's windshield at the moment, and I resolve to clean it, and my glasses, and my body, as soon as I make it to the station. The jeep and I stay well below the island's ten-mile-per-hour speed limit, even though there's a cold IPA waiting for me at home. I don't pop it open until I've gently inspected inside the bracts on a dozen fennel stalks, coming up empty each time.

July 13

The foxes woke me up last night at what had to be the witching hour.

I had dozed off while reading the annual supplement published by the checklist committee of the American Ornithologists' Union. Imagine that.

---

20. I look this up when I return to the field station, and sure enough, caterpillars are a main staple of the yellow jacket diet. I add this to my store of knowledge about *Vespula* natural history.

The checklist comes out once per year to denote which species have been split apart, which have been lumped together, and what birds simply received a new name. Of note, the western scrub-jay was split into two new species, the California scrub-jay and Woodhouse's scrub-jay. Which means not only that the brand new field guide I purchased a month ago is now out of date, but so are the field notes I wrote earlier this month at Hastings. Also of note is that the sooty shearwater, referenced earlier in this chapter, is no longer *Puffinus griseus*. Now it's *Ardenna grisea*. In essence, the entire puffinus genus was split. There must surely have been a reason for this.

Back to the foxes.

At first it sounded as if two foxes were gearing up for an altercation. After listening for a while, however, it seemed less as if the foxes were expressing displeasure with each other, and more as if they were raising a joint alarm about a third party. But who could that be in a neighborhood such as this. A gopher snake?

I fell back asleep pondering this query, and was awakened shortly thereafter by a single fox barking directly outside my window. Quite loud, quite close. Remembering that I was the only person occupying the field station dorms these past two nights, I found myself wondering whether I was the source of foxly concern. Did they want me out of the field station? Had they grown weary of my clumsy attempts to photograph them?

Once more, sleep.

Perhaps due to the disruptions, my internal clock allowed me to sleep in this morning, almost until 6:00. I read through the BBC while still in bed; today they get a new prime minister. But when I emerge from Room 4 to head up to the kitchen to put on the teakettle, I discern the faintest hint of skunk, not as if a skunk has sprayed, but clearly indicating that one is in the neighborhood.

I recall a conversation with Carson, Kathryn's college-bound son, a week ago about what had changed since he was a boy visiting this field station. He told me that before the foxes came back, skunks would often den beneath the station. It could get pretty ripe, according to his childhood memories.

The island spotted skunk is endemic to the two largest Channel Islands, Santa Cruz and Santa Rosa. Unlike the foxes, the skunks have not formed separate species on each island, which suggest relatively recent colonization. They are only about one-third the size of the foxes, weighing in at less than a kilo. This is another case of dwarfism; the island spotted skunk is considerably smaller than the mainland species from which it descended.

The skunk population expanded on this island when the fox population dropped during golden eagle predation, probably because the skunks are nocturnal while the eagles only hunt during the day. It is thought that the skunk population is currently at carrying capacity here on the island, which would normally be around a dozen skunks per square kilometer. This capacity has likely diminished during the drought.

Island foxes and island spotted skunks are the only two terrestrial carnivores on this island, and they compete for the same food resources: deer mice, lizards, large insects, and fruit when it's available.

It occurs to me, while I write this, what may have been the bone of contention last night. There is an apple tree on the other side of the wet lab across from Room 4. This tree is the halfway point between my room and the restrooms. Several times, over the course of the past few days, I've seen a fox foraging there. Yesterday, I saw a fox pick up a fallen apple and trot off with it a good hundred yards down the path before turning left and disappearing into the oaks.

My conjecture about last night, based solely on what I heard then and what I smelled this morning, is that a skunk may have ventured into the neighborhood hoping to harvest apples, but the foxes defended their trove of fruit by barking loudly enough to wake me up.

I make a mental note that if I have to visit the restroom this evening, I should take a headlamp to light my way. And perhaps a camera.

This will probably be my last full day on the island, and although I've enjoyed dozens of fox sightings, both around the field station and beyond, I haven't yet gotten an excellent photo of one. This will be my priority today.

Although I decide that my best strategy will be to set up under the apple tree, when I emerge from Room 4 I notice a fox foraging in the field below. While I suspect that this is a fox I've tried to photograph before, the same fox that always turns its tail toward me, I head toward the field, like Charlie Brown running up to kick the football, ready to give it another try. I avoid looking directly at the fox, and choose a path that is merely passing by, not directly aimed toward it. Out of my peripheral vision I can see the fox give me a low look, as if to ask, "Really?"

Yes. Really. I kneel down on one knee, raise the camera to eye, focus, frame, and shoot a fox with the most bored expression projected by any mammal this side of a house cat. I don't move, thinking that surely it will improve its disposition. Thirty seconds pass by, and then the fox closes its eyes.

My recurrent secret fantasy over the years has been to run off and become a wildlife photographer. The problem, however, is that I seem to bore predators.

Within a few minutes the fox seems to forget that I'm stalking it, and resumes its foraging. I remain still, and as I watch I realize that there is nothing about the behaviors I'm observing that would make me characterize it as "sly." Or even "clever." Cautious, perhaps. And patient. A lot more unflappable than a coyote would be in a situation like this. But how does one measure a fox's insight, let alone its brilliance?

The personality of these animals seems more feline than canine in many regards. They will certainly approach humans at times, and will often tolerate our presence, but they distinctly don't want to be approached by humans. Everything has to be on the fox's terms. The other morning I was sitting out in front of the station house, munching on my granola, when a fox jumped up on the barbecue grate to investigate whether any good flavors had been left behind. The fox was less than two meters from my knees at one point, and it completely ignored my presence. I was just another granola-eating environmentalist, as far as it seemed to be concerned, nothing to worry about.

Of course, I didn't have my camera at that moment.

I get off a few dozen shots before the fox ducks into thick underbrush, abruptly ending our session. I retreat to the apple tree to set up shop and await portrait customers, but there's already a fox there, chomping on a fallen apple the size of its head. While I shoot, I notice that the mouth of an island fox doesn't really open wide enough to accommodate fruit much larger than a golf ball. It takes about five minutes for the fox to gnaw the top half of the apple. During this time a raven lands nearby, and I wait patiently for the raven to come close enough to the fox that I can include them both in the same frame. This never happens, of course, but it would have been a great shot nonetheless, because of the scale it would have provided, with the raven standing taller than the fox.

The fox wanders off a few minutes later, apparently having had its fill. I wait to see whether the raven is interested in the apple, but it seems that the raven is there merely to observe. After another minute, it flies off, no doubt bored with wildlife photography.

Clearly, I should have followed the fox.

It's midmorning now, the time of day when I seldom see foxes out and about. I should see them again once it cools off, this evening. I grab a chair from the library, an ice tea from the kitchen, and park myself outdoors, near the apple tree, to catch up on my notes, keeping the camera at hand just in case. Sure enough, after I've scribbled for perhaps half an hour, a fox drops by. I'm able to switch my notebook for the camera without being observed as the fox searches the grounds for a fallen apple. The only one on the ground is the half apple left behind a while back, which this fox sniffs at but doesn't eat, making me think that I'm seeing a different fox than the one before. Just as I'm wishing I'd pulled an apple down, the fox leaps up into the tree, catlike, and begins climbing, hugging the tree with its front legs while using the rear legs for propulsion, almost a shimmying motion.

I'm out of the chair now, hardly believing what I'm seeing, shooting away although I haven't really got a clear shot. The tiny fox climbs higher into the branches, obscuring itself from my lens on the far side of the trunk, in search of the perfect apple. I keep shooting and keep inching closer to the tree, realizing even without checking that all I'm getting here are shots of apple leaves with maybe a bit of fur in the gaps.

The fox climbs higher and higher until it's out on branches no thicker than my thumb. It snatches an apple, climbs down tailfirst for a couple of meters, and then switches to a head-down descent seemingly without any hesitancy, picking up speed as it descends and then leaping to the ground once it reaches the thick part of the trunk, an apple firmly in its mouth. It scampers away, no doubt aware of my presence.

This, of course, is the damnedest thing I've ever seen. I head back to Room 4, hook into the Internet, and search on foxes climbing trees. Sure enough, I discover that gray foxes can climb trees in ways that red foxes cannot. I discover that gray foxes have curved claws that are semiretractable, and rotatable front legs that contribute to their climbing ability. And I learn that they not only climb trees to get fruit, but also to escape from coyotes, which cannot follow them up a tree.

Of course, climbing a tree would not be much of a defense mechanism for an animal being preyed on by a golden eagle. I suddenly understand how the population of foxes on this island diminished to a hundred animals as recently as 2004—they must have been easy prey for golden eagles if their best defense was to climb trees. After all, they are not particularly swift, nor are they wary, and they wouldn't appear to be menacing even if they hunted in packs, which they don't.

We should be happy that they bounced back so quickly, and that the captive breeding program only needed three years until the population stabilized, once the golden eagles were removed from this island. But despite the enormous success of this conservation story, it's not yet time to breathe a sigh of relief. This drought has me concerned; it's gotten beyond the point where relief is a few good rainy seasons away. If the ecology shifts to something a bit more arid, a bit more desertlike, the carrying capacity for island foxes will diminish considerably.

If there's enough will—demonstrated in terms of sufficient funding—a great deal can continue to be done to put this island's ecosystem back together. Just as honeybees were eradicated and just as golden eagles were replaced with bald eagles, a lot of cool stuff is in the works. We can probably eradicate the Argentine ants, restore endangered plants like Hoffmann's rock cress, and restore endangered birds like the island loggerhead shrike. And there are people working on the kelp beds as well. While we're at it, I'd love to see someone get rid of all this damned fennel. Let's hope that solutions to such pernicious invasive plants are just around the corner for restoration ecologists.

Even though I know better than to fixate on charismatic fauna, I ultimately came to this island to write about the foxes. I ended up getting sucked into concerns about plants, insects, and geology. This is as it should be today; ecological concerns consider the interactions between organisms and their environments. And this is why field stations such as this one have such enormous value. Convergence happens here, and the research is based in curiosity rather than specialty. As one becomes enamored with the island ecosystem, one gets drawn beyond specialized concerns and begins to synthesize different ways of understanding the system. First, you share a refrigerator with a botanist, and the next thing you know . . .

July 14

I begin my last full day on the island in the field station library. There is apparently some controversy as to whether sycamore trees are native here, or whether they should ultimately be taken out. Lyndal is aware of a historical source, Charles Frederick Holder's 1910 edition of *The Channel Islands of California: A Book for the Angler, Sportsman, and Tourist,* which indicates that Holder observed mature sycamores when first coming to the main ranch from Prisoner's Harbor. I e-mail Lyndal a preliminary opinion that, using the tools of historical ecology, we can make a strong case that sycamores are native to the island. I'm guessing that whomever wants these trees removed has confused *Platanas racemosa,* which is native to California, with *P. occidentalis,* which is not.

The field station's recent silence—I've been alone here the past two nights— is shattered by the arrival of three rambunctious volunteers who are here to install metal siding to the dorm and lab buildings, which have suffered greatly the abuse of woodpeckers. In anticipation of the noise that is sure to come, for which the workers have already apologized, I have dragged the laptop computer outside, setting up shop at the picnic table from which I'd watched a woodpecker take its dust bath last evening. I'm never as productive transcribing field notes outdoors—too many creatures create too many distractions.

Sure enough, there's a splash of yellow overhead. A huge butterfly—a swallowtail!—is heading down toward the field where I've been investigating the fennel. Without pausing to save my prose on the computer, I grab the camera and begin running after it. It has a significant head start, and disappears over the dorm. By the time I circle around the buildings, it's nowhere in sight.

I'm determined not to give up despite the absurdity of looking for a yellow swallowtail in a field of yellow fennel. I push ahead, scanning from side to side, and I finally see the swallowtail at the far edge of the field in a small patch of narrow-leaf milkweeds, *Asclepias fasicularis*, that I've been watching in the hope that monarch butterflies might be attracted. I come as close to a sprint as a sixty-two-year-old man can while wearing full leather hiking boots and carrying a superzoom lens. The swallowtail moves to a neighboring milkweed, and I slow down, careful not to scare it away. Stop. Zoom. Focus. Frame. Snap!

Even as I click the shutter release, I can see that this is not an anise swallowtail. It's the pale swallowtail, the other resident swallowtail of this island. Still, it's the first member of its genus I've seen during my stay, and I interpret it as a harbinger of hope. Its beauty is undiminished by the fact that it's a different species than the one I sought.

I move back to the picnic table and get in not quite a good hour of writing, but when Lyndal offers to take me and the new fellows down to the ranch museum for a tour, I stash my field notes.

Our tour of the ranch buildings is lubricated by Mexican *cervezas* that have been smuggled along and that go down all too quickly. When we return to the station, I'm informed that a fourth is required for horseshoes, and that if I can handle a bit of competition I'm welcome to partake of a steak-and-potatoes barbecue they are planning afterward. I donate tomatoes and celery for the salad, and dig out a bottle of cabernet that I've been saving for emergencies. It is the only bottle of wine I'd brought along, and it's a miracle it lasted until now.

We draw straws to form teams, and I'm linked up with a pleasant, soft-spoken building contractor. An environmental contractor from New Zealand and a commercial boat captain make up the opposition. I suggest naming our team "the Good Guys," and suddenly we have a classic confrontation between the forces of light and darkness. The Bad Guys take the practice game thanks to the boat captain's late-in-the-game run of ringers, but my consistency ends up carrying the day once we get down to championship play. The Good Guys emerge as island champions just as dusk descends. I light the charcoal while others argue the feasibility of a tiebreaker played in the dark, but the discussion ends when I open the wine. The steaks are all the better served by firelight.

July 15

The Internet news is grim in the morning as I mop out the showers and sweep Room 4. Someone has driven a refrigerated lorry into Bastille Day revelers in Nice, France, and the death toll is expected to be high. Two tragedies thus bookend my stay here on the island; five Dallas police officers were murdered by a sniper on my first full day here. Now this. Whatever enthusiasm I felt about returning to the mainland suddenly diminishes, and I pack up my laptop computer without reading through the rest of the news.

Lyndal is occupied this morning, so I drive myself back to Prisoner's Harbor in the white jeep, having plenty of time to survey the sycamores that Holder wrote about. I'm given instructions on how to take the old route rather than the new one that follows the valley floor. My route will follow a stream whose name I cannot locate on my map, and I know from the drive out last week that I will cross through this stream numerous times on my way to Prisoner's Harbor.

I drive along slowly, content with second gear at idle speed. I'm amazed at how much more thoroughly I'm seeing this riparian stretch of the island than I was on my drive out. All I seemed to notice on my first day here was the pervasive fennel, but now I'm noticing the mountain mahogany with its fruit feathers, the monkey flowers and paintbrush blooming everywhere, the Catalina cherry . . .

The sycamores, whose leaves, to my eyes, transform from green to yellow when the sun strikes them, and whose bark, again to my eyes, moves from white to a pinkish gray to something of a sun-bleached tan, stand out among the oaks and cottonwood. Did I notice these trees on the drive in? How could I not have? They seem to call out to me.

How could anyone believe they don't belong here?

Epilogue: August 11

Today, less than a month after I returned from Santa Cruz Island, the United States Department of the Interior announced the delisting of the San Miguel, Santa Rosa, and Santa Cruz Island subspecies of island fox. This represented the fastest successful recovery for any mammal listed as endangered under the auspices of the Endangered Species Act, bringing the total of delistings due to recovery up to thirty-seven over the course of the act's forty-three-year history. During that same time, there have been ten delistings due to extinction.

Santa Cruz Island bird list, July

California quail
Mourning dove

White-throated swift
Allen's hummingbird
Black oystercatcher
Pigeon guillemot
Cassin's auklet
Brant's cormorant
Pelagic cormorant
Bald eagle
Red-tailed hawk
Acorn woodpecker
Northern flicker
American kestrel
Pacific-slope flycatcher
Ash-throated flycatcher
Black phoebe
Island loggerhead shrike
Hutton's vireo
Island scrub-jay
Common raven
Horned lark
Barn swallow
Bushtit
Pacific wren
Bewick's wren
Varied thrush
Spotted towhee
Chipping sparrow
Channel Islands song sparrow
Dark-eyed junco
Western meadowlark
Black-headed grosbeak
Hooded oriole
Northern mockingbird

3

Notes from the Golden Gate Raptor Observatory

Citizen science is not just an expression of an achieved democracy;
it is a vehicle for creating more democratic transitions.

MARY ELLEN HANNIBAL, *Citizen Science: Searching for Heroes
and Hope in an Age of Extinction*, 2016

A hawkwatcher with the Golden Gate Raptor Observatory (GGRO) commits to a rotation during the fall migration, basically mid-August to early December, participating on a team at least one day every other week. My team is the second of the two Saturday teams, better known as "Saturday II." Our team has an exceptional level of experience; it seems that half the crew on any given Saturday have earned ten-year pins, and you don't really get bragging rights on this team until your twenty-year pin has been affixed to your hat. I will be awarded my five-year pin in another year.

It started out innocently enough. One of my students wrote a paper on citizen science, and mentioned the GGRO as an example of how citizen-science efforts often generate long-term data sets that would be prohibitive for conventionally funded scientific studies. My interest was piqued because Hawk Hill is a fifteen-minute drive from where I moor my sailboat in Sausalito. I was lucky enough to visit the hill on an exceptional day, which for Hawkwatch purposes can be defined as any day where over five hundred birds are identified in a six-hour period. I assured myself that with a bit of study I could do this.

I was up-front about my color blindness on my application, and again during my interview. My interviewer was not overly concerned about a lack of color vision as long as I was committed to the GGRO process. "We work as a team," he assured me, adding, "If you focus on learning the silhouettes and the jizz,[1] you'll be able to make a contribution."

The training was rigorous, but the GGRO style was reassuring. The rule for beginners is "When you see a hawk, start to talk." We had to learn not only the field marks of the nineteen species we might encounter, but also the local topography, where every landmark goes by a distinct name. On Hawk Hill, you might hear someone on the west quadrant saying, "I've got an accip stooping left on the lobster," while someone on the north quadrant sings out, "There's a kettle of TVs forming above Elvis," while someone in the east quadrant yells, "South, we're passing you an undoc coop at mid-span." You can be a long-time birder and still not have a clue on Hawkwatch.

After a summer of training, one becomes an apprentice for six months, graduating to unofficial novice status during the second year. My apprentice year was tough, and it was all I could do to identify genus and species. When that. I didn't really start working on aging and sexing birds until my novice year, and didn't feel that I was making a real contribution until my third season. Even then, I was striking out on the hard birds, unable to do much with birds more than a couple hundred meters away. The time had come for me to start using a scope to augment my binoculars, a straight scope rather than the angled scopes I used for teaching and fieldwork. This meant more work honing technique, not to mention a significant cash outlay, but now, in my fourth year, I am starting to be able to identify raptors with which I previously struggled. That feels good, especially when my day leader started teaming me up with apprentices so that I could put my teaching skills to work.

Even now, I still make mistakes, and it's always embarrassing when a more skilled hawkwatcher has to correct me, especially when I blow an ID that's obvious to someone with good color vision. Last time out I identified a northern harrier incorrectly as an adult female because I didn't notice the pumpkin breast coloration that was so prominent to everyone else, which marked the bird as a juvenile. When will I learn?

I have chosen this project, going out with all fourteen Hawkwatch teams through a complete rotation, for purely selfish reasons. Every year I have noticed that our interns, although they receive only a bit more training than the apprentices, rocket past them in terms of expertise. In essence, the apprentices

---

1. Jizz—sometimes GISS, from a military acronym for "general impression of size and shape"—is birder lingo for learning a bird by developing a mental image of a species' morphology, behavior, flying style, and the general vibe it gives off. More than just gist, jizz is an appreciation of the bird's gestalt.

only apply their training once every other week, while the interns are on the hill five days a week.

After fourteen straight days on watch, I'm hoping to develop some serious talent.

Saturday II

We meet together at 8:30 a.m., at Fort Cronkhite, in an army barrack built during World War II as part of the coastal defense system. This wood-frame "temporary" building, built in 1942, supported soldiers whose job it was to man sixteen-inch caliber casemated guns capable of firing 2,100-pound shells twenty-five miles. Nowadays, the building is no longer considered temporary; GGRO Headquarters supports National Park Service volunteers who count birds. Otherwise, little has changed: the floor is still bare wood, the rafters have been uncovered, and the windows still rattle in a breeze. I'm guessing it's still the same color paint they first applied seventy-four years ago.

The banding team has already met, but not yet dispersed. (I should probably mention that there are fourteen banding teams in addition to the fourteen Hawkwatch teams. They work in blinds while we work outdoors.) The banders are all business this close to peak migration, and we pretty much ignore each other around headquarters unless there are leftover brownies from their meetings. We hawkwatchers are briefed that adult accipiters are now showing up in force, so we should age these birds carefully. Then we receive a quick refresher on ferruginous hawk field marks. We are also briefed about the heat—it's expected to get nasty. Because we're official NPS volunteers we have to be warned about the hazards of sunburn and dehydration on days like today. It's policy.

Up on the hill we get going at the stroke of 9:30, and almost immediately someone spots a spider kite, about two meters long, drifting by on the gentle easterly breeze. We call this a "balloon spider," all the while knowing that this is not a scientific description since multiple species employ this technique for migration. We don't see the actual spider—more accurately a spiderling—which is almost certainly tiny. What we see, instead, are the gossamer strands of silk that were released when the spiderlings decided that conditions were ideal to migrate. One of the hawkwatchers says that this behavior is triggered by high pressure, and predicts that we will soon be seeing other ballooning spiders float by.

Sure enough, another floats by. And another. And . . . I stop counting when I get to fifty, and shortly after that we see no more ballooning spiders. I conclude that this must be a morning phenomenon, a strategy that works best before a sea breeze kicks up. On the other hand, given the light easterly breeze this morning, it seems that most of these spiders will descend into the ocean. Mortality associated with this form of migration must be high.

I am partnered up with one of our two Saturday II apprentices, Lisa, a field biologist who works in the local county park system. She's young and wonderful and is still unsure of her accipiters; we're assigned to the north quadrant for the first hour. Our day leader, Brian, prefers a NEWS rotation—North > East > West > South—so that no group ever has to face the prevailing northwesterlies two hours in succession on cold days. I've visited a few other teams in the past, and have been surprised to learn that they don't practice this sensible approach.

As a general rule, the more northerly the winds, the better the hawkwatching. The birds, after all, are heading south, and most of them are smart enough to avoid migrating into a headwind whenever possible. But we know from experience that on calm, hot days the hawks will climb the thermals, and will transit our hill high overhead, adding to the challenge of identifying them. There will be a lot of stiff necks for Saturday II tonight.

While we wait for raptors, we start seeing wave after wave of violet-green swallows; flocks of at least fifty birds penetrate our airspace every few minutes. One of the irregulars—a person from another team who is joining us for the day—complains of the swallows creating "static" in his binoculars. Large numbers of dragonflies add to the visual confusion.

We will have a lot of irregulars joining us today, and they will inevitably camp out in the north quadrant, freely "poaching" birds from east and west quadrants as well. Per standard policy, we do not mind the extra help: some of these irregulars are regular irregulars, and I have personally learned a good deal from the most stalwart among them. However, we anticipate being joined by an unusual number of irregulars today because it's Fleet Week. Even though the United States Navy no longer maintains a base in San Francisco Bay, the Blue Angels Flight Demonstration Squadron still shows up most years, and one of the better places from which to watch them, arguably, is Hawk Hill. Fortunately, the park service will shut down the road once there's no more parking left up here, this happens fairly early on days like today.

The violet-green swallows continue to pass by, bigger flocks than I've ever seen, and I worry that some of them might get sucked into a jet-engine intake once the air show escalates. I consult with one of the irregulars who is our most experienced hawkwatcher, and we estimate that five hundred are passing through each hour, which means that we will see several thousand migrating through today. As far as I'm concerned, they've completely stolen the show, not only from the birds of prey, but also from the warbirds as well.

For me, the highlight of the day comes when Lisa and I finally move to the west quadrant. The temperature has climbed into the 90s at this point, and despite the fact that I'm wearing a high-tech shirt with an SPF 30 rating, the sun feels as if it's doing its level best to burn my back. But we're far enough away from the commotion that we can take our time with the occasional accipiter, giving Lisa enough leisure to work the problem of whether the current bird is a sharp-shinned or a Cooper's hawk. Side by side, binoculars attending, we discuss the corners of the tail, the projection of the head, whether the bird gains altitude with each flap of the wing. It drives the irregulars crazy that we're so slow with our identifications, but the day leader intervenes, and asks them to give us time to study the birds. It doesn't help, after all, if someone calls out, "West, did you ID that sharpie yet?"

Lisa gets it, finally, calling a juvenile sharp-shinned hawk in to the person keeping the tally.

It's all about investing the time.

Total sightings: 452
Total species: 11[2]
Hawks per hour: 75.33

Sunday II

I almost arrive late, and Sunday II has already dispersed into quadrant teams when I get to the top of the hill. There's a westerly breeze and some distant fog spreading to the ocean horizon below. After yesterday's heat it feels merciful.

I find the day leader, a genial fellow who I've worked with before. Horacio. I ask him whether he wants me to join a quadrant—the alternative is to become an irregular myself—and Horacio asks me to join the team in the east quadrant. My two partners include an apprentice, Joey, who works at Point Reyes National Park as an NPS intern, and Christine, an IT developer who works with large-system medical records and who describes herself as a novice in her second year on Hawkwatch. They are a joy to work with, and I immediately feel as if I've been adopted by a new team.

Shortly after shifting to the south quadrant after the first hour I am approached by four Canadians who I instantly recognize as serious birders— they are all sporting high-end binoculars that cost as much as a decent horse. What I do not realize is that they'd all been attending a professional conference

---

2. Including two osprey and a golden eagle. And fourteen northern harriers!

on monitoring bird populations. Their leader, unable to hide the mischief in his smile, asks, "How do you know you're not counting the same birds twice?"

We get that question a lot. I launch into the usual explanation, saying, "We use a quadrant system where we pass . . ."

I am interrupted by Canadian laughter. Then, the one who had laughed the loudest explained, "That's exactly what Allen said you'd say."

Allen Fish, the Grand Pooh-Bah of the GGRO, has just celebrated his thirtieth anniversary on Hawk Hill. As soon as my new Canadian friends have formally introduced themselves, I spot Allen puffing up the hill. An affable, barrel-chested man with a beard fuller than my own, he comes to me immediately, shakes my left hand, and apologizes for the bee sting I'd suffered a week ago. (A yellow jacket had crawled into my sandwich while I was paying attention to a male northern harrier, and stung me on the side of my tongue once I took the next bite. What was funny about the whole situation is that after I'd gone to the first aid kit for some Benadryl, I was approached by the Hawkwatch director, Step Wilson, who asked, in his most sympathetic voice, "You gonna finish that sandwich?")

Today turns out to be Allen's fifty-fifth birthday. One of the interns, Violet, leads us in a round of "Happy Birthday to You." I note that most of the hawkwatchers are singing with their backs turned to Allen while they continue to monitor their respective quadrants. We've all been trained—by Allen himself—to keep our eyes on the sky. This piece of Hawkwatch etiquette is vital enough to have been mentioned twice in the Hawkwatch manual.

It's turning out to be a tough day for counting raptors. Things will nearly shut down for ten or fifteen minutes, and then we get a spurt of activity where it is almost impossible to count quickly enough. But I will remember today for our sighting of ferruginous hawks.

The largest of the buteo genus of hawks, *Buteo regalis* is truly regal. We look down on this juvenile as it forages above the coyote brush below, and the ventral view is striking because the tail glows with a whiter-than-white hue, almost matched by white patches in the primary feathers at the end of each wing. A particularly beautiful bird. One of the irregulars comments, "That hawk makes the whole day," and I realize that, up here on Hawk Hill, the Blue Angels, who are flying again today, will not make nearly as lasting an impression.

We will end up counting three juvenile ferruginous hawks—I mark them in my field notes as FEHA—during the watch. Two of them were close birds in the west quadrant. One was distant, in the east. Joey eyeballed that bird first, saying that he was on a buteo that wasn't a red-tailed hawk. That was a pretty good call for an apprentice, and I quickly got the bird in my scope, able to ID and age the FEHA.

It felt good to work as a team with members of another team.

Total sightings: 428
Total species: 11[3]
Hawks per hour: 71.33

Monday I

It was sunny in Sausalito when I left my boat, but I could hear foghorns from ships out on the bay, so I packed an extra layer at the last minute. I was engulfed in fog about halfway up the hill, so I drove down to Fort Cronkhite to meet up with the team who, I assumed correctly, would be in a holding pattern.

My Saturday II day leader, who will earn his twenty-year pin this year, doesn't like sitting around in the fog, so when we're delayed by poor visibility we tend to go off for a hike, diverting ourselves with shorebirds, quail, owls, or whatever else proves interesting on a foggy morning. The Monday I day leader, who will earn his twenty-five-year pin this year, takes a different approach, generally preferring to get to the top of the hill and wait until the fog burns off. Less wasted energy this way.

One of the team members asks whether she can carpool with anyone, and I offer her the shotgun seat in Little Dog. Her name is Nelia, and she's a recently retired environmental scientist who trained as a vertebrate zoologist but later became a restoration ecologist specializing in riparian zones. She worked most recently for the water district, doing a lot of spatial analysis. While loading her gear she spots the Baja sticker on my scope case, and we discover that we know many of the same people in the smallish world of Baja natural history.

We are the first two to reach the top of the hill, and it's cold. Breezy. My glasses fog up, and it's a lost cause to wipe them clean. There's nothing much to see anyway. Visibility is somewhere from forty to fifty meters, depending on the optimism of the person making the estimate.

As soon as the full team gathers, the topic of long underwear pops up. A pattern emerges: the older hawkwatchers are either wearing long johns, wind pants, or both, while the millennials are woefully unprepared, a few of them even wearing blue jeans. The youngsters drop down on the lee side of the hill, huddling together in generational solidarity. Baby boomers remain on top.

It's 10:00, and the day leader promises to call off the watch if it doesn't clear up by 11:00. It doesn't. But we spend a fine hour together, chilly but congenial,

3. A good falcon day with one peregrine, four merlins, and five kestrels. And a whopping 182 sharp-shinned hawks!

and when I descend the hill I feel an emptiness that I didn't get a few hours of birding in with this group.

But that's Hawkwatch.

Total sightings: 0
Total species: 0
Hawks per hour: n/a

Tuesday I

A grand day on the hill.

The Tuesday I day leader, Tim, is not only one of our most active hawk-watchers but one of our most expert as well. If we were to designate a Grand Irregular, it would be Tim; he is on the hill more days than not, and inevitably sets up his well-worn spotting scope on the east edge of the north-quadrant platform. Indeed, the only times Tim won't regularly be found at this spot is when he's working as day leader or when the 49ers have a home game.

I arrive on the hill a couple minutes after the team, and ask Tim which rotation group he wants me to assist. He has other ideas, however, and asks me to set up my scope in his usual spot, spending the day there since they're short on scopes. I'm not only honored but a bit intimidated by this, and I say a quick prayer to the raptor gods that I don't make any egregious mistakes.

Although the horizon is clear of fog, the day starts slow. It's a bit chilly, there's a high marine layer blocking the sun, and there's no wind, so most of the hawks are content to remain perched and await better conditions. However, a birding club and a birding class both join us, and by noon there are at least forty people atop the hill with binoculars around their necks. The group has a convivial feel, but the amount of chatter makes it difficult to hear what birds are being identified.

An irregular named Jim has taken a position across from me on the west edge of the north platform. He is reputed to be one of the best raptor ID guys in the state, and was active in Hawkwatch before moving south to Paso Robles a little more than a decade ago. He's here for a week during what's supposed to be peak migration, and this is the third day this season I've worked with him. He works without a scope, happy to leave distant birds to me. A notorious poacher, he has no qualms about identifying a bird in someone else's quadrant, but only if it's a worthy bird. If there's a falcon in the neighborhood, Jim will probably get it. Or an eagle, an osprey, or any of the more rare hawks. Working on the same platform as him invigorates me, strangely.

Over the course of the next few hours, Jim will poach three ferruginous hawks from the west quadrant—this ends up being our quota of FEHAs for the day. They are gorgeous birds, however, without exception, and the team is appreciative that they are identified quickly enough to give everyone a good look.

Meanwhile, I make the mistake of being overcautious. I spot a falcon high overhead, moving south, but I am not 100 percent certain which one. I have been trained to say something along the lines of "I have a falcon high in the fifth quadrant." Instead, I hesitate, just for a moment until I am confident of the ID. Normally, I would have gotten away with this, but the falcon spots its prey just as I feel confident that it's a merlin, *Falco columbarius*. The dark, chesty bird goes into a steep, fast stoop, easily exceeding one hundred miles per hour as it streaks downward, its wings folded in. An observer in the west quadrant sees the dive, and tentatively misidentifies the bird as a peregrine. I have to go over and confess that I had it as a merlin. Thus deadlocked, we have no choice but to ID the bird as an "unidentified falcon."

Had I been confident enough to ask for Jim's help at the outset, that bird would have been properly ID'd. Lesson learned.

Late in the afternoon we have a rush of good fortune, identifying a subadult bald eagle, a dark-morph redtail, a broadwing hawk and a peregrine falcon all within a two-minute window. This brings our number of species up to thirteen, which is agonizing. GGRO awards special pins to the team with the season's high species count at its annual banquet, but that award usually goes to a team with fourteen or even fifteen species.

During our last hour I move over to stand by Jim, saying, "Let's get a golden eagle." These big birds often come late in the day when the breeze is stronger. Jim replies, quietly, that he and Tim had watched a distant bird in the west that they suspected was a GOEA, but that it was entirely dark, silhouetted by an ocean backdrop, and that it glided the entire time he watched it go by. "If it had flapped even once," he lamented, "I'd have had it."

Ouch.

I compliment Jim on opting to go with "unidentified raptor" rather than GOEA. The integrity of the count, after all, is more important than being awarded a silly pin. He agrees, but somewhat glumly.

With ten minutes left in the count, I follow a Cooper's hawk below Mount Tamalpais, trying to age it, when it crosses in front of an osprey, a species no one has seen today. I blurt out, "Ooooh! Oooooh! . . . Below the golf ball!" Jim follows my clumsy directions, spots the osprey, slaps me on the back, and shouts, "Well, ID it!"

Tuesday I currently holds the honors for the high species count this season. There's still a lot of hawk-watching to go, but as we pack up our gear at 3:30, everyone agrees that fourteen species might be enough to win a pin this year.

Total sightings: 338
Total species: 14[4]
Hawks per hour: 56.33

Wednesday I

It's foggy again, so I show up at Fort Cronkhite at 8:30, careful to bring along an anthology so that I can occupy myself productively. I'm reading *Forest under Story: Creative Inquiry in an Old-Growth Forest* in final preparation for my visit to the Andrews Experimental Forest in a couple weeks.

The team is smaller: nine people not counting interns. Two members are missing, and something is said about them grieving.[5] Two of the members, Terry and Dennis, are introduced as having been part of the original Hawk-watch in 1986. It boggles the mind that these two gentlemen have been contributing to this effort for three decades. I scan the other name badges, and see a familiar name attached to an unfamiliar face: Mary Ellen Hannibal. It takes a few moments to place the name before I realize that Mary Ellen had a book come out last month. Allen had recommended that I read it, and it sits there, back on my boat, conveniently downloaded on my reading tablet: *Citizen Scientist: Searching for Heroes and Hope in an Age of Extinction*. I kick myself under the table for not having read it last weekend. Ah well, something more to read in the Oregon rain.[6]

We sit through a slide presentation about rough-legged hawks. In GGRO we call these "pizza birds" because the first team to identify one each year is treated to pizza on their next watch. As a devotee of all things cheesy, I pay rapt attention. Afterward, Allen descends from his upstairs office and engages

4. The subadult bald eagle was the second BAEA seen this year. We ended up with four kestrels, four merlins, three peregrines, and one "unidentified falcon."

5. It goes without saying that the cause of grief is the fact that the San Francisco Giants were knocked out of the playoffs the night before. Fans have come to expect the Giants to win the World Series on even years, as they've done three times consecutively. It has come as something of a shock to the city that this isn't our year.

6. I have been monitoring the Oregon weather since I'll be heading that way soon. This particular month will go on record as the rainiest October in Oregon in the past sixty years. When I finally arrive, Oregonians will wonder aloud where I got my tan.

us in a conversation about avian speciation that we would not be having were the sun shining. The chat is interesting, however, if you don't mind a bit of genetics with your birding.

The Wednesday I day leader, Christine, takes a different approach to fog delays. She directs us to assemble at a parking lot that hawkwatchers call "the Annex" about two-thirds of the way up Hawk Hill. The fog often dissipates here first, and we'll be able to keep an eye on the hilltop to determine when it clears. We can practice our raptor identification skills from the Annex even though none of those birds will count.

Although the fog clears all around us other than for one short, nasty drizzle, it never clears from the top of the hill. By 1:00, when the watch is called off for the day, we have managed to ID seven species: American kestrel, Cooper's hawk, sharp-shinned hawk, northern harrier, red-tailed hawk, red-shouldered hawk, and turkey vulture. All the usual suspects, with no sightings of pizza birds.

Total sightings: 0
Total species: 0
Hawks per hour: n/a

Thursday I

Both times I've been fogged out so far, someone on the team has said, "Oh well, at least we're not Thursday I." It is common knowledge that Thursday I hasn't even gotten up to the top of the hill this year, either because of fog or rain.

When I roll out of bed I immediately fire up the Internet and check one of the webcams looking north from the Golden Gate Bridge toll plaza. It shows that there is indeed fog atop Hawk Hill, but it doesn't look like deadly fog. I figure that with any luck it will burn off by 11:00.

On the other hand, Thursday I isn't known for its luck.

I meet the team at Fort Cronkhite at 8:30 and discover a few old friends. Natasha, a former GGRO intern, is now an interpretive ranger at Point Reyes National Seashore; she and I worked together recently on a pilot project to survey raptors up on Mount Tamalpais. She has great eyes, and her lively approach to birding makes the time pass quickly.

The day leader, Josh, is only twenty-nine years old, but has been active on Hawkwatch for twenty-one years. Yes, he was eight years old when he "officially" began. He points out that he was actually six years old when he started, but he wasn't considered part of a team until he'd proven himself for a couple years.

He's good.

At the briefing we get a serious talking to about the protocols of being fogged out. There has been a great deal of buzz going around GGRO the past few days because the Monday I day leader called off his watch the other day at 11:00. It turns out that things cleared up at noon, and by 12:30 a rough-legged hawk had turned up at one of the banding blinds. Had the bird been counted, it would have been the earliest roughie appearance in our thirty-year database.

Step, the Hawkwatch director, speaks gently to the team about the importance of sticking with our protocols so that we generate reliable data. He encourages us to find ways to stay motivated, even if we're going to be fogged out yet again. We discuss ways to pass the time productively here at Fort Chronkhite, and one suggestion that seems to generate interest is that we can visit the skin room, where deceased birds have been preserved, and study feather topography. Josh follows up Step's speech with stronger words, about how teams who quit early are not being fair to other teams who stick it out on bad days. We need to be committed to our science.

Josh leaves the room when the interns start showing the rough-legged slides, and returns a short minute later with the news that Hawk Hill seems to be clearing up. He suggests that we skip the rest of the slides and get up the hill. We scramble like fighter pilots.

On the hill, I team up with David, a man who graduated from college the same year that I did. He works as a golf-course superintendent, which means he works four days per week, with Thursdays always off. "It's a great career for birding," he assures me. He's been a GGRO volunteer for nine years.

It's slow for the first ninety minutes, with only the small accipiters bothering to fly. The range of hills to the north is still covered in fog, but we can see low-flying birds. After two hours Natasha, who has been keeping the tally, asks who wants to take over. She looks directly at me.

My dirty secret is that I missed the training session on how to score the tally sheets—it's never really been an issue on Saturday II, where we have so many willing data recorders that my services are never required. However, when Natasha and I were working together on Mount Tamalpais, there were only four people working the mountain that day, so everyone took a turn at the book. Including me. Things were slow enough on Mount Tam I could teach myself how to tally.

Natasha is still staring, so I volunteer. After all, it's a slow day, so it shouldn't be too difficult. Right?

Natasha takes my spot in the rotation, and I situate myself in the center of the four quadrants so that I can hear. Josh comes up to me and quietly suggests that I should visit each quadrant, tell them that I've got the book, and remind them that my name is John. I do so, ending up with the north quadrant, where one of the irregulars comments that it was starting to clear around Mount Tam, and that we might soon be getting a jailbreak.

I didn't sign up for a jailbreak, I think to myself.

Big Alaskan birds like bald eagles don't mind flying in the rain—it's what they do for a living. But less robust birds tend to hit the migratory pause button in inclement conditions. Many of these birds were sitting tight through all of yesterday. It's possible that they even knew there was a storm moving down from the north, and therefore they want to get out of here while the getting is good. That constitutes a "jailbreak," in Hawk-watch lingo.

I've been on the hill during a couple jailbreaks over the years, and I find them invigorating. Fun for everyone except the dude with the book.

Over the course of the next hour we count seventy-six raptors, mostly Cooper's hawks and sharp-shinned hawks. At one point I run out of space for undocumented sharpies, in other words for sharp-shinned hawks for which it was not possible to determine age for one reason or the other. Often this happens because the bird is too distant, or the viewing angle isn't right. Other times this happens because there are too many birds coming too fast to spend the time it takes aging a single sharpie. I call out at one point that I'm running out of room for undocumented birds, a gentle way of asking for greater diligence at determining age. Then I remind myself that it is Thursday I's first time on the hill this season; these rusty hawkwatchers must be feeling the strain.

My second hour isn't so bad. There is time to chat with a visitor who turns out to be a pilot from British Airways on layover. He is a bird band-er in his spare time, and is delighted to discover that I'm fluent in British birding, where blinds are called "hides," banding is called "ringing," and the closest thing they have to a National Audubon Society is the Royal Soci-ety for the Protection of Birds. I lend him my binoculars after letting him in on the secret that I earned my PhD in Scotland, and was able to sneak away from exams to get in some birding in the Hebrides islands and the Cairngorm Mountains. When I ask whether he's ever read the work of poet and nature writer Kathleen Jamie, who was my doctoral supervisor, he re-sponds, "Of course."

I return to the quadrants after my second hour, working again with David. Our camaraderie was strengthened by the absence, and by the end the watch I feel as if I've truly become a member of Thursday I. I can only hope that some of their steadfast cheerfulness has rubbed off on me.

Total sightings: 313[7]
Total species: 10
Hawks per hour: 55.2

Friday I

Our first major autumnal storm was forecast to arrive just after midnight Friday morning and to continue through 10:00, at which point it should turn into occasional showers. Step, the Hawkwatch director, counsels that I should hold off until 10:00 to come in to Fort Cronkhite. I'm awake at 4:30 anyway, awakened by a southerly gust that hits the boat square abeam, and I make my tea while listening to the rain bounce off the deck above. While I love sleeping on a sailboat, it's much more difficult to ignore a storm in the forward berth of a sloop than in a brick-and-mortar domicile.

I arrive at Fort Cronkhite at 10:00, only to discover that the team just decided to delay until 11:00. I walk in as Teresa Ely, the banding program director, finishes presenting a paper on declining populations of American kestrels that, judging from the conclusion, I would love to have heard in full.[8] Everyone disperses soon afterward, leaving me to myself in the conference room.

A central tenet of my father's philosophy was "Never get stuck without a good book." Like his son, Dad had attended grad school later in life than the norm, using it as a transition into a career as an academic. Like my father, I relish the idea of an uninterrupted hour with the book I'm currently reading. I lay it on the table beside my field notebook, and, other than the lack of a roaring fire and a fresh cup of tea, I am perfectly content. Indeed, it's not until 11:30 that I notice that the team never showed up.

The rain subsides as soon as I'm back in Little Dog, so I decide to take the long way home via the summit of Hawk Hill, figuring that as long as I'm wearing my foul weather gear, I might as well see whether there are any hawks about. Before I get to the parking lot below the summit, however, it becomes

---

7. Of which 131 were accipiters! A tough day for Thursday I's first day on the hill.

8. I was able to read the paper later online, and found it disturbing. It can be downloaded at Teresa E. Ely, "Population and Morphological Changes in American Kestrels through Space and Time" (master's thesis, Univ. of Nebraska, Lincoln, 2016), http://digitalcommons.unl.edu/cgi/viewcontent.cgi?article=1085&context=bioscidiss.

clear that there will be no hawking today. Perhaps not even tomorrow. The fog is more dense than I've ever seen it on this hill.

Total sightings: 0
Total species: 0
Hawks per hour: n/a

Saturday I

I've stood watch with Saturday I numerous times in the past. Their day leader, Bob, is the former director of the Santa Clara Valley Audubon Society, so I've known him for years. He's a stickler for protocol, and his team is more skilled at scope usage than any team I've been with to date, a high percentage of them bringing in their own scopes. Saturday I is a well-oiled machine. Unfortunately, the machine may have gotten a bit rusty today.

The rule these days in California, especially given the recent wildfires, is that no one is allowed to complain about inclement weather during a drought. It grows wearisome, however, to be missing so many days during my rotation.

Total sightings: 0
Total species: 0
Hawks per hour: n/a

Sunday I

Showers are forecast, but a ground fog covers the coast for the first time this week. The fog is dense enough that I drive slower than the thirty-five-mile-per-hour speed limit on Bunker Road, worried that I won't see a bobcat or a coyote until it's too late.

Only six banders show up, but their protocols are different because, for the safety of the birds, they can't use wet nets. I'm almost surprised—and I shouldn't be—that a full complement of twelve hawkwatchers shows up, not counting me and the two interns.

The day leader, Dennis, begins our briefing with a strong statement about the protocol of not calling the watch off until 1:00, explaining how what happened on Monday I was problematic. His message, in essence, is that Sunday I is going to do what it's supposed to do: sit tight until 1:00 despite fog and rain.

Showers are forecast, and one of the team members has an app that tells her exactly when each shower will hit our location. It turns out to be accurate to within a minute.

By 10:00, when the drizzle turns into a solid rain, the banders leave, followed shortly by the telemetry team, since they can't do their work unless the banders have provided them with a bird to track. Now that we have the building to ourselves, we shift gears: some of us read, others chat quietly. We share snacks. I only read for half an hour, and then pull out my Moleskine notebook to catch up on my field notes.

While I am in the process of writing this sentence, I am interrupted by an apprentice, Julia, who wants to know about the book I'm writing. I quickly discover her to be knowledgeable about the role of long-term ecological studies, and then learn that she earned a master's of public administration from Columbia with a concentration in environmental education.

We continue to chat while a number of the team members congregate with their smartphones or tablets, comparing weather apps and live weather radar images. Our conversation, which I'm enjoying entirely, is cut short. At 11:05, the day leader, having become convinced of the futility of waiting for a break in either the fog or the rain, let alone both, calls the watch over for the day.

So much for protocol.

Total sightings: 0
Total species: 0
Hawks per hour: n/a

Monday II

Light pouring through the hatches of my sailboat wakes me up around 2:00 a.m., shortly after a squall blows through. It is the moon, and I realize that it's been a while since I last saw it. The skies have cleared. I am excited to return to my sabbatical this morning, and I have trouble getting back to sleep, as this writing attests. I lie abed, dozing off and on, listening to blissful silence coming from the foghorns on Golden Gate Bridge.

Hiking the steep pathway up to the summit I do not see any hawks, but I spot at least a dozen western bluebirds, which appear absolutely electric when backgrounded by fog. The breeze is southwesterly, which probably means that we won't see huge numbers of migrants today. Not only would they prefer something out of the north, or at least the northwest, but they'll probably need to forage today to make up for the past few days when they've been hunkered down because of the weather. For a hawk, migration on an empty stomach is death.

I arrive on Hawk Hill five minutes before Monday II shows up, and the hilltop is clear although there are some low clouds to the west. By the time the team gets to the parking lot, however, those clouds blow in, and visibility is reduced to a hundred meters or so. This is to be the theme of the day: the vacillation between fog and sunshine slows us down but never defeats us. As one of the irregulars was later to state, "There's just enough fog to be annoying." But many of us, those of us who take longer to ID a bird, will be frustrated to have birds vanish even though we are staring right at them through our optics. It sometimes feels as if the birds are blinking existentially.

Monday II is the smallest team in the GGRO, and I have no idea why. They are delightful, at least the six of them I meet. Their day leader, Laury, has an infectious humor that takes a few moments to figure out. When I ask how long she has been on Hawkwatch, she replies, "Twenty-two years," and then jests, "I started when I was five."

Our first bird of the day is not a bird at all—it's a bobcat. It traverses the next hill over, perhaps a 150 meters below us, and seems to be enjoying the post-storm sunshine. We all gather on the north quadrant platform to gawk through our binoculars, and when I offer a view through my spotting scope there are numerous takers. Meanwhile, thousands and thousands of termites are swarming atop Hawk Hill, pouring from holes in the mineral soil that we didn't even know were there. Termite swarms take place, at least here in California, after a rain, and they break off their wings after they've mated. This is probably not a reproductive strategy that would work for *Homo sapiens*.

The ground is soon littered with silver wings, each one a testament that sex has been happening up here. A lot of sex.

We watch as a nearby California scrub-jay devours minuscule snacks, easily snapping up twenty just-emerged termites each minute for at least ten minutes. It hops as if its legs are built of spring steel, and when I squint I can trace how it descended from dinosaurs. To these termites, velociraptors still exist. Above us, white-throated swifts, hundreds of them, swarm in a feeding frenzy of their own, chattering incessantly. One of the irregulars, Herb, suggests that the chatter is a collision avoidance system to keep swallows from running into each other. I think he's serious about this.

Herb is precious; he retired after forty years working for the phone company—he claims to have been a pole climber all that time—and he rides his mountain bike from San Francisco across the Golden Gate Bridge and up to the summit of Hawk Hill almost every day. Almost. Every. Day. I've never caught him making a mistake on a bird even though he takes half the time I need to make an ID. But that's birds. It was Herb who first noticed the bobcat, but he misidentified it as a coyote.

You've just gotta love Herb.

Our first buteo[9] is a leucistic red-tailed hawk. Leucistic birds are not complete albinos, but grow some feathers that don't have color pigment. This bird's dorsal coverts, both primary and secondary, are white; its flight feathers and tail feathers are normally pigmented. In short, it appears from above to be wearing glow-in-the-dark shoulder pads. With a red tail.

Of course, I had decided to lug my camera up the hill tomorrow, not today.

No loss—Herb describes it perfectly: "That bird looks like it lost a paintball fight."

At 3:30, the steep trail back down to the parking lot is littered with termite wings.

Total sightings: 255
Total species: 11[10]
Hawks per hour: 44.35

Tuesday II

I arrive on Hawk Hill a few minutes late because, during the drive up, I pulled over to chat with two of our telemetry team members, Max and Ron, who are also members of my Hawkwatch team, Saturday II. They are excited to be tracking a female Cooper's hawk broadcasting on a new, smaller transmitter that we're experimenting with to allow us to track smaller birds. This bird's name is Paula—the telemetry teams name their birds in alphabetical order, just like hurricanes. The next bird will start with Q, and the top vote getter so far is Quixote. The telemetry team hopes that Paula leads them all the way to Mexico, but for now she's perched in some trees within a mile of where she was released yesterday. It's axiomatic, here in the GGRO, that birds won't fly until they're ready to fly.

I'm greeted at the top of the hill by a flock of cedar waxwings, the yellow tips of their tails glowing as if each bird is being chased by a shooting star. Beautiful birds, but awfully screechy when they migrate. Back on campus these

---

9. The buteo genus is characterized by a robust body, broad wings, and a broad, relatively short tail. When most Americans use the word "hawk," what they are really referencing is a buteo.

10. Including two ferruginous hawks, a fabulous peregrine falcon flying close to the summit, and four merlins.

gregarious birds are among my favorites. They flock year-round except when nesting, and they love to perch shoulder to shoulder with other members of their flock. If you're fortunate, you'll see a well-fed waxwing land on a branch near its kin with a berry in its bill, and pass the berry along. If the next bird has already had its fill, it passes the berry along to the next, until someone is finally hungry enough to swallow it.

The day leader, Mary, has been active in Hawkwatch for twenty-two years. She expresses appreciation that I'm going to help out for the day. I've noticed that the weekday day leaders tend to do this, but not the weekend day leaders—probably because the weekend teams are so large that an extra pair of eyes in the sky doesn't make that much of a difference. Or perhaps the weekday day leaders are just nicer. I'd need to conduct more rigorous research to determine this.

The air is clear with almost no fog and smallish puffy clouds scattered above, but the gentle southerly breeze, at least at hilltop, is contrary. The expectation among the more knowledgeable team members is that many raptors will spend the day foraging, still making up for the recently passed rain front, and won't get serious about resuming migration until tomorrow. It is generally agreed that with the right wind, tomorrow could be epic.

The red-shouldered hawks didn't seem to read the memo about not migrating into a gentle southerly, and we see an unusual number of them, six juveniles and five adults, most of which come through early in the day. I feel a particular affinity for red-shouldered hawks; I'm not sure why. Maybe it's just the how the white commas at their wrists seem translucent when you look down on them from a hilltop. Watching a red-shouldered hawk from above is always a privilege.

There's a lot of chatter about yesterday's leucistic red-tail, and about a northern goshawk that was seen by a smaller hawkwatch group up north in Jenner. We are hopeful that the goshawk will show up here today or tomorrow. The Jenner hawkwatchers, reportedly, were unable to document the goshawk's age, which makes some of our members skeptical of the sighting. One of the irregulars asks, "How can you be sure it was a goshawk if you couldn't age it?"

As heads nod, I resolve to brush up on goshawk identification tonight at home. The last one I saw was a nesting female up at Tuolumne Meadows in Yosemite National Park a couple of summers ago. I remember it to be a large accipiter with a distinctive supercilium,[11] but I don't exactly remember how to age the birds other than to look for the heavily streaked breast of

---

11. To humans the supercilium appears to be a large white eyebrow, although it's not technically an eyebrow at all.

juveniles. Like many other hawks, the breasts of adults are barred rather than streaked. The female we saw in Yosemite dive-bombed us aggressively on the trail, apparently defending her nest, which we never saw. It was one of those I-wish-I'd-brought-my-camera hikes.

The day's most memorable moment for Tuesday II comes when two merlins threaten to go into the near blind while a small peregrine takes a few swoops at a blind farther up the ridge. In our excitement it is hard to know who we are cheering for, the birds or the banders.

During our last hour someone points out, a couple miles away, a flock of more than a hundred white-fronted geese moving from left to right across the north quadrant. They are so far away that they're not visible without binoculars, and not identifiable without a scope. The Vs this particular species forms always seem disorganized, but are fluid and alive, and I found this flock particularly mesmerizing. I stay with it in my spotting scope for several long minutes. On a normal hawkwatch with my own team I would never allow myself these self-indulgent minutes monitoring birds other than raptors. But I feel, somehow, that I've earned the respite. This is, after all, my sabbatical.

I am fatigued when I return to the boat to transcribe my field notes, almost as if I need a day off from Hawkwatch. Even though the watches are never longer than six hours, it's difficult to maintain an appropriate level of attentiveness hour after hour, day after day. My face seems a bit more sunburned than usual even though I applied serious sunblock and wore my broad-billed Tilley all day. And my eyes are fatigued even though my binoculars and spotting scope are the finest optics available, each costing thousands. According to the literature, that sort of investment is supposed to ward off eyestrain.

I resist the temptation to check e-mail or my news app before attending to my notes, but I am unable to forego opening a beer before I finish typing these sentences.

Total sightings: 278
Total species: 8
Hawks per hour: 46.33

Wednesday II

When I share with the irregulars how drained I felt at the end of yesterday's watch, they agree wholeheartedly. "Nobody realizes how much stamina this takes," one says. "You get better at it the more you do it," says another.

The day is absolutely gorgeous. It's the first crystal clear day since two Saturdays ago, and there's a consistent breeze out of the east that is supposed to turn northerly by afternoon. It's strong enough to make me zip up my field vest, but not strong enough to necessitate a windbreaker. Perfect conditions for migration.

When the group hears that five of my twelve days so far have been fogged out, the regulars want to know whether the irregulars think it's been as crazy a year as it seems. There haven't been many days with more than five hundred sightings, and species counts have tended to be low. Could this be because of the drought?

The irregulars point out that patterns seem to be shifting. For example, we're getting many more merlins and peregrine falcons than we did historically, but fewer American kestrels. We discuss the kestrel situation at great length, our eyes always on the skies, but no one has heard anything definitive about why kestrels are in decline.

Our first falcon of the day is a Peale's peregrine. This subspecies is fairly common worldwide, but we don't see many of them on Hawk Hill. We take it as a good omen of things to come.

One of the telemetry team members, Phil, is up on the hill this morning with all his gear, including a Yagi antenna that looks like something left over from a black-and-white era science documentary, or maybe the death-ray prop from a 1930s science fiction film. It seems funny, as he sweeps the antenna in an arch, his arm out stiffly, that we haven't yet come up with something more sophisticated. The Cooper's hawk they've been trailing has been sticking around, moving from grove to grove without ever leaving the headlands. When I ask what Phil does when he's not involved in telemetry, he answers that he's a field biologist who specializes in seabirds. He switched from banding to telemetry, he tells me, because it was easier to structure the time commitment around his work.

Around midday a news helicopter flies overhead, which somehow leads to a discussion about tonight's final presidential debate between Clinton and Trump. Bob, the day leader from Saturday I, who is here today as an irregular, complains, "Darn it, you guys, I just went three hours without thinking about that mess." Jon, the Wednesday II day leader, adds, "We come up the hill to escape!"

There is no more talk of politics.

Bob doesn't end up staying the whole day. He leaves a little after 2:00, claiming that he's going to "take one for the team." This is something of a Hawkwatch joke, because when someone leaves early there is usually a late eagle or a rare bird that comes as soon as they've given up the watch. Sure enough, we get a good look at a juvenile golden eagle within twenty minutes of Bob's departure. While the people from the north quadrant are still watching it disappear into the south, I spot a second golden eagle coming from the north. This one's a subadult, and also gives us a good look. Then, around 3:20, with only ten minutes to go in the watch, we spot a Swainson's hawk, only the second one of these to be spotted this season, and my first one this year.

As we hike down the hill there's a great deal of joking about what Bob will say when he reads the daily hawk count on the website[12] this evening. Although we didn't get the epic day that most of us were hoping for, we got some really fine birds.

I'm able to type out my filed notes today without first pouring a beer.

Total sightings: 385
Total species: 13[13]
Hawks per hour: 64.17

Thursday II

I'm climbing the hill slowly today, feeling a bit more weighted down than usual, perhaps because I'm carrying the camera and a huge lens. Step, the Hawkwatch director, comes up behind me, snatches the scope case from my hand, and proceeds up the hill at a faster pace than I can match. Robert the intern trails behind him.

In addition to being the Hawkwatch director, Step serves as day leader for Thursday II, begging the question of whether he transmogrifies from scientist to citizen scientist ten times each autumn.

I start out in the north quadrant, teamed up with Nancy, a veterinarian who specializes in horses. Once again I'm shoulder to shoulder with a citizen scientist who has some serious scientific credentials. Not that Hawkwatch doesn't include its share of teachers, retired postal workers, and software developers. It would be interesting to study the professional credentials of our three hundred volunteers to determine whether there's a pattern here, at least in terms of the scientific literacy of our crew. How many of our citizen

12. http://www.parksconservancy.org/conservation/plants-animals/raptors/research/daily-hawk-count.html
13. In addition to the usual suspects, this includes one osprey, four white-tailed kites, two ferruginous hawks, nine red-shouldered hawks, two golden eagles, five merlins, six peregrines, and one Swainson's hawk.

scientists moonlight as professional scientists on the side? Might there be a paper in there somewhere?

Morning is slow even though a northerly breeze is blowing. The highlight of the morning is when Bob shows up and all the irregulars, myself included, thank him for leaving early yesterday so that we could get the two golden eagles and the Swainson's hawk. Bob gets even, cracking jokes all day, starting with his first ID, when he chants, "I've got a bird moving left on North Slacker Ridge . . . It's a buteo . . . It's a red-tail . . . It's a juvenile . . . It's a Taurus!"

One of the irregulars immediately responds, "Are you sure, Bob? From here it seems to be a Gemini."

Despite the slow start, we expect a glut of raptors as soon as the wind pipes up. It dies at noon, however, almost as if the United States Park Service neglected to pay its wind bill. Herb, the irregular (and former day leader) who once again rode his bike up the hill from San Francisco, recites the rule for anyone who hasn't heard it, "No breeze, no birds."

The accipiters keep coming, but little else. Big birds are not going to wing it in these conditions. There's just not enough food en route to make migration a sensible option on a day like today, especially given the drought.

In midafternoon an irregular drops in who just came back from the Hawk Ridge Hawkwatch in Minnesota. He describes days when they saw upward of three hundred bald eagles, and how at any moment there would be at least ten birds visible. During this conversation, one of the team members looks over at me and suggests, "Maybe you should have taken your sabbatical in Duluth."

Sigh.

The temperature climbs. Although it tops out at 83 degrees Fahrenheit, it feels warmer given the lack of wind.

We finally see an intermediate-morph red-tail, which one of the irregulars calls a "speckle-belly" because of the distinctive mottling throughout its breast and belly. I comment that it looks just like the speckle-belly that came through here yesterday, at which point an intern asks, "How do we know it's not the same bird?"

This intern has apparently forgotten an important part of her training, which is that we're not actually counting raptors. Instead, we're counting raptor sightings. If a raptor is sighted today and is sighted again tomorrow, that's two distinct sightings. This is important for our data—as long as we're consistent with our protocols about what constitutes a separate sighting, the data are useful.

After this is explained to the intern, Herb interjects, "The protocols are not to be confused with science."

Such is the way, I'm coming to understand, with Hawkwatch. The slower the birding becomes, the faster the jokes come.

Irregulars start trickling out around 2:30; the old-timers intuit that there's little chance for a significant bird showing up without a breeze. I spend the last hour in the east quadrant with Robert the intern, chatting in between birds about his plans, his future. Robert has a bachelor of science in biology, but would like to move into the public policy arena regarding conservation issues. He's applying for internships with conservation organizations, thinking that one more good internship is in order before he considers graduate school.

I concur that this is a sensible plan, especially if it's a paid internship.

I leave the hill feeling good that we had five kestrel sightings today. Even though it was a shame that Thursday II wasn't able to get into the double digits in terms of total species, and even though the biggest bird we saw was an osprey, a single osprey, I would not have wanted to go a third consecutive day without sighting an American kestrel.

Total sightings: 354
Total species: 9
Hawks per hour: 59

Friday II

There is fog inversion today, so the top of Hawk Hill is clear and sunny, but the valleys to the north, the bay to the east, the ocean to the west and the Golden Gate itself are choked with fog. This could potentially make our observations more difficult, depending on whether some of it burns off. But it's a beautiful sight, one that could tempt a fellow to turn to landscape photography.

The day leader, James, instructs the team to put on extra sunscreen and to protect their eyes. Many hawkwatchers do their birding without sunglasses because they can pick up subtle plumage hues better without them. But on a day like today, with all the extra light reflecting up from below, and all the glare, one has to worry about eye sunburn, photokeratitis.

When I ask James how long he's been on Hawkwatch, he chuckles, explaining that at the day leader meeting this year he turned out to be the least experienced of all fourteen team leaders. It turns out that he's only participated in Hawkwatch for seventeen years. In day leader years, this makes him something of a subadult.

It takes this group longer than usual to set up in their initial quadrants. At first I'm not certain why they are slow, but then I notice that we've got twelve spotting scopes set up once everyone is in place. For my own team, Saturday II, we're lucky to have a scope in each of the quadrants!

It quickly becomes apparent that this is going to be something of an accipiter day. Accipiters are birds of the forest, having evolved to prey on other birds. They have relatively short wings and long tails in comparison to buteos such as red-tailed hawks, which tend to have long, broad wings and short, broad tails. With this fog inversion we won't have the wind or the thermals that buteos and larger, heavier birds need for migration. Accipiters, which tend to soar less and to move about with a flap-flap-glide pattern, and which tend to be lighter birds, won't be as put off by this inversion.

The problem with identifying accipiters is that the farther away they are, the more difficult it is to pick up the field marks that distinguish them from each other. The tails of sharpies are less rounded than coops because there is a smaller delta between the fifth and sixth rectrix feathers on each side. Usually. And the heads of coops tend to project farther beyond the wings than sharpies while soaring, usually. The eye of a sharpie takes up more of its head than the eye of a coop, and its legs are thinner, and the white terminal band on the tip of its tail is narrower, and its tail is proportionally shorter, and the bill isn't as aquiline, and the cap of adults isn't as dark, nor is the nape as pale, but this sort of detail can be difficult to discern on days like today.

The banders are especially busy whenever there are large numbers of accipiters. Because of the system GGRO uses to lure in birds, accipiters tend to be more easily enticed into the bow nets.

Once a bird is trapped, it is quickly released from the bow net, and then assessed prior to being banded. It gets weighed and measured, and sometimes there is even a blood sample taken, depending on what our scientists are investigating at the moment. And how they are funded. The bird then receives its leg band so that if it's ever recaptured or if its body is found after it dies, the person finding the band will contact us with information that helps us determine where it breeds or where it winters.

Then comes the fun part, at least for the hawkwatchers. If the bird was captured in "Hawk Blind," the blind closest to the summit of Hawk Hill, the banders will radio us and ask whether we want a "study bird." If we're so busy identifying birds that we can't spare a minute for the study, we'll decline the opportunity and they'll release the bird privately. But that rarely happens. If we accept the opportunity for a study bird, one person will stay behind in each quadrant while the rest of the team, especially the apprentices and novices, will head over to the north quadrant to participate in the study.

There's a small stake with a tiny orange flag at the release point. We are not able to see the banders during the release, but they count down on the walkie-talkie—five, four, three, two, one, release—before letting the bird go free.

Some birds are uncooperative, and dive out of view within a few seconds, certainly not giving the less experienced hawkwatchers time to study the bird, especially if the only view was tail feathers. Other birds will fly around for a bit, giving us views from different angles and showing us different flight patterns. These birds, even if they are accipiters, tend to be easier to ID.

The protocol on the hill is that no one is allowed to talk about the bird except for one of the more experienced birders who will describe where the bird can be seen, landmark by landmark. Then, once the bird is out of sight, there's a discussion, usually starting with apprentices, about what you're able to say about this bird. If you couldn't identify a bird to species, it's okay to identify its genus.

Then, after the group has decided to the best of its ability everything it can about the bird's natural history, the day leader will call on the radio and ask the banders for a description. What comes back will be impassioned, something along the lines of "Hatch-year male sharp-shinned hawk."

These study birds provide a way for us to determine the accuracy of our data collection, both as individuals and as teams. For example, over the course of the past two weeks I've probably participated in fifty studies, and I've gotten them all right except for one. There was a coop that was flying away from me and disappeared after maybe five seconds, and I guessed it to be a sharpie. I should have called it an "unidentified accipiter," which is what one of our more experienced hawkwatchers said. It was a humbling mistake even though I've been able to identify 98 percent of the study birds I've seen this year.

Today, with our lovely fog inversion, there are more study birds than I've ever seen. Hawk blind seems to be releasing a bird every fifteen minutes, and they have all been accipiters except for one merlin.

I decide to sit for a study, and hear myself making an old-man noise as I settle down to dangle my legs over the edge of the concrete slab. Embarrassing. It's late in the watch, however, and I've certainly earned my fatigue. When they release the bird I immediately, silently identify it as a sharpie. It climbs more sharply than a Cooper's hawk would, then it mutes and veers left, crossing a nearby coop. I decided to stay with the coop, already having aged the sharpie. It crosses the other direction, and out of the corner of my binoculars I see a flash of white. A ferruginous hawk! I scream, "I've got a ferruge!" and every hawkwatcher on the north quadrant shouts, in unison, "WHERE?"

We never did get back to identifying that study bird.

We end up seeing two ferruginous hawks this afternoon. Both are juveniles, and both were discovered and identified by yours truly. Loudly. The second of these came during the last half hour of the watch, after most of the irregulars had left.

It's the closest I've ever come to feeling heroic.

Here's what the interns, Chase and Emily, posted in the GGRO daily hawk count blog afterward:

Today was a lovely symphony of foghorns and raptors. The hill was still and sunny, and the hawkwatchers were only slightly blinded by the reflection off the fog that hung below the hill. The team was challenged by the lighting; lots of "dark morph" accipiters were recorded, and lots of individuals showed a false orange tint. But with good communication and collaboration, all the birds got the attention and tallies they deserved. A westerly wind picked up later in the afternoon and brought a nice flurry of harriers, a red-shouldered hawk, an adult peregrine, mystery kestrel, and two juvenile ferruginous hawks!

Total sightings: 417[14]
Total species: 10
Hawks per hour: 75.82

Postscript

In terms of peak migration, the two weeks I attended during the autumn migration in 2016 may have been an all-GGRO low for that time of year. Six of the fourteen days were either fogged or rained out, which is unusual for October in these parts. The highest daily total, 452, occurred the first day, when I counted hawks with Saturday II, my own team.

On one hand, it must be noted that over the fourteen consecutive days I participated in this project, we counted only 3,211 raptors. Compare this with the fact that the GGRO has had days when over a thousand hawks were counted. It was a fairly slow couple of weeks, especially during theoretical peak migration.

On the other hand, Oh my god! I saw more than three thousand raptors in two weeks! Really, how many people on this planet can say that and still be disappointed?

14. Of which 218 were accipiters!

4

Notes from the H. J. Andrews Experimental Forest

I am alarmed when it happens that I have walked a mile
into the woods bodily, without getting there in spirit.

Henry David Thoreau, "Walking," 1862

Day 1

As Little Dog winds its way up the placid McKenzie River, I listen to National Public Radio via a satellite channel. First, NPR reports that the seven defendants who occupied the Malheur National Wildlife Refuge here in Oregon were just found to be not guilty. Following that comes a report that the World Wildlife Fund just released the latest edition of the Living Planet Report, which claims that the global wildlife population is less than half as large as it was when I was in high school. I'm not certain which report to find more shocking.

The deeper I get into logging country, the more "Drain the Swamp" signs I see by the side of the road. It occurs to me that an environmentalist ought to enter into this discourse with a sign saying, "Preserve the Swamps & Restore the Wetlands."

I have the feeling, when I finally exit the highway onto USFS Road 15-130-132, that I've arrived late for the party. But it's sunny here, and the fall colors along the river are spectacular. From where I park it's hard to imagine that anything could be wrong with nature. The river was full, wasn't it?

I am issued a bright-yellow hard hat, which the United States Forest Service prefers me to wear when I'm out and about, especially since it's elk season, and a heavy USFS radio, which I am "urged in the strongest terms to always pack and keep on while in the field." I'm also issued a spare battery and written instructions on how to call for help.

Getting here was something of a whirlwind. It's Friday, not yet a full week since I left Hawk Hill for the last time this year. After driving home on Saturday, I flew to Wesleyan University in Connecticut on Monday, gave a six-hour workshop there on Tuesday, flew home on Wednesday, and drove off for Oregon on Thursday. In the process, I forgot to pack shirts, so I purchased three flannel shirts at an outlet store in Reading, California, in the hopes that FedEx could catch me up with the rest of my clothing soon.

I am assigned to a three-room studio in the "Green House"—nothing fancy, but nothing lacking. Cement floors, radiant heat. I unpack the same plastic tubs and cooler I used on Santa Cruz Island, plus an additional duffel bag, and this time I've packed enough beer to start a fraternity.

A smaller spotting scope this time, my travel scope. Better for hiking. Six field guides and a Kindle full of literature. Several pairs of thermals, two pairs of rain trousers, a British waterproof parka—moss green—suitable for birding in Scotland, three pairs of gloves, two scarves, gaiters, and two pairs of ankle-high waterproof boots, the "regular" ones and the extras I purchased while at Hastings. I'm all set, other than for shirts.

I pause, finally, and remind myself that rain is heading this way. Lots of rain. The food in the cooler can stay there for now. I return to the headquarters, recruit a "buddy" to make certain I check in by 6:00, and then guide Little Dog up Lookout Ridge to get some sense of the Andrews Experimental Forest's scope. Once we get more than five miles past where the pavement ends, I feel glad for the heavy Forest Service radio I'm carrying. I also make a mental note to toss a blanket in the back next time I wander up one of these roads. A rockslide or a fallen tree could cut me off for the night, and even though there's always a foam camping pad back in the camper shell, it would be a chilly night there without the solace of a cover.

The forest is entirely unfamiliar, and yet its eerie first impressions live up to my expectations. Having lived in Colorado, New Mexico, and Arizona prior to my current sojourn in California, my sense of at-homeness leans toward something more arid. This forest has the feel of abiding precipitation—a place where it has rained recently and will soon be raining again. Steam appears wherever sunlight breaks through the forest canopy for more than a few moments, and drifts skyward. I ask myself whether I could ever live in a place such as this.

Nine miles beyond pavement's end I finally come to a small clearing, perhaps thirty meters in diameter, surrounded by second-growth firs and hemlocks. A former clear-cut. It's windy here, which surprises me because down in the old-growth sections there was no appreciable breeze. I stand outside

Little Dog for a while just taking in the soundscape. The noise is clearly being generated by the top two or three meters of each tree; it crescendos down on me, sounding sharp, as if a thousand foils are being slashed. The sylvan orchestration fluctuates, rolling around this little glen, animating it gratuitously.

To the south, through the trees and across the valley, the opposite hillside is such an aquamarine blue that at first I think I'm seeing ocean. I snap a wide-angle lens on the camera and proceed to wade through the thick understory beyond the clearing. There is no trail, and yet I can tell that someone—if not a person then a perhaps a bear—has bushwhacked through here before me. Tough going.

I come to a steep drop-off, and the forest again plays tricks on my eyes, seeming to stretch my vision unnaturally. I realize that as someone accustomed to more open landscapes, I lack some of the visual literacy I need to make sense of the expanse before me. Even the colors don't make sense because the conifers have a way of absorbing light without reflecting it back. The washed-out sky has no brilliance, and the depth of the forest below seems extreme. Clearly, the trees I'm looking down on are taller than I think. I would like to come back here again, or someplace similar, with my chair and writing table, and spend a day just watching this valley absorb sunlight.

The only birds I see are ravens. They seem a better fit here than they did back in the Marin headlands, more able to scheme and cavort under the cover of this forest.

I keep my fog lights on the whole way down the hill, just in case I encounter another vehicle coming the opposite way in the darker sections of the forest. I do not encounter anyone or anything—I have this unpaved road all to myself. Judging from the lack of tire tracks, I'm the only vehicle to have come up here since yesterday's rain.

I make it back to headquarters forty-five minutes ahead of schedule, and immediately go to the whiteboard where I had originally signed out. I move the magnet next to "Dr. Farnsworth" from the "out" column back to "in," and I erase my destination info. This checkout procedure, which seemed a bit overly cautious when I was first briefed about it, makes a lot more sense now that I've been out in the forest. Before leaving the board to inform my buddy of my return, I erase the honorific before my name.

Day 2

The rain stops, almost suddenly, at 7:15, almost exactly at dawn twilight. It's still dark, with first light filtering down from above, almost blocked by the tallest firs, but not entirely. In Sausalito this morning the sun will rise at 7:34, hitting the top of my masthead first, but here at latitude 44 it will not come until 7:42, so there's time to make tea. It would be a perfect morning to build a fire, but the studio for visiting writers has no fireplace. I cannot detect warmth through my leather moccasins, but when I put my hand to the cement floor it seems that some attempt is being made to warm things up. Hot tea is my salvation.

All I see of the trees outside are their silhouettes, but that provides me sufficient information to distinguish one species from another. The Douglas-firs have a triangular crown, and the tips of the branches flare up like the primary flight feathers of a soaring red-tailed hawk. The western hemlock has a narrower crown, and the branch tips tilt downward, each branch spreading in a green cascade. The western red cedars have a cone-shaped crown, and the branches point upward at the tip. The Pacific silver firs have an oval crown, and the needles droop vertically from flat branches, hanging like the leather fringe on a western jacket. There are still a few trees out there I can't identify, but they are no less distinctive than the others, and I hope to recognize them all by the end of my first week here.

The rain comes and goes as I enjoy my tea, and I can judge its intensity by the apparent opacity of the trees on the far ridge. They grow more silver, and faint, when the precipitation increases, greening up significantly when it abates. This tonal shift, I decide, will be my rain gauge each morning.

It's light enough now that I can use my spotting scope to examine cones and bark, but I'm aware that I'm cheating a bit, studying the great outdoors from indoors, keeping dry on a day when I'm meant to get wet.

Before I venture outdoors, it may be wise to describe my task. I've been awarded a two-week residency in this forest through the Spring Creek Project,[1] which is administered through Oregon State University. The project began in 2003 and will continue until 2203, fully funded. Indeed, I will receive a small stipend for staying here, enough to cover gas, groceries, and the cost of shipping my shirts from campus. Our mission is to keep a "Forest Log" of our ecological reflections for two centuries. This chapter will become part of that log.

The list of those who have preceded me reads as a who's who of US nature writing: Barry Lopez, Linda Hogan, Robert Michael Pyle, Alison Hawthorne Deming, Thomas Lowe Fleischner, Jane Hirshfield, Scott Slovic, Kathleen

---

1. The full name is Spring Creek Project for Ideas, Nature and the Written Word. The project recruits "creative writers whose work reflects an appreciation for both scientific and literary knowledge," and its goal is "to create a living, growing record of how we understand the forest and the relation of people to the forest" over a two-hundred-year period.

Dean Moore, Scott Russel Sanders, Robin Wall Kimmerer, Laird Christensen, Pattiann Rogers, David James Duncan, Emma Marris, John McPhee . . .

It was intimidating when I read through *Forest under Story: Creative Inquiry in an Old-Growth Forest*, an anthology of the first decade of the "Forest Log," to wonder what I can possibly add to the mix of poetry, nature essay, and literary natural history that had already been composed. Will my writing expose me as someone who hasn't quite made the A team? As I type out this question I realize the need to brush aside the imposter syndrome, and I decide, finally, to engage in exactly what I've spent the past decade teaching collegians to do: description. Accurate, honest description.

My recently retired course, Writing Natural History, required students to keep field notes in which they would record two observations and one reflection each day while in the field. There was a final writing prompt, to be completed toward the end of the ten-day field experience down in Baja, which functioned as the course's final examination. Students were instructed to place themselves in the littoral zone—in other words, on the beach—and to describe a stretch of the intertidal in such detail that were they to return to that same site ten years later they could reassess it, and, comparing it to their original field notes, determine what changes had taken place in terms of the abiotic structure, biotic diversity, and health[2] of the site.

I have decided to attempt similar descriptions of the four reflection sites designated by the Spring Creek Project, but to describe the sites in ways that might be useful in scales of centuries rather than decades.

The sun comes out, and so do I, shortly thereafter, my new field guide to the trees and shrubs of the Pacific Northwest in hand. It's rare for me, outside of wildflower season in the California springtime, to be ignoring the birds, but I hone my attention treeward other than for the momentary distraction of a varied thrush, which I identify by call but cannot locate visually because it seems to be hiding in the dense understory. The varied thrush has arguably the least haunting song of all its family, just a single, fluted note drawn out for a full two seconds, but it seems to be calling to me. I scan the ground, but instead

---

2. Ecosystem "health" is something of a metaphor. Because the metaphor represents a value-laden construct, some critics worry that it misrepresents, as science, that which is not fundamentally scientific. Others, myself included, find it a useful metaphor to communicate the ecosystem's ability to maintain ecological processes and to support viable populations, especially of native species.

of locating avian fauna I discover a newt, which seems very close to a California newt except that the eyes are wrong. Smaller than our newts back home.

There is a nice collection of field guides in a conference room in the headquarters, and I've been shown where the secret key is hidden. I capture the newt gently and it curls up its tail in a defensive pose, but relaxes quickly and begins to explore my forearm. I transport it to headquarters, there to discover it to be a rough-skinned newt, *Taricha granulosa,* fairly common in these parts. Had it not been common, and had I discovered a new species, I'd probably have named it the rough-skinned newt anyway, *Taricha farnswortha,* because of its bumpy skin tubercules. Or maybe I'd have named it the Halloween newt because of its seasonally orange underbelly.

Unable to resist, I cross the conference room to where books written by my fellow writers in residence are stored under the banner "Nature Writing." I limit myself to checking out a single volume, which isn't that hard because most of the volumes in this library are already stacked close to each other in my office library back on campus. I choose a book from a writer unknown to me, Michael Lannoo, called *Leopold's Shack and Ricketts's Lab.*

The great naturalist Louis Agassiz had a sign on his Harvard office door that instructed, "Study nature, not books." My departmental office back on campus has a different sign on the door that says, "Study nature; read books." Today I study nature outdoors, learning to identify the trees of this rainforest. And a newt. This evening I will study nature as well, by reading Lannoo's book.

When I return to my studio for lunch I look up Lannoo on the Internet, and discover him to be a professor at the University of Indiana. His biographical sketch informs me that he trained as a herpetologist, his PhD thesis having been concerned with lateral line topography in amphibians. How appropriate that my encounter with an amphibian led me to his book!

An afternoon hike with my two field guides, trees and birds, yields a new-to-me bird, the golden-crowned kinglet. They were foraging actively in a mixed flock with black-capped chickadees, and I was able to bring them down to my level by making pishing sounds, an old birder's trick.[3] I've never been a great pisher, but there I was, the only fellow in that particular stand of forest, so it was me or nothing.

---

3. Pishing is a way of engaging the auditory curiosity of songbirds, attracting them to come out of the foliage and reveal themselves. The best pishers seem to almost whistle the word "pish" without enunciating the *i* sound. For ethical reasons, pishing should be curtailed or avoided completely during the breeding season, especially in heavily birded areas.

I knock off "early" at 4:00, crack open a pint of beer and a tub of my secret-recipe[4] gorp, and begin reading about Aldo Leopold's shack and Ed Ricketts's lab. I am fully invested in the book by its fifth page, where Lannoo informs me that the concept of "shack," which is fundamentally a frontier structure, works as "metaphor for a grounded, bottom-up, facts-based approach to thinking and to living."

Not for the first time, I muse that I need a shack of my own.

Day 3

It's the sort of day I'd expected every day to be up in these mountains, especially this close to Halloween: drizzly and gray without breeze or birdsong. The fog seems to rise up out of the forest itself, rather than blowing in from ocean waters in a manner to which I'm accustomed. It rises, like steam. I decide to focus on the understory, and it's maddening how much one leaf looks like the other.

I begin by identifying some of the easier plants. Low Oregon grape is distinctive, even without its flowers or fruit, and it seems to hold up well to the gloom. And there's trillium everywhere, an old friend easily recognizable, even without its bloom, by its three broad leaves. And then there are plants for which I shouldn't make a definitive identification until spring, at best, when they flower. Among these is *Linnaea borealis*, better known as "twinflower" because of how two blooms share the same stalk. But there are no blooms to speak of here at the end of October.

One fairly common plant drives me near mad, because I'm almost certain I've identified it in the past, perhaps during my writing retreats in Mendocino County during the past few winter solstices. The alternate leaves are somewhat lanceolate, although not sharply pointed, with simple edges. I pluck one and measure it at fifteen centimeters using the ruler on the back cover of my field guide. The shrub grows in small clusters, seldom gaining more than a meter in height.

At the point where I've checked every shrub in my 447-page field guide, I march back to headquarters, leaf in hand, to check the field guides and floras there. It's no use; I waste at least an hour on a single leaf.

---

4. Two-parts blister peanuts, one-part raisins, and one-part smokehouse almonds. Absolutely no M&Ms, freeze-dried banana chips, cashews, or anything else that clashes with cold-lagered, cold-filtered beer.

I retreat back to the forest, having temporarily given up on plants. Pulling out my phone, I quietly listen to the call of the spotted owl, attempting to mimic it in my own voice. Spotted owls are reputed not to be wary of humans, and they are easy to find in the forest, say the field guides, because they will return your calls. However, I can't seem to summon the appropriate falsetto, and the spotted owl's airy "hoo, hoo-hoo, hooooo" comes out of my throat sounding more like ribbits and croaks.

I wander a while, hooting now and then, looking for yew trees, listening for woodpeckers. Pileated woodpeckers have been reported in these woods, huge pileated woodpeckers, and seeing one would make my day. For that matter, even hearing one drum, at this point, would make my day.

I listen, and while I listen the glen in which I'm standing seems to darken a click or two. A more concentrated rain surely can't be far away.

One can walk silently in old growth like this, and even if one's footfalls were to make noise, it would quickly be absorbed by the surrounding biomass. This is not to say that an old-growth Douglas-fir forest is silent, as I've read several places. While there is no wind noise down this far from the canopy, there is always the noise of water. It seems that one is never far from a river or a creek here in the Andrews, nor far from the noise of rain, and this supplies a constant background, white noise that's actually silver. It's no wonder the owls can't hear me.

Day 4

Halloween, and it's raining this morning even though the forecast envisioned a dry spell until late this afternoon. Regardless of the prognostications, I'm guessing that there won't be any goblins visiting this deep into the woods after sundown.

I've decided to take the morning "off." I'm supposed to be oriented to the reflection sites today, and I look forward to meeting Dr. Frederick Swanson, a retired geologist who animates this project. Meanwhile, a handful of former students have requested recommendations for graduate school, and I can't rightly claim that my sabbatical excuses me from the responsibility to help worthy students pursue advanced degrees.

The afternoon comes none too soon, and with it, Fred. I've been warned that, given half a chance, he'll talk my ears off. My ears are ready for a good talking to, however, after a morning of writing recommendations. I head to the headquarters a little before my tutor is scheduled to arrive, there to finish the final two chapters of Lannoo's book and return it to the library. Fred, who has also read the book, arrives in the parking lot just as I finish reading.

Fred is tall, slender, energetic, and has a full white beard. He has been associated with the Andrews Forest since 1972, the year he earned his PhD. That's the year I graduated from high school, and yet when we begin to hike, his top speed is faster than mine, as if he's been equipped with superior gear ratios.

You miss a lot of nature hiking this way, but Fred's approach to the forest seems perpetually frenetic. He continues to lecture no matter how far I fall behind, mostly about the history of American forestry. I had read a couple books on the subject that Fred had recommended when I was first awarded the residency, one of which was his own, but I'm getting the full spiel here on the trail as if I hadn't bothered. Through it all, I can't shake the surreal impression that I've teleported back in time to hike with John Muir.

My guide claims not to be strong at botany, but when I ask about a few of the understory plants, he can readily identify them. And his familiarity with American nature writing is outstanding. He has read the work of most of the writers who have been part of the long-term ecological reflections, and that includes the greater part of the pantheon of living, well-published nature writers. And he's probably dragged most of them along the same hike that I'm currently undertaking. I want to ask whether he made Robert Michael Pyle hike this fast, or Scott Russel Sanders, or . . .

Our objective today is to familiarize me with the four reflection plots that the visiting writers are asked to visit and then write about. The first one is close to the forest headquarters, but the other three require us to jump into Fred's car and drive. Two of the four plots are located beyond the boundaries of the Andrews Forest itself.

I will describe the plots later, when I visit them alone and have time for leisurely descriptions. Suffice it to say that they are interesting. And I hope I can find them again on my own.

November 1
Reflection: Lookout Creek gravel bar

I situate myself below the north[5] bank of Lookout Creek in a young stand of red alders, none more than twenty years old, on a flat bar directly upstream of the reflection plot. Were the creek to rise another fifty centimeters, my boots would be submerged. While I set up my stool and stow away my daypack I am greeted by a Pacific wren who bobs almost formally with each two-note call.

---

5. This is called the "north bank" in common parlance, given the general east-to-west flow of Lookout Creek. However, my compass indicates that from this point the creek is east-northeast of where I've set up my writing station.

Chee-chee, chee-chee. Down up, down up. The bird is clearly aware of my presence, and seems to want me to know that it owns the timber rights to the pile of logs on which it perches.

There are four large Douglas-fir snags above me on the bank, and it could be perilous on a windy day to encamp where I currently sit. Any of six snags from the north bank would add to the gravel bar's topography were they to collapse downhill, which judging from the deadfall around here would be the logical direction, and most of them are already leaning downslope. There are likewise two snags on the far side of the creek whose tips, at least, will someday add to the bar's mass.

The creek runs clear despite the recent rains, and when I look upstream from the bar I can clearly make out the round rocks all the way across the bottom. From the bank I cannot see fish or any other aquatic fauna.

A cluster of large logs—I can count seven from here but there are certainly more—the largest of which are more than a meter in diameter, form a partial dam on the upstream edges of the bar, bifurcating the water to create a fairly stable island. With the exception of a large Douglas-fir that serves as a bridge from this bank, the other logs seem to have flowed here from upstream during a flood. Both channels form ripples and rapids just loud enough to make it impossible to hear ambient birdsong from the forest. Twice as much water flows to the far side of the bar than the near.

The downed log that serves as a bridge has a stile built over it to facilitate crossing. The log is covered with moss uphill of the stile, but not on the side leading to the bar, where it appears that human traffic has worn away any growth. The logs on the gravel bar, likewise, are not mossy, which may attest to the thoroughness of my colleagues' explorations here. After all the rain in the past few days, the bridge log does not appear safe to cross.[6]

Three separate alders grow on the bar, the largest being approximately ten meters tall and about twenty centimeters in diameter at the base. They have shed most of their leaves by now, and appear to be flourishing. Younger hemlock and Douglas-fir saplings crowd together in the center of the bar, none having exceeded two meters in height.

I leave the security of the bank to climb along the logs atop the bar, moving from mossy stepping-stones to slick logs that have long ago shed their bark. To say that these logs are slippery is to understate the peril, and I'm glad no one can see me straddling them and crawling along the more precarious sections.

---

6. When I drop by headquarters later this afternoon I mention the slipperiness of the logs and I'm told that, yes, a professor recently slipped off the bridge log, which crosses the shallows a good three meters up, and was lucky she wasn't seriously injured.

The largest of the logs is a bit spongy, and I keep an eye out for rot while I cross it. The transit was well worth the effort, however: one understands a gravel bar imperfectly from the bank.

I can now count fourteen logs thick enough to have been the trunks of centuries-old trees atop this bar. None of the logs appear to have been lumbered; their ends are snapped rather than sawn. There are six large tree-trunk logs immediately downstream, visible from the outside of the gravel bar. A lot of timber went into the creation of this reflection plot. There is an S curve below me as the water runs past this bar and then left into the next group of three giant logs on the southern bank. Clearly, these trees are altering the course of the stream within its traditional banks.

After returning to the alder grove, I hike downstream a few hundred meters. More logs have aggregated here, at least a dozen. Indeed, the number of huge logs that this stream has transported boggles the mind, and I'm having a hard time getting my head around any upheaval large enough to have resulted in what I'm seeing. Heading back upstream, I am unable to access the creek a hundred meters beyond my study site. There is a larger gravel bar upstream, quite overgrown, that may have contributed to the formation of the bar I've been describing. I would need a chain saw to transit the upper bar, or at least an ax.

I return to the alder grove where I started. The opposite bank has been cut away by floodwaters, in many places three to four meters high as the water squirted past the upper bar. It appears that during the flood the upper gravel bar may have been created in an eddy below where the floodwaters dug into the far bank, thus aggregating the substrate on which the second bar was built. I would like to have witnessed that, especially with all the logs flowing downstream. Although this flood occurred two decades ago, in 1996, it seems like a more recent event: the evidence is still fresh. Time itself slows in old growth.

As I begin to gather up my kit, two American dippers fly by, low over the water, heading upstream. The one behind is vocalizing loudly, a sharp ZEET, and seems to be chasing the one ahead. How I wish they had stopped by to forage at my gravel bar! They are North America's only aquatic songbird, presently, and all their food comes from under water. I look again for signs of aquatic life in the water above the gravel bar's rapids, but can see nothing from this vantage. Ah, for a D net and a pair of waders! But I can at least infer the presence of aquatic insects from the occurrence of the dippers, not to mention the fact that one of them would defend this territory so aggressively—there has to be food here for that to happen.

The Pacific wren reappears on the logs, deus ex machina, as if to defend its turf from the dippers. It's been at least an hour since I last heard it, but the presence of another species seems to have inspired its rhetoric.

I head downstream one last time. There is a second gravel bar—a smaller bar—some forty meters downstream of the reflection plot at the completion of the S curve. No logs lie atop it. Although vegetated, it does not support tree saplings or shrubs. It doesn't have nearly the gravitas of its upstream cousin, but the noise of the water flowing around it is more intense, almost musical. I find it quite pleasing to sit on the bank above it, gazing upstream at the more famous gravel bar, a hydrologic celebrity that has already inspired numerous poems. The sun comes out as I sit here, absolutely transforming the morning. I check my watch, and discover that it's already afternoon. I've been here longer than I thought.

I hike slowly back up the hill; there are newts everywhere along the trail. It takes effort not to step on one, and I come very close to skewering one accidentally with my hiking stick. Once I'm out of the newt zone I start searching for a possible entry for the biggest big-leaf maple leaf contest back at headquarters. Yesterday Fred warned me that anything under nineteen inches won't have a chance of winning.

Day 5 postscript

Shortly after I finished transcribing the field notes above, I decided to head out for a walk. No destination, really, no Forest Service radio, no field notebook, no rain gear, not even binoculars. Just a walking stick. I hoped to come back carrying the biggest big-leaf maple leaf in the forest.

I didn't get far before bumping into a postdoc, a relatively new postdoc who was awarded his PhD this past spring. We had met, briefly, earlier this afternoon but couldn't remember each other's names. When he asked where I was heading I told him about the contest, and he asked whether he could join me (even though I was headed in the direction from whence he'd just come). I assured him that I would welcome the company.

As we strolled through the forest he spoke about his recent journey in life, how he'd moved to a faraway university, how that had been stressful in terms of a relationship with a girlfriend, and how he missed the community he'd left behind, especially with his dissertation adviser.

We reflected, together, that many young academics experience a postdissertation letdown. One misses the intensity of the research, the focus, the collaborations. I told him how I'd wept after I finally defended my doctoral thesis and realized, suddenly, that my supervisor was no longer my supervisor. I shared how I had not even been aware up to that moment of how fond I'd become of her.

And then, your career trajectory rips you away from the campus that had become your home, alma mater, and now you're in a field station on the other side of the continent with no one to talk to.

Yes, my new friend confided. That's it. That's exactly it.

And now you need to find new sources of funding for your research, and a tenure-track position at a university that may be even farther from home, and build new relationships as if you're starting your life over from scratch.

Yes . . . That's it!

We found a fabulous leaf, finally. Yellow with bright red splotches. The petiole was at least a foot long, and I couldn't imagine anyone finding a better leaf anywhere. This one was not only huge, it was aesthetically perfect. No insect holes, no rot, no shriveled lobes.

We continued our conversation until we arrived back at the lodge where my new friend was staying, and we made plans to chat again sometime soon. It was growing dark, and I wanted to get my leaf to the headquarters building before they closed for the evening.

The leaf was put into a press between newspapers in the library, and labeled with my name. As we leafed through the other leaves, I was astonished to see one not only larger than my own, but nearly twice its size. Green. A monster. It had been collected in June by a research assistant named Sarah who had left the forest to begin a master's program this fall.

I wish her all the best in graduate school.

Day 6

I spend a pleasant hour today with Dr. Steven H. Acker, a senior faculty research assistant in the Department of Fisheries and Wildlife at Oregon State University. He runs the owl team here at the Andrews and shares an office with the other researchers on his project. He sports a full beard and wears a mud-brown hat advertising Mud River dog products. The hat makes him seem eminently trustworthy.

Steve clarifies, right away, that his program isn't considered a part of the long-term ecological research schema of the Andrews. When I ask how long he's been doing this, he answers, "Sixteen years." I laugh, and inquire how long it's going to take for his project to lose its short-timer status around here.

When I ask whether he thinks the spotted owl will be delisted during his lifetime, Steve shakes his head "no" emphatically, and a research assistant, Andrew, doing data entry at a nearby computer quips, "The only way that will happen is if they go extinct."

From the perspective of Steve's demographic analysis, the problem is three-fold. First comes habitat loss, because the spotted owl needs old-growth forest to flourish. Put a spotted owl into a less protected environment and it will either be eaten by great-horned owls or freeze to death. Second, barred owls have emigrated from eastern North America to the Pacific Northwest, and they are outcompeting their cousins.[7] They are one-third larger, have greater environmental adaptability, and they don't play nice with spotted owls sharing their turf. Finally, there is climate change. The spotted owl does best when rainfall and temperatures are moderate, and it's not yet known how the changes that are in store for the Pacific Northwest are going to affect this species.[8]

The spotted owl is one of the most studied birds in the world, and I ask Steve what we don't know about it at this point. He knits his eyebrows before replying that we're not sure about the effect of the barred owl on our ability to locate and monitor spotted owls. Scientists have traditionally located *Strix occidentalis* by hooting. Spotted owls hoot right back, and often come to visit the scientist who was hooting because they are not intimidated by humans. Indeed, some birders think of them as a tame species. However, anecdotal evidence has been gathered recently indicating that spotted owls don't return hoots when barred owls are present, perhaps because they don't want to advertise their presence to their aggressive cousins. This seems to be a new behavior, an adaptation the owl might be making to the invasion of barred owls, and if so it will make the spotted owls much more difficult to locate and monitor.

When I ask Steve how this affects him, he pushes back his hat and answers, "Sleep deprivation. I spend a lot more time trying to hoot them up in the middle of the night."

This leads to a conversation I really want to have, about my current inability to get the owls to answer my hoots. I feel a bit sheepish as I demonstrate my hoot, but Steve kindly suggests that part of my problem is that I've chosen a particularly tough time of year to interact with spotted owls, especially during the daylight hours. He doesn't think that my hoot is all that bad, opining that he's seen them come to naturalists with far worse hoots, and he shares that when he first got hired there were dozens of what he calls "field trip sites" where he could take people for a guaranteed spotted owl encounter. But those days are gone.

---

7. Both species are members of the same genus of true owls, *Strix*. The spotted owl is *S. occidentalis*, and the barred owl is *S. varia*.

8. The National Audubon Society considers the spotted owl "climate endangered," and projects that the species will lose 98% of its current winter range by 2080. See http://climate.audubon.org/birds/spoowl/spotted-owl.

Andrew, the research assistant, comes over with a folder of topographical printouts of an area that he thinks might be a good spot to find owls right now. It's more than an hour's drive from the Andrews, but it has had a fairly active concentration of spotted owls during the past breeding season.

I thank them both, grab my binoculars and my Forest Service radio, and head out into the greater Willamette National Forest. It's a great drive (snow-capped peaks!) followed by a lovely uphill hike, and I come pretty close to perfecting my hoot after the first twenty minutes. Regardless of the progress, my efforts don't generate a response of any sort.

The forest seems fairly empty these days.

Day 7

I meet Dr. Chris Walter and his research assistant, Colby, at precisely 8:30 a.m. at their rental SUV. They do not have access to a Forest Service truck because they are conducting research compliments of a National Science Foundation grant through the University of Minnesota. Chris is a biogeochemist, presently working as a soil scientist, and Colby is taking the fall semester off from his undergraduate studies in environmental engineering, and has been working at the Cedar Creek Ecosystem Science Reserve, another long-term ecological research site. Chris is precisely half my age, and I worry about keeping up with these lads on the uphill sections of our hike.

We will be carrying full packs. For my part I've packed both the camera and binoculars, and the Forest Service radio, of course, but no field guides in order to save weight during our long uphill trek. They are carrying tools, PB&J sandwiches, and soil. Yes, they are carrying dirt that they transported down the mountain two days ago. This is how science is done.

The day is nearly as gorgeous as the landscape through which we hike. Early on we transit through a glen of trees whose trunks are covered in soft, loose lichens, and Chris wonders whether these were the trees that inspired the Truffula trees in *The Lorax* by Dr. Seuss. Then, when we pass a particularly large patch of rhododendrons, he exclaims, "I can't believe that people work here!"

Chris earned his PhD at the University of West Virginia.

We quickly regret the fact that I'm not carrying my field guide to trees and shrubs of the Pacific Northwest. Chris wonders how many different types of rhododendrons there are in these woods, and I assure him that there might be as many as half a dozen.[9] But the shrub he thinks might be a rhododendron is

9. Actually, there are only five, if my field guide is to be trusted.

actually *Ceonothus cordulatus*, better known as "snow brush." A few minutes later, when we pass by an actual patch of rhododendrons, he says, "I feel like I fell asleep and woke up in a Bob Ross painting." I can't help but wonder what he'd be saying if these rhododendrons were in bloom this time of the year.

At one point we need to leave the trail and bushwhack through tall bunches of bear grass, straight up a steep hill to get to the meadow where the study plots are located. I can tell that this hill will be much more difficult to descend than it is to climb, and now I regret leaving my hiking stick behind. Ah, the treachery of packing light! I keep wanting to photograph the distant snow-covered mountains that we can now see off to the east, but Colby, from above, assures me that there will be better views once we get to the top. We are all breathing hard now, none harder than me, and I ask Colby whether he knows how high we've climbed. He pulls out his iPhone, activates the compass app, and reports that we're just under five thousand feet.

I'm feeling it.

We top out around 10:15 into a gorgeous natural[10] meadow fringed by silver fir, hemlock, and Douglas-fir. To the east, a crisp view of three volcanic peaks known as the Three Sisters, snowcapped, triangular, and splendid. To the north stands Mount Bachelor, rugged and solitary, but at just over nine thousand feet[11] it stands a good thousand feet shorter than any of the Three Sisters.

The meadow turns out to be well worth the climb despite the numerous plot markers that testify to where science is being conducted. This meadow is part of a worldwide study called "the Nutrient Network," which is hosted by the University of Minnesota, and has been fertilized with nitrogen, potassium, and phosphorus. I can't imagine how they lugged all that fertilizer, not to mention the fencing, tools, and markers, up here.

Chris and Colby get immediately to work installing root ingrowth cores. They removed the dirt from these cores a few days ago, transporting it down to the lab to sift the dirt and remove any root material. Chris will return a year from now to this site, pull the cores, and then determine the subsoil productivity by observing root ingrowth. This is one of nine sites on which he will be conducting this study, the others being in Colorado, Minnesota, Nebraska, Kansas, Illinois, New Mexico, and Texas. He hopes to get a better understanding of how grassland soils function as a carbon pool across a range of grassland aridity.

---

10. This meadow is the result of natural processes rather than logging.

11. Herein lies one of the problems of keeping contemporaneous field notes. I did not know the actual elevation of Mount Bachelor when I wrote this up in the field, and therefore had to resort to rough figures from memory, using the imperial system. For the sake of accuracy, the summit of Mt. Bachelor is 9,068 feet high, or 2,764 meters.

While they labor in the dirt I busy myself with the camera, recording the distant mountains and the bear grass bunches, the latter being a difficult task because I left my wide-angle and macro lenses in the SUV. Oh, to be in my fifties again and not have to worry about how much weight I'm lugging up a mountain!

We pack up an hour later, my partners relieved no longer to be carrying so much soil. We find bear scat—a copious amount of bear scat—at the top of our descent. Colby, who will be starting his junior year when he returns to college next semester and is therefore nearly immortal, has the Forest Service radio now. I instruct him that if a bear attacks, he is to bludgeon the bear with the radio while Chris and I run away. We pass by a five-meter high Douglas-fir, and Chris snaps off a needle, instructing me to sniff it because it smells just like orange peel.

There's a lot you can learn from a biogeochemist.

November 4
Reflection: Log decomposition site

One doesn't notice how narrow and overgrown the trail into the log decomposition plot is until one carries a camp chair and writing table its length. Yew saplings, *Taxus brevifolia*, are attempting to close this trail, pushing up through the moss and ferns, turning the old growth back into wilderness despite the best efforts of the United States Forest Service.

I set up my writing camp in the one place where sunlight breaks through the canopy, but even while sitting in the sunlight it's cold enough in this glen that I can see wisps of my breath. I dig my British, moss-green birding parka out of my pack, and when I slip into it I feel as if I've just donned an invisibility cloak. I now match pretty much everything in this forest.

I make a little trip around the grove with my camera. I've got the wide-angle lens attached today, and the macro lens in my pack. Each time I squeeze the shutter release I realize how poorly equipped I am to capture the gestalt of this stand: the intricate foliage of the forest floor juxtaposes with the enormity of the trees themselves on a scale that photography just can't handle. The mavens of digital photography haven't yet invented a lens that will do this landscape justice. Because I'm supposed to be focusing on logs today, I focus my photographic attention on the understory.

There are mushrooms everywhere here—a variety of species considerably beyond what my untrained eye can identify. I see no chanterelles, however, which I know from several conversations this past week to be the most sought-after fungus in these woods.

Other than for the anck-anck of two Steller's jays harmonizing poorly, this grove exudes silence. I can hear the occasional jet overhead, and the low distant swish of Lookout Creek, but the pen-scratch of my own writing is strangely truncated. If this grove wants me to feel transitory, perhaps even inconsequential, it's doing a good job.

I take a slow, off-trail hike, heading north-northeast from my writing table, leaving everything behind but my binoculars. I would estimate—and I'm trying to be conservative here—that at least 20 percent of the forest floor is covered by downed trees. Many of the logs are soft and spongy. All are moss covered. I can see why loggers used to consider old-growth stands to be inefficient; all this downed timber going to waste! And yet this is what the Andrews has taught us over the years, that old-growth forests are far more vibrant and productive than any tree plantation. These downed logs contain more living cells than they did when they were vertically alive.

The forest makes me sleepy as it slowly warms up, and I can't help wishing I'd brought a hammock rather than a camp chair. Or at least a thermos of tea.

The longer I stay in one place, the more detail I notice. For example, after the first hour I become aware of how the forest floor is littered with lichen, *Lobaria oregana*, which has either blown down or been knocked down from the canopy. It's everywhere, fixing nitrogen into the forest soil that it extracted directly from the air. I notice red cedar saplings growing up beneath a Douglas-fir even though there are no mature western red cedars in the vicinity. I look this tree up in my field guide, and discover that "seed is produced copiously and wind-dispersed." I notice how the upper branches of the truly huge Douglas-firs emerge from the trunk in a fan-shaped spray. I've read before that this is characteristic of old growth, but now I'm observing it firsthand.

I notice that even past the noon hour, when a shaft of sunlight hits a new log, it steams.

What am I not noticing, as morning turns to afternoon?

- I have not seen a mammal of any sort, nor the spoor of any mammals. Flying squirrels, weasels, and wood rats are supposed to abound in this forest, providing a food source for the owls, so where are their nests? (As I finish writing this I hear the far-off chatter of a squirrel. If one listens intensely enough . . .)
- I'm not seeing any raptors. Of course, it's the first week of November during a presidential election year and many diurnal raptors will have already migrated. But all of them? I haven't seen so much as a turkey vulture in the week I've been here.

- There is absolutely nothing in bloom right now, nor signs of recent flowering, and there probably wouldn't be any pollinators available if something were to blossom. I wonder whether this will be the case two hundred years from now. Will climate change extend the flowering season of the temperate north? Will there be an early November when these rhododendrons are all in bloom?

I listen to a distant red-breasted nuthatch toot its tin-trumpet notes. The call sounds lonely and exotic in these woods, and none of its conspecifics answer. Birds can sound so sad this far from spring, but perhaps I'm listening too hard, and watching in wonder too wide-eyed.

Feeling completely drained, I pack up a bit earlier than I'd planned to, resolving to move at a snail's pace as I pick my way back down the trail. On the way out I step across an eighteen-centimeter-long banana slug, and realize that this is the most charismatic nonavian wildlife specimen I've encountered today.

November 5
Reflection: Clear-cut site

Unlike the previous two reflection sites, this plot is not within the limits of the H. J. Andrews Experimental Forest. It lies on the other side of Lookout Ridge, where I hiked with Chris and Colby a couple days ago. Although it's physically close to the Andrews, it is existentially distant.

When one arrives at the clear-cut site, one no longer sees a clear-cut. Instead, one sees a Douglas-fir plantation where a clear-cut once happened.

I wish I could report on how ugly the plantation is, but it's really not. While it's clearly not as beautiful as the old-growth grove I visited yesterday, it's no less beautiful than a Kansas wheat field or a Nebraska cornfield. The trees are all roughly the same age, as you'd expect with monoculture, and the top two meters of the branches radiate a silvery hue this morning, laden as they are with moisture from a morning fog that doesn't disperse until 10:15, when it begins to rain gently.

One of the skills a boy must accomplish to become a First Class Scout, at least back when I was promoted, is to be able to measure the height of a tree. Using the method I was taught fifty years ago, with the aid of a hiking stick that's exactly a meter long, I estimate the height of three separate trees, and they all turn out to be twelve meters tall. They are planted so tightly together, however, that they create a tight tangle, and it appears impenetrable for someone my size.

The birds don't seem to mind the tangle, at least not the golden-crowned kinglets, which are noisily foraging for insects. For a moment I'm tempted to give things a try and see how far I can penetrate the tangle, but a hairy woodpecker working an alder behind me on the south side of the road distracts me, all for the better. It takes the better part of five minutes to locate the woodpecker, but a few seconds after I've finally framed her in my binoculars, she flies off.

I hear a wrentit somewhere up the hill. It probably appreciates the dense tangle as much as any bird would.

I find a brambly draw in which no trees have been planted, and attempt to climb it. Thorny, nonnative Himalayan blackberries have colonized the draw, making progress difficult even when I employ the hiking stick to move the prickles aside. The draw closes off after no more than a hundred meters, and rain begins again, so I retreat back to Little Dog to catch up on field notes while waiting the shower out.

When precipitation stops I drive to the west end of the plantation; I plan to climb up its west flank so that I can view it from above. This time I take my full pack, correctly estimating that the climb will take longer than it seems it would from the road.

The going is rough. This site has been logged twice and burned at least once. Numerous huge stumps, greatly weathered now, testify to an old-growth era prior to the first logging operation that would have taken place seven or eight decades ago. This site was no doubt clear-cut at that point. The logging of second-growth timber evidently followed a selective-cutting protocol where a certain percentage of trees of all species were left behind, as were a number of logs and branches. Red cedars and hemlocks are interspersed with Douglas-firs, but it seems a strange sort of forest. The logs left behind are not moss-covered for the most part, nor do I see much fungus helping them to rot. The ground is not strewn with lichens like yesterday's plot, and I can't help but wonder how much the soil has been depleted by the two rounds of logging.

Across from me, on the steeper sections of the plantation, the trees only seem to be two-thirds as large as they were in the flat. They are still densely packed together, however, and I will have to return downhill the way I came up. I descend cautiously; it would be easy to break a leg slipping between logs.

A fresh apple awaits me back at Little Dog, and I pull out my writing table and camp chair for the third time today, but this time I set it up so that my back is to the areas that have been disturbed by logging. The woods I'm facing now, to the south of the logging road, are notably different. There are alders here, the largest of which is a full meter in diameter at the base of the trunk. And there are snags—I count half a dozen without leaving my seat. There is a great deal more moss on the branches of trees.

My comparison is not entirely fair; I can hear a creek nearby, so this is more of a riparian ecology than the hillside behind me. Still, there is a mystique south of the road that the hillside lacks. The feeling over here is that the forest is controlled by its own systems, not ours.

Feeling ready to be finished with this disturbed landscape, I decide to head farther out the logging road just to get the lay of the land outside the Andrews. The drive is not encouraging. Stumps blacken the landscape everywhere, and even though the trees through which I'm driving have been growing back for decades, this forest lacks a certain vitality that the Andrews still exudes. It is truly disturbed, and somehow in the process of its perturbation, this forest seems to have lost significant portions of its magic.

Day 10: Day off

I take a needed Sabbath this Sunday, profaning it slightly by going into town to shop. I head into REI to pick up a summer basket for my hiking stick, which sometimes sinks twenty centimeters into this old-growth duff. I'm also hoping to pick up a hunter's safety vest, to make up for my refusal to wear the yellow hard hat I've been issued. REI can help with the basket, since I originally bought my hiking stick from them, but they send me to Cabela's for the safety vest.

I am surprised to discover myself to be the only customer not wearing camo in Cabela's. Customers are crowded around the weapons counters, and I pretty much have the clothing section to myself. Over by the handguns you have to take a number and wait to be served, and I hear a sales representative call out, "Number 82! Number 82!"

I ask the sales rep in the clothing section whether they're having a special sale on guns, and he replies that they are not. The reason that so many customers want to purchase a gun today, he informs me, is that the FBI just announced that Hillary Clinton will not be indicted for the additional e-mails that were discovered a week ago. The lads at the gun counter are worried that Trump is going to lose at this point, and Clinton is going to try to take their guns away.

I discover that they sell orange hunting vests in camouflage patterns. Fleece. The oxymoronic concept of high-visibility camouflage strikes me as being so wonderfully bizarre that I purchase one to wear in the field for the rest of my time in the Andrews. A shame I didn't have this to wear on Halloween when I was hiking with Fred.

November 7
Reflection: Blue River face timber sale unit

I am near the top of Blue River Ridge, just beyond the Andrews, at an altitude of nine hundred meters, facing northwest. Although the morning is overcast, a stunning vista opens before me, and the forest is thin enough here that I can see across to the far side of the Blue River watershed. Using the Forest Service map, I search for names of the distant hills: Twin Buttes and Gold Hill sound familiar—déjà vu from other national forests in other states—but I'm taken with "Tidbits Mountain," and make a note to look it up once I'm back on the Internet.[12]

The site is difficult to penetrate; no trail provides access through a barrier of bracken, snowbrush, and Douglas-fir saplings. Not only does this barrier keep out the casual investigator, it limits what is visible from logging road 1508. Were this site part of the Andrews, a trail would probably have ushered me to its bowels. I would have liked to have such a trail this morning—Dr. Walter dropped by after dinner last night to deliver his farewell and helped me polish off a modest pinot noir.

I'm looking for birds today, and I set up my travel scope at the observation site I've selected near the logging road, which gives me the most unobstructed view of the timber sale unit. Sure enough, the first bird to announce its presence, a Pacific wren, lands directly behind me, and were it not for its agitated chirp I would never have been able to identify it. It plays its usual wrenish game of hide and seek, and I'm happy to concede my defeat since it's not technically inside the plot I'm monitoring. One needs to resist such distractions.

A number of mature Douglas-firs stand at the top at the top of the plot, a couple dozen trees that were spared the harvest. The original plan was to leave 45 percent of the canopy intact in this site, which was logged in 2002 and then broadcast burned in 2003 to create deadwood snags since previous clear-cutting had left it "snag depauperate." I have no basis of measurement here, but it seems that less than 45 percent of the original canopy remains today, especially in the central section of the unit, which has a handful of snags but is somewhat tree depauperate. No matter how much you stretch the term, there is nothing here that I would currently call a "canopy."

A western hemlock stands solitary in the middle section, and seems well on its way to becoming another snag. Its needles droop as if it has recently died, and I ponder whether it's had too much sun during the recent drought

---

12. I learn, once back in my studio, that the name comes from the tidbits of rock pinnacles along its ridge. Climbers, no doubt, must have originally come up with this appellation.

conditions. I wish I could tell whether the needles are brown or green, and I'm suddenly missing Carol, the love of my life, who usually fills in these color details for me. The tree is thick with cones, and perhaps seems all the thicker due to the diminished condition of its needles.

I hear, but do not see, the usual suspects: Steller's jays, red-breasted nuthatch, black-capped chickadee. But it's not possible to tell whether the vocalizations are coming from within the timber sale unit or from the far side. They sound distant. Listening closely, I hear the soft, rhythmic purr of a Pacific chorus frog—it's the call referred to as a "land call" used by frogs away from the water. I must assume that it comes from a confused youngster who doesn't realize that it's November, not to mention the middle of the day.

The sun breaks through the thin, high layer of clouds just before noon, and I apply sunblock for the first time in many days. The sun seems to perk up insect activity: gnats hover over the bracken while an unknown species of fly inspects my writing table. Moments later, a western conifer seed bug, *Leptoglossus occidentalis*, lands, and I reach for my camera but it doesn't stick around long enough for a portrait. Putting the camera down, I notice strands of spider silk streaming off my spotting scope as a gentle easterly breeze pops up.

It occurs to me at first that maybe these insects will draw in some birds. Then I realize the fact that although I've been scanning the vista to my west for several hours now, I still have not spotted a bird on the wing. When I hear close birds, they inevitably come from behind, from the timber that was not cut in 2002. I realize, as I write this, that I saw significantly more avian fauna two days ago at the clear-cut reflection plot than I'm seeing here today.

This site represents the pinnacle of modern timber practice. The loggers not only left behind mature trees, but left snags and downed logs. And yet, in more than four hours of monitoring this site, I have not seen one bird fly within it, through it, or over it.

The birds have not been fooled.

Encouragement so often follows disappointment, and today is no exception. On the drive down the hill I encounter the pileated woodpecker for which I've been searching ever since arriving in the Andrews. Because of the white wing bars—I had a dorsal view of the startled bird flying away down the road—for the first fraction of a second I thought I might be seeing an old friend, *Melanerpes formicivorus*, the acorn woodpecker. But this bird was too big for that, and I quickly realized it for what it was. I would guess its wingspan to be at least seventy centimeters, and yet it still followed the undulating flight pattern characteristic of woodpeckers, beating the wings quickly at the bottom of the lower arc and then folding its wings back on the rise, finch-like but seemingly more playful. It's hard to be discouraged about forestry practices when you share a logging road with such a wonderful animal.

Day 12

I have arranged to spend the morning with two researchers affiliated with INSTAAR, the Institute of Arctic and Alpine Research, both of whom are based out of the Colorado School of Mines. Jackie Randell is a field technician with considerable expertise in data-logging systems. Ryan Harmon is a brilliant hydrologist disguised as a second-year PhD student. They've come out for a short stay to repair, maintain, or upgrade some of their data-collecting equipment and to download the data loggers that have been steadfastly monitoring experiments in a watershed just outside of the Andrews boundaries.

Leaving from the Andrews main entrance, we are surprised by a loaded logging truck barreling down the road. He is driving in the center of the road, which is paved but doesn't have painted stripes to divide lanes that may or may not exist. Braking at the last possible moment, at which point my life has already flashed before my eyes, Ryan says, "Huh. I wonder where they're logging up here."

We find out soon enough. The logging operation is across the valley from Watershed 10, which is where INSTAAR has located its research. It will not be a quiet morning in the forest.

I don't have to worry too much about keeping up with Jackie and Ryan this morning. They are carrying deep-cycle twelve-volt batteries, computers, desiccants, et cetera. This is their second trip today; early this morning they carried inverters to replace two that had ceased to function in the recent rains.

A short hike—a short, ridiculously steep hike—takes us up into the most incredible Swiss-family-Robinsonish infrastructure of scientific paraphernalia I've ever seen out in the woods. A nameless creek has cut deeply downslope, resulting in hillsides that are between sixty and seventy degrees, on average. Ladders have been strung together, pegged into the soil and augmented with climbing rope, similar to how Sherpas set up the transits of ice fields on Mount Everest. Only muddier. Wires run along the ground everywhere connecting sensing equipment with data loggers.

Ryan has installed electrodes everywhere, using an experimental method called "electrical resistivity tomography," ERT for short. In essence, since resistivity is the mathematical inverse of conductivity, and since water increases conductivity in soil, he can chart how water flows at various depths downhill, and is able to account for the amount of water the trees draw up through their roots. He speaks of the trees turning on and off during the day when they photosynthesize, and how that influences the hydrological flows in the forest. Of course, he uses a more conventional system using soil moisture probes as a second data point to confirm what he's discovering about soil resistivity through his ERT study.

I ask whether he's able to do spatial analysis with this data, and after a moment's hesitation he answers, "That's the goal." They are apparently in the early stages of trying to develop a program to accomplish this, but Jackie pulls a computer out of her pack and says, "I can pull up an image." So here we are, in the forest primeval, analyzing how a computer image is attempting to capture the hydrological cycle of this very forest in full color. Ryan criticizes where the image still fails to capture the true extent of what's going on in nature, saying, "It's not quite this smooth a few meters down."

The more Ryan explains the intricacies of his research, the more animated he becomes. While Jackie begins downloading a data logger belonging to another researcher, he takes me from instrument to instrument, including the ERT central control unit, which originally cost $70,000.[13] But he also shows me how and where he is saving money by building his own data-collection cables and such parts of the physical infrastructure as the stand supporting a solar panel. "That stand could have cost me $200," he says, proudly, "but I built it for free out of materials from the scrap heap back at Andrews headquarters."

Facing outward, Ryan descends an interconnected series of three ladders, a method that can't possibly be safe. Clearly, he's bopped down these ladders a thousand times. I descend properly, and it takes me quadruple the amount of time it took my young hydrologist friend.

We finally reach the bottom of the creek, which Ryan calls a "bedrock creek" because it's washed away all the soil down to the volcanic bedrock. This creek, however, isn't where Ryan encounters mystery. "I'm shocked at how little we know about how trees work," he complains. He speaks about how hydrologists tend to oversimplify the "plumbing network" of trees, considering them as nothing more than sophisticated straws that suck water up so that the trees can transpire it into the atmosphere. He begins to lecture me and the forest about the ways in which it's more complicated than this.

Jackie, meanwhile, has been having trouble with the data logger, and returned to the truck to pick up another battery. This turns out not to solve the

---

13. Ryan's research is being underwritten by the National Science Foundation. He explains that the CRT controller was designed for oil and mineral exploration, and an oil company won't shrug at paying for equipment like this. Ryan is convinced that he could develop an instrument of his own for far less if he had the time to do so.

problem, however, and she discovers, after opening up the case that holds the data recorder itself, that the wiring has become a chaotic tangle of multicolored wires. "This is what you should be taking pictures of," she tells me.

While they consult about possible solutions, I frantically try to catch up these field notes. I'm having the usual difficulty writing productively while standing, however, and I ask whether it's OK for me to sit down on what appears to be an abandoned instrument case from a bygone experiment. It's OK, but I should be careful, I'm warned, because that experiment has been over for quite some time, and as a seat it may be sketchy.

This leads to a discussion about "research trash," as it's called here in the Andrews, which Ryan also refers to as "science trash." He tells me that he's personally hauled out a couple truckloads of abandoned research equipment from this site, but admits that it's almost a losing battle in these parts. He thinks that this may be a downside to long-term ecological research (LTER) sites, but I assure him that the biological field stations I've visited have also been struggling with this problem.

We hear a tree crash across the valley at the timber operation, and Ryan notes the irony that we're concerned about science trashing the forest while, less than a kilometer away, trees are being systematically ripped out of the ground.

Our field time is cut short by Jackie's need to return to the Andrews and download wiring diagrams. Ryan and Jackie will have to return here in an hour and rewire their colleague's data logger, a process that may consume the better part of the afternoon. Realizing that my continued presence will only slow things down, I thank them for letting me experience a morning in their field site, and I excuse myself for the afternoon to attend to my field notes.

Day 13

The showers this morning had not been forecast, so I feel no particular compunction to venture out into them, especially given the vexations of last night, which was election night. I spend a couple hours setting things up for the next residency, to which I will proceed directly from here. And another letter of recommendation has been requested to help yet another recent graduate find gainful employment. The forest staff hold an all-hands meeting throughout the morning to plan and prepare for the winter season, after which they attempt a festive taco luncheon, to which I am invited. The tacos are great, but the festivity is a bit muted by the results of last night's presidential election. No one seems to want to talk about it, but there is a lot of headshaking going on. One of the staff members takes solace that at least Oregon had gone for Clinton.

"California too," I remind everyone.

"And Washington," another chimes in.

It doesn't need to be said that we are all worried about what this means for the environment. And education. And the US Forest Service. And science itself.

I spend the afternoon pursuing the endangered spotted owl along an old-growth trail where I'm told there's a chance of finding one. During my trip into town last Sunday I purchased one of those self-contained, portable Bluetooth speakers the college kids use to turn their smartphones into concert halls. It was pricey, but I'm considering it a research expense because I can use it to play hoots via one of the field guides stored on my smartphone.[14]

The plan is to stop every two or three hundred meters and spread some owlish cheer. I rarely make it more than a hundred meters without stopping, however, because the mushrooms today are fantastic, and I mean that literally. I'm not carrying a mushroom field guide, of course, so I decide to photograph the more fabulous ones for later identification. Some seem to be blue, almost a metallic blue, and I would guess others to be purple, a color I've never been able to distinguish. And a reddish brown? Some are toothed, some are veined, some are billed, many are cupped. Most represent the classic bolete morphology, with its convex caps, some of which are huge, others tiny. Mycologists claim that there are fifteen hundred different kinds of mushrooms in the Pacific Northwest, and that's easy to believe after a couple hundred meters into this bewitching stand of trees.

I'm still not accustomed enough to this Douglas-fir old growth to think of it in anything less than magical terms. If ever there was an enchanted forest, it must have resembled this one in most ways, especially with all these mushrooms. The light plays tricks on muggles like me with a camera in hand. At one point I see a spider web gloriously lit up by a ray of sunshine that seems to be focused solely on the web's water droplets. The only problem is that there are two huge, moss-covered logs between me and the one with the web, and by the time I drop my hiking stick, set down my pack and climb over both logs, the sun has moved just enough that the web is not so brilliantly lit. Were I a professional photographer, I'd make note of the time and come back to this spot

14. The use of digital audio devices is controversial among birders. During the use of this speaker I was careful to follow the guidelines outlined by David Sibley in "The Proper Use of Playback in Birding," found on the Sibley Guides website, www.sibleyguides.com. Speaker volume was never amplified beyond the normal volume of the spotted owl itself, and playbacks were short, with pauses between them of at least a minute.

tomorrow to wait for the perfect moment I missed today. Sabbaticals, however, are too short for that sort of perfectionism. I content myself with compiling a photographic record of mushroom morphology.

I can't help but wish I'd been here in this exact spot a century ago, at a time when spotted owls were common and logging activities had not made this sort of grove the exception rather than the rule. There were grizzlies then, if we're to believe the journals of the Corps of Discovery expedition. Would Lewis and Clark have found a grove such as this as magical as I currently do? Would it have been more frightening to them, or is it more frightening to a college professor nearing retirement who sometimes hikes alone and isn't carrying a rifle?

Over the course of the hike, which should more appropriately be considered a ramble, I stop at least a dozen times, get out my new research toy, and attempt to initiate a conversation with an owl.

No response.

Day 14

The big hike, today, now that I've completed all the requisite elements of this residency. Big hike, solo hike, no rain in the forecast.

The Lookout Creek Old-Growth Trail has its own brochure. It also has its own booster club; everyone even remotely associated with this forest has told me that I've got to "do" this trail. The trail map on the brochure is so low scale that it doesn't show most of the switchbacks. But the last sentence in the brochure reads, "Because of the rugged nature of the trail, you should expect at least a two-hour hike one way."

I am advised that for older knees it's easier to climb the trail from the lower trailhead to the upper, descending on the logging road thereafter. I'm also told that it usually takes Spring Creek Project writers at least three hours to climb the trail one way, regardless of direction.

I'm stoked. I pack light. Only one liter of water, since I haven't been consuming as much on these cool, humid, November days.[15] Only my compact 10×25 binoculars, and only the wide-angle lens for the camera. I still bring along the recently purchased Bluetooth speaker, but I have a new plan for how that's going to work. And I'm still carrying that loathsomely heavy USFS walkie-talkie.

---

15. This turns out to be a mistake, and I will return to headquarters with a very empty water bottle. Indeed, if I had bothered to leave the second water bottle in the truck at the lower trailhead, I probably would have drained it as well before returning to headquarters.

Yesterday, whenever I wanted to hoot, I had to remove my pack, pull out the speaker, turn it on, and then play the audio from a digital field guide app. Today, however, I'm going to carry the speaker, which is shaped like an oversize suppository, in one of the water bottle holders on the outside of my pack. I'll leave it on since the battery is supposed to last twelve hours. That way I can hoot every few minutes without having to stop, just by pulling out the smartphone and hitting the play button.

The modern high-tech naturalist enters old growth. Look out, Nature.

I'm using Sibley's digital field guide today, since I struck out yesterday with the recording from the Audubon Society field guide. Sibley includes two spotted owl recordings, one recorded in Utah, the other in Colorado. (This seems a little parsimonious. I grew up in Colorado, and love the state dearly, but when I think "spotted owl," I think "Oregon." Are you reading this, David Sibley?)

The forest is incredible, and it may be that the riparian section where the trail first crosses the creek is the most scenic mile of hiking in these United States. And the footbridge itself gets an A plus from this educator. The walkway is made from a single log, milled flat at the top, protected with handrails. Spectacular. With the balance issues that have come with increased age, water crossings on wet logs have become a concern. But if this first footbridge is any indication of what is to come . . .

The digital hooting system works—which is to say that it functions, not that it produces immediate results—but I have to remember to hoot every few minutes because the speaker turns itself off after a period of inactivity. Maybe five minutes? And there aren't as many mushrooms as on yesterday's hike, probably because I'm now carrying a mushroom guide. Otherwise, I'm missing my wife terribly during this hike, because she would so love it. And she loves pointing out things that I'm missing. "Oh look over there. Purple."

I force myself into a faster pace than I usually prefer, and it feels a bit as if I'm jogging through Westminster Abbey. During Evensong. But if I want to make it back to headquarters by the 4:00 check-in time I scribbled on the checkout board, I'm going to have to scoot.

Within the first mile the trail begins to ascend up out of the riparian zone, and I begin perspiring heavily. It's not raining, but the humidity here has me thinking that my sequence of layers needs to be reexamined. I've spent the greater part of my hiking career learning how to stay cool in arid and semiarid environments. But I'm learning that sweat doesn't tend to evaporate here in Oregon—it just sort of works its way down to your knees. I have never in my life had perspiration soak the entire bill of a baseball cap and then begin dripping from the tip, but my hat starts doing that before it occurs to me that I really don't need a hat in an old-growth forest. The sun's just not going to get into my eyes today. I take it off reluctantly, however; it's the red-billed H. J. Andrews Forest hat with the rough-skinned newt embroidered on the front, and I've never been shot by an elk hunter while wearing it. Good thing I'm wearing my orange camouflage vest!

As I transcend the riparian ecology, I note an increase in the number of huge western red cedars. It gets to the point where there are as many of these giants as Douglas-firs, and the forest is transformed for their dominance, which I understand is rare in old-growth, since red cedars tend to be scattered into a mix of trees. My field guide, Turner and Kuhlmann's *Trees and Shrubs of the Pacific Northwest*, explains that "very wet places are the exception, and here western red cedar often rules."

Yes. These trees rule.

I finally have my owl encounter. Unfortunately, it's a barred owl rather than a spotted owl. I've continued to hoot, of course, electronically, but the last hoot was several minutes ago. I'm looking down, mostly, making note of the density of the small seed cones from the red cedars, and how distinct they are from Douglas-fir cones also littering this section of trail. I'm still hiking hatless, and I somehow I sense the owl before I actually see it. By the time I see it, blasting away from a low branch, it has decided that it wants nothing to do with me. It startles me as much as I seem to have startled it, and flies away to the west.

Catching my breath, I assume that the owl had heard my speaker broadcasts and was investigating whether a spotted owl had invaded its territory. I don't think it was expecting a sweaty naturalist representing the Spring Creek Project. I've read, in numerous places, that spotted owls are tolerant of human presence, often appearing tame when humans approach. If this barred owl is representative of its conspecifics, the species has the complete opposite personality.

The owl quickly flies out of vision. As I resume my hike, I hear a mob of Steller's jays, off in the direction where the barred owl fled, squawking raucously. It seems that at least five birds are ganging up on someone, and I must conclude that they are objecting to the presence of the barred owl I just flushed. Good for them.

There's little more to report from this hike. A half-dozen feeder streams present crossing challenges, mostly in the last mile, but I manage to lose my footing in only one of them, and am delighted to discover that these boots are as waterproof as advertised. Right now my feet are the only thing dry. I'm also happy to report that in three hours on this famous trail, I didn't encounter a single fellow primate.

I emerge from the upper trailhead three hours and ten minutes after having set out. And I honestly feel I was moving fast, despite what the brochure might imply. As it is, there's no time for a late leisurely lunch at this point, and I must consume my Philadelphia burritos on the hoof as I descend the logging road. It's sunnier out here on the road, and when I withdraw the map from my pack I put the hat back on. The Andrews Forest map doesn't show mileage markers, and the USFS map is back on the coffee table in my studio, but I estimate that I'll be back to my truck in another three miles.

Almost two miles later, I hear a diesel pickup coming down the road. I turn around, stick out my thumb, and it stops. The window rolls down, and the driver, a white-bearded gentleman a bit older than myself, says, "We don't usually pick up hitchhikers, but you're wearing the right hat."

His buddy moves over, and I scramble around to the passenger side, explaining that I only need a lift to the lower trailhead. They seem impressed that I've just done the trail, and the driver says, sympathetically, "That's a tough one!"

"Takes longer than it looks," his buddy agrees.

They seem impressed that I made it in just over three hours. We discuss the merits and perils of the trail, and what I'm doing here, and when they discover my affiliation with the Spring Creek Project, they become downright supportive.

"A damned fine program, that one."

"They bring some good writers up here."

They ask my name, and the name of this book, and promise to watch for it.

Little Dog appears all too soon, sitting there obediently right where I left it. Before I hop out, I tell them to look for themselves in chapter 4.

I hope they read this someday.

Thanks to the lift, I return to headquarters with an hour to spare. After signing back in on the checkout board I say my farewells. Even though I'm sticking around another day, the staff here, regardless of whether they work for the Forest Service or Oregon State, have tomorrow off to commemorate Veteran's Day. Everybody wants a goodbye hug. I object that I'm far too sweaty to hug, but we all hug anyway. It's Oregon.

Back in the studio I switch to a dry sweatshirt, crack open a beer, transcribe these notes into the computer, hit the save button, and then steer the computer to my favorite news aggregator to see what the world's up to. There's a fresh article from *Time* magazine: "2 Oregon Residents File Petition for the State to Secede from the US."

I'm in. And I'm wearing the right hat.

Day 15

I wake up to a surprise: my body is not at all stiff from yesterday's exertions.

How did that happen?

Even though the forest staff has the day off to commemorate Veteran's Day, Terry, the campus supervisor, bustles with activity. First a snowcat appears, a blade attached to the front. Then a blade suddenly appears on Terry's pickup, ready for winter duty. Then a second snowcat appears. Where were they hiding these machines?

When I leave my studio with a final load of laundry, I ask Terry how come he doesn't get Veteran's Day off. With a wink, he replies, "I'm a veteran."

I thank him for his service, and he replies, "Nothing to it, I do this every November." I tell him that I'm thanking him for his military service to our country, and he breaks into a wide grin, saying, "That's the first time I've ever been thanked for that."

It will take me hours to pack up and then clean the studio—the place looks as if an entire scout troop spent the summer camping here. It always amazes me how someone as neat as me can make such a mess when his wife isn't around.

I can't apply myself fully to the cleanup detail yet, however. Yesterday, the professor who is running my department's proseminar this year wrote to our faculty about the class session last night. The students wanted to talk about the election results from the day before, which she had anticipated would be the case. But what came up was a surprise: a few of the students were wondering whether they should change majors, given the new administration's hostility to environmental issues.

And these were all seniors!

I shared in my colleagues' collective surprise—none of us had seen this coming—and yet we all seem to understand why our students would be so distraught. And it's been difficult, being up here at the Andrews, to shake the feeling that I should be available to my advisees for office hours. So since that wasn't going to happen, I decided that rather than wander off on one last hike to spot a spotted owl, I would do something constructive by blogging a perspective they might find useful.

Here's the blog I just posted:

Post-election thoughts for Environmental Studies and Sciences students

11/11/2016

I write from the H. J. Andrews Experimental Forest in Oregon. I will be conducting sabbatical research for another month in the Pacific Northwest, and I regret that I cannot be with you during the turmoil. I will return to campus on December 16th, after having spent a month at the North Cascades Institute, where I look forward to working with grad students interested in field-based education.

Yesterday I learned that students attending our proseminar on Wednesday were concerned about whether they should switch away from majoring in Environmental Studies/Environmental Sciences, given the recent presidential election. This question has weighed heavy on my mind the past twenty-four hours, and, while I tend to be cautious about dispensing career advice, I would like to share a few perspectives.

I first voted in 1972, the year that eighteen-year-olds were extended the privilege of voting for the first time in this country. I was a freshman at the time. That was the famous Watergate election, which Richard Nixon won. During his first term Nixon had expanded the war in Vietnam to include a supposedly "secret war" in Laos and Cambodia, and these campaigns were highly unpopular with college students. Most of us had former high-school classmates who had already been drafted into military service, and many of us had lost friends and family members to the war. Nixon's opponent, Senator George McGovern, ran on an antiwar platform, and was supported by nearly every college student in America. But he lost in a landslide. We were devastated, in part because we considered Nixon's victory to be something of a death sentence for many people our age, because the war would inevitably continue past the point when we would lose our college draft deferments.

By the time I graduated, however, President Nixon had brought the war to a close, accomplishing something that the two previous Democratic administrations had been unable or unwilling to do.

I'm hoping that the Trump administration will surprise us in similar ways. Even if that doesn't happen, I feel that there are solid reasons for environmentalists like you and me to stay the course.

During my sabbatical, I've spent time in field stations that are invested in long-term ecological research. The project with which I'm involved up here in the Andrews, the Spring Creek Project, is funded to extend through 2203. That wasn't a typo; it's a 200-year-long investigation. What I'm finding, out here in the field, is a vibrant research agenda that is providing enormous opportunity for recent graduates to gain experience as field technicians and research assistants. And what I keep hearing, over and over as I work with these young people, is something to the tune of "I can't believe I'm getting paid to do this work."

Granted, I would not want to be starting a career with the EPA during a Trump administration. But that's not where the great majority of the ESS alumnae preceding you have been getting jobs. Rather, they seem to be finding work everywhere from the Sierra Club to Tesla. Indeed, I know of a couple ESS alumnae who are working to make the wine industry more sustainable. And, folks, people are not going to stop drinking wine just because Donald Trump was elected president. As a matter of fact . . .

Finally, I want to share with you my personal perspective on being an environmentalist. I didn't go into this work because it offered attractive job prospects. Rather, I have always seen my work as a personal response to issues about which I care deeply. My first job, during my collegiate summers, was at a Boy Scout ranch in Colorado. I taught two merit badges, hiking and nature. I made $35 a week, plus room and board. The pay may have been low, but the job satisfaction was enormous, and that's become the story of my life. Is my job satisfaction truly enormous? Well, yesterday I hiked a six-mile loop through old-growth forest, solo, hoping to see a spotted owl. Taking that hike was actually part of my job—it's something I was paid to do, even though I only ended up getting close to a barred owl. And today I get paid to write a blog for some devastated kids I care deeply about.

Hang in there. Cry if you need to. And when you hear Rudy Giuliani complain, as he did yesterday, that you college kids are a bunch of crybabies, go ahead and cry some more because the haters will always be out there, and sometimes they win elections. In the end, however, I'm all the more committed to our present course. I'm not going to become a billionaire, and I'm okay with that. And even if I'm fighting for a losing cause, which I sincerely hope is not the case, I will continue doing what I do because it's the right thing to do. And knowing this provides me with enormous job satisfaction.

Please join me. It's the right thing to do, and deep down you already know why. Let's make a difference together.

H. J. Andrews Experimental Forest bird list, October–November

Varied thrush
Gold-crowned kinglet
Yellow-rumped warbler
Red-breasted nuthatch
Hammond's flycatcher
Black-capped chickadee
Pacific wren
American dipper
Common raven
Steller's jay
Hairy woodpecker
Pileated woodpecker
Barred owl

5

Notes from the North Cascades Environmental Learning Center

A period recourse into the wilds is not a retreat into secret silent sanctums to escape a wicked world, it is to take breath amid effort to forge a better world.

BENTON MACKAYE, "A Wilderness Philosophy," 1946[1]

When I left the Andrews Forest a couple days ago, the McKenzie River that led me back toward the coast was flowing at a rate of just under three thousand cubic feet per second. Although placid, it seemed like an implacable river doing a steadfast job, successfully draining a watershed where a tremendous amount of rain has fallen recently. A serious river. But now, driving away from the coast along the Skagit River, I perceive more than mere hydrological competence—I get a sense of power. The Skagit is running at just over thirty thousand cubic feet per second, and that's after having been "tamed" by the three hydroelectric dams up ahead. This river doesn't appear to be much wider than the McKenzie, but it seems a lot more muscular.

In another hour I will be driving over one of those dams on my way to the North Cascades Environmental Learning Center. The center was built as mitigation for the environmental harm caused by the dam when the dam was relicensed in 1989. It was a unique idea, to mitigate environmental damage with environmental education by building a world-class field campus. But the idea

1. Benton MacKaye, a cofounder of the Wilderness Society, is also considered the founder of the Appalachian Trail.

was supported by the National Park Service, the Forest Service, local tribes, the North Cascades Conservation Council, and the city of Seattle, which owns the hydroelectric project. The city owns the campus buildings, having invested $12 million in their construction, and leases them to the North Cascades Institute for a dollar a year. It's a tidy arrangement for the environment.

I stop at the North Cascades National Park Visitor Center, hoping to pick up some maps and a bird checklist, but there's a sign at the entrance that says, "Closed for the winter."

Uh-oh.

It begins to rain, and I realize that I've passed beyond the rain shadow cast by the Olympic Mountains. I've been warned that it will rain much more up here than it did down below where I'm more familiar with the terrain. Once I pass the first dam, just past the town of Newhalem, the valley's sides steepen. Feeder streams became cascades, and then cascades became waterfalls, and at one point there seem to be at least a dozen waterfalls per mile, equally dispersed on both sides of the river. The Cascade Range is explicating its name.

Although I've visited the Cascades a number of times, mostly down in Oregon, this is my first stay in the North Cascades. Copywriters associated with these mountains want to call them "the American alps," but being from Colorado, I've tended to discount this as boosterism. After all, the higher peaks here seldom exceed ten thousand feet, which doesn't stack up to Colorado's impressive fourteeners. Right? But now that I'm engaging with these mountains, I understand what generated all the ballyhoo—it's not so much high summits as low valleys. The delta between peak and valley is often six thousand feet, and the terrain is remarkably steep. The landscape indeed takes on an alpine feel, although this version of alpine is more heavily forested than any of the European montane habitats through which I've trekked. I am forced to admit to myself, finally, that this topography is more alpine than the Southern Rockies in which I grew up.

The rain stops but the gray skies persist, and then I finally get to the dam. Diablo Dam. I wait for an enormous Seattle City Light pickup crossing in the opposite direction to clear the narrow roadway, not aware that these drivers consider the road atop the dam to be wide enough for two pickups to pass if they're traveling slowly. He passes with a friendly wave, undoubtedly noting my California plates. Little Dog wants to bark, but I shift back into gear and drive slowly along the dam's high curve, looking to the right with expectations of the sublime. I've read that the water is a brilliant turquoise in this reservoir. Geologists attribute the color to the fine powder resulting from the glaciers above grinding up rock, a powder so light that it stays suspended in the lake after being washed down in the creeks.

I don't really see any turquoise, but from the gravel parking lot I can see glaciers.[2]

There's an apple tree at the far side of the dam, laden with golden apples. I almost decide to stop and pick one, but then I notice movement in the tree. A bear. A really, really enormous black bear, its coat thick, its body fattened up for winter. Munching on apples.

Deciding that it would be prudent to leave the apples to the bear, I drive on.

I hike up to the office, and am disconcerted to find a sign saying, "Office closed." I can only hope it's not closed for the winter.

The clouds part, briefly, and sunlight careens off the high peaks above. I make a mental note that I should learn the names of these brilliant peaks immediately. It would seem sacrilegious not to.

My residency here is termed a "creative residency," and is scheduled to last a month, from November 14, today, through December 14. This gives me a full cycle of the moon, starting with the supermoon tonight, which will be the largest full moon of my lifetime.[3] The residency, however, gets off to a rocky start when I am informed that a monthlong EMT training program that was scheduled to coincide with it was canceled, which means that there will be no food service except for a few days when other groups are around. This was something I was really looking forward to, having cooked for myself during the months I've spent at field stations writing this book so far. Not that I can't spend another month eating soup, hot dogs, chili con carne, and some really fine mac and cheese, to which I always add green olives, carefully sliced. But it would have been nice to know about this when I was remotely close to a grocery that sold olives.

I assure myself that there must be a store around here somewhere, but the vexations don't end here. I'm informed that my apartment won't be ready to occupy for "a day or two," the previous occupant having not yet moved out. So I won't really have a kitchen until then. Fortunately, I brought way too much gorp for a primate my size to consume over the course of seven weeks. And there are still cans of soup in my larder that I never had to resort to eating in the Andrews. And there are always the apples. And all that cheese, and all those crackers. I will not starve here, I keep telling myself. An angel lets me in on the secret that they make their own granola here, and that I'm welcome to help

---

2. I am informed, later, that the turquoise water color is really a spring phenomenon. The glaciers are not all that active at this time of year.

3. A supermoon happens when the full moon coincides with its closest approach to earth in its orbit. The last time a supermoon was this close to earth was in 1948. The next time will be in 2034. Since I was born in 1954, it's possible that tonight's full moon will be the most spectacular one of my life. It's even more possible that it will be obscured by clouds, although, as I write this, the sky is mostly clear.

myself to the supply. And there's a refrigerator full of leftovers in the staff room that I'm welcome to plunder. Sometimes lasagna shows up in it miraculously just to keep the grad students alive. They are apparently in the same metaphorical boat as me, suffering an equal loss when the EMT program was canceled.

I'm temporarily assigned to a room with four bunk beds in a lodge that's not currently in use. One can almost hear the echoes of Mountain School, a glacier-fed river of fifth graders that has flowed through here since the beginning of the school year. My residency begins just after the last group of campers departed, a move that seemed so sensible when I thought there would still be food service.

I write for a while, distractedly, and then decide that a short hike would be elevating. Or at least redemptive. It is, but I'm a full ten degrees higher in latitude than when I left home, and sunset, which should be happening at 4:29 at this latitude, for all practical purposes happened a good hour earlier because of the mountains that surround this place. By the end of my short ramble along the lakeside I decide never again to hike during this residency without carrying gloves. And perhaps a headlamp. But at least it's not raining. In an attempt to cheer myself up, I remind myself how nice it is to hike without that heavy Forest Service radio.

Despite the cold and the dark, I resolve to continue to approach this residency optimistically. I remind myself that this is supposed to be an adventure. I knew, going into the project, that my best-laid plans would sometimes unravel, if not completely go awry. This is the nature of the venture, and adventurers unwilling to subject themselves to the vagaries of mislaid plans should perhaps never write a book in remote field stations staffed by people more invigorated by natural history than the mechanics of scheduling and communications.

For the most part, the North Cascades Environmental Learning Center is shutting down for the season. Boats are being pulled out of the water, gear used for Mountain School activities is being cleaned and inventoried, one of the walk-in freezers has already been cleared. The staff seem a bit tired, ready to head elsewhere the moment they are furloughed. The program manager is spending her day conducting exit interviews with the naturalist staff, and when those staff are not thus involved, they are packing. Most hope to return in April when the school opens up again. Many will be heading for the ski slopes, replacing one form of seasonal labor with another.

I'm told that the pass to the east is not yet closed for the winter, but this is expected to happen any day, and then things will get really slow around here. I'm also told that last month was the rainiest October in the past sixty years, which helps explain the level of staff fatigue I'm sensing, and perhaps also explains why the waterfalls were so spectacular on the drive up.

I am invited to dine with the program manager, who will not be furloughed for another week. She will orient me over quesadillas. They will be amazing.

They are supposed to get eight inches of snow up on the pass this morning, but it's raining down here. Pouring. The rain awakened me numerous times last night, thrumming on the steel roof of this lodge. I delay going down to "breakfast" until what appears to be a lull between downpours, but it's a short lull and the next gush gushes before I make it halfway down the hill to the dining hall. I resist the impulse to hurry—there's no advantage here to marking myself as a Californian unaccustomed to precipitation.

The homemade granola turns out to be as delicious as promised. And there's a bowl of fresh Washington apples—not the golden apples from the bear tree—on the table. No sooner do I sit down in the staff room than a young academic with tousled hair comes along and scoops himself a bowl. I judge him, correctly, to be an associate professor, and he turns out to be from Western Washington University. Doctor Nicholas Stanger will be conducting this morning's session with the MEd in environmental education graduate students that spend their first year of studies on this field campus. I ask about his topic. He tells me that he'll be working on transformative inquiry, and I express interest even though I've never heard those two words linked together. After all, it sounds as if they should be. He invites me to attend, and I immediately accept the invitation, viewing it as a superior alternative to my original plan, which would have me slogging through old growth in the morning deluge. He warns that first he'll ask the students whether they mind having a visitor around, especially since they'll be talking about establishing safe spaces in the classroom as part of today's conversation. He may have to kick me out if the students are feeling snarly.

This is a risk I'm happy to take.

I'm jumping with both feet into what this field campus is about: environmental education. While the previous field stations I've visited have been mostly about research, providing a smattering of enlightenment on the side, this institute takes the opposite approach, and is primarily an educational enterprise. In the case of the WWU master's program, the signature program up here, they're actually helping to educate the educators. A former student of mine got her master's here about five years ago, and she raves about the program.

A sign on the seminar room instructs all who enter to remove their boots. Please. The room is set up with plastic chairs in a horseshoe formation, and it's a bit chilly where I take my seat near the door. About a third of the students have broken out Mexican blankets that are stored in one of the side closets, and have spread them on the hardwood floor to create a warm space. I note that all the students taking advantage of the blankets are female, and I do a quick count: there are four males in this class, and ten females. Three of the four males are wearing knit caps, and only one female is wearing any sort of head covering, something of a Western hat, but without the huge brim all the country singers are sporting these days.

When Nick follows up his opening exercise, what in my classes I call a "free write,"[4] with a short opening lecture on today's topic, I automatically shift into student mode, perhaps as a conditioned response left over from the ten years I spent pursuing advanced degrees. We sat around enormous seminar tables at Stanford, which stimulated note-taking and rigorous debate, but there's a feeling of intimacy here that I never experienced at the Farm. I find myself wishing I was back in grad school, here in this place, here with these people, this time engaging in a process of transformative inquiry.

There's another exercise, this one conducted in dyads, and one of the students asks me to serve as her partner. Huge fun. After that, another professor, Gene, takes over. Gene is closer to my age, clearly a full professor, and he somehow causes me to make the mental shift from student mode to teacher mode in terms of how actively I listen. Indeed, I have to force myself, consciously, not to jump into the conversation, especially when he wanders into areas of my scholarship.

The constant rain on our roof vacillates between downpour and deluge. I find the cloudbursts distracting, but the group must be habituated to them, for I'm the only one glancing out the windows during the bursts. Or perhaps it's just me. The comments section from every report card during grade school says something like, *"Johnny gets distracted if he sits by the windows."*

And to this day I refuse to teach in a windowless classroom.

Nick takes back over, and critiques the movement toward safe space in the classroom, claiming that it's often a false sales job. His term. What he says we need are "safe-enough spaces" to accomplish what we're supposed to accomplish in the classroom, which often requires moving students beyond their comfort zones. I tend to resonate with everything he's saying at this point, and take furious notes for a few minutes before deciding to relax and just take

---

4. I instruct my students that there are three rules for a free write: (1) don't stop writing; (2) don't stop writing; (3) no scratching out.

it in. He's preaching to the choir here, and one doesn't take notes during the sermon.

I'm finding the library to be a welcoming space, although I wish it had a fireplace on days like today. But the light here is far better than in my lodge, and on rainy afternoons like this I feel a need for light. A couple of the grad students warned me about SAD, seasonal affective disorder, which I've been assured is a real thing at this latitude the closer we get to the winter solstice. Between the deep forest and the thick layers of clouds, the morning gloaming seems to run directly into the afternoon gloaming without it ever getting bright in between. An all-day dusk where the only evidence of noon comes from your wristwatch.

I've learned a trick from the grad students for the next time I visit the library. Keep your moccasins in your daypack so you can wear them in the library, where we also have to remove our boots at the door. The light is good here, but the floorboards are cold.

I see the grad students, at least some of them, on my way to breakfast. They are already on the way out. They seem excited. Anticipatory. "Did you see the snow?" I'm asked.

The snow level descended overnight. Even though it rained on our roofs down here at twelve hundred feet, the snow made it to the two-thousand-foot level, or perhaps a bit lower. I am assured that this is terribly exciting, as if Christmas is almost here.

It suddenly occurs to me that I can play carols on the new speaker I bought for my spotted owl investigations. This prospect brightens my mood considerably.

There's an undergraduate class from Evergreen State College[5] here for a few days studying the geography of polar regions, taught by two geographers, Doctors Martha Henderson and Peter Impara. I'm happy to hear this, for it means

---

5. ESC is a public liberal arts college that I've always admired for its innovative curriculum and its catchy motto, *Omnia extares,* which is Latin for "Let it all hang out." School mascot is the geoduck, the largest burrowing clam in the world, which has a normal lifespan of 140 years.

I'll be fed. I've been asked to give a guest lecture this evening about the scholarship in which I've been engaged during my sabbatical. It's time, finally, to put some slides together. Because I've been asked to speak on the same topic when I return to my own campus in January, I give my full attention to the images. This takes several hours during the afternoon because it's the first time I've looked through many of the shots I took at the various field stations preceding this one. It's fun to look back on shots of Natasha climbing oaks back in the summer heat of Hastings, and to remember the efforts I went through to keep my head wet back then with the soaker hat. Now it's all I can do to keep my head dry.

I have dinner with the WWU grad students, and they take great delight in hearing that I spotted the bear who has been feeding on apples down by the dam. His prehibernation binge. They speak of the bear as "him," and I ask whether they know for certain that it's a male bear. One of them, an outdoorsy fellow from Vermont who seems to know a lot more about bears than I do, tells us that he's certain that it's a male because of the size.

When I concede that the bear was huge, my new friend invites me to dinner sometime. I reply that he's too kind, and then he replies, "No worries, I've got elk." Impressed, I offer to bring a nice bottle of wine.

The conversation turns to their afternoon activities. They all went up into the snow, some hiking, others skiing. A few of them saw a buck with only one antler, an unfortunate state of affairs for an ungulate. One of the students cracks me up when she observes, "That dude's season is over."

The Evergreen students huddle around a bonfire outside the dining hall, and I feel a pang of guilt when they're called in for the lecture. They come without hesitation, however, and don't smell particularly smoky, and I'm encouraged when they scoot their chairs forward toward the screen. Once I've been introduced, I suggest that we douse the lights, which shifts the focus more toward my photography and less toward me.

The hour flies by, and I'm asked insightful, challenging questions at the end, starting with why I regard the trope of the solitary nature sojourner as being outmoded. I answer about the motif's inherent maleness, and how it feeds off the narrative of self-reliance, the Emersonian roots of which I question. Heads nod, which I take as a good sign.

I emerge from the experience energized to return to the classroom in January. I needed this reminder of how much I love teaching, for I've been dreading this sabbatical coming so soon to a close.

In midmorning, during a pause in the rain, I hustle down to Little Dog to retrieve some gear. The door sloshes when I open it. Although there's no water in the cab, the door itself has filled with water, probably from rain flowing down the windows. I trudge up to borrow a drill from the maintenance shed in order to install a drain hole, but the facilities manager, who grew up in Washington State, assures me that vehicle doors are built with weep holes that should deal with this. Before drilling, I'm advised, I should check to make certain my existing weep holes have not clogged up with dirt.

Having spent my formative driving years on the Colorado plateau, in the Upper Sonoran and the northern New Mexico high desert, this is the first I've heard of an automotive weep hole. But when I slog back down to the parking lot to inspect Little Dog for such orifices, I discover two small plastic panels at the bottom of each door. I pop open the one on the driver's side, and water gushes out. When I pop open the one on the passenger side, I get the same result.

It occurs to me, as I hike back up the hill, hood up and my jacket zipped to the throat, that I've lost touch with seasons. I recall how, when we first moved to California, my wife purchased all sorts of fresh produce from farm stalls in autumn, intent on canning vegetables for the winter. Little did we know that those vegetables would be available whenever we wanted them in California's year-round growing season. Before long, the word "autumn" would lose the greater part of its meaning, other than for being the season when they also sell pumpkins on the roadside.

When I attempted to set things up at this field station, I'd completely forgotten that there are places where things shut down for the winter. During the planning phase, I'd inquired with a Park Service geologist who monitors glacier activity whether I could tag along during my residency here. Here in the mountains, at latitude 48, in November. When he replied that he was interested in my project and would love to have me along but that he would not return to the field until April, I was astonished, at least for a moment. We arranged for a hike closer to sea level.

So. Weep holes. Important things to know about this time of year in certain latitudes.

There are at least thirty brush piles in the woods just below my cabin, each one the size of a Volkswagen Beetle. This morning a three-man crew from the Park Service, clad in heavy rain gear and yellow hard hats that make them look like fire fighters, is attempting to ignite the piles using driptorches. These devices, commonly used to start backfires and prescribed burns, look like a giant oilcan with a flaming spout. They don't shoot fire out like a flamethrower, but rather pour it out, nice and slow, as if we have finally controlled fire itself.

This is a process I cannot ignore. I go out on the deck in my moccasins, mug in hand, and sip tea while watching. The process has its comical elements, if properly viewed. Whenever one of the Park Service fellows gets a good blaze going, he moves to the next brush pile, and as soon as he starts torching the latter pile, the former goes out. I'm following one fellow in particular, and by the time he moves to brush pile number 3, the first pile he'd torched was no longer even smoking.

I look up "driptorch" on Wikipedia, and therein learn that they contain a fuel of 30 percent gasoline mixed with 70 percent diesel. This makes sense: there's just enough gas to keep the concoction lit when it pours, yet not enough to blow up Park Service personnel. Totally cool. I'm overwhelmed by the urge to rush out and consult. Surely someone with my experience, having worked four summers at a scout ranch where we built a bonfire every night . . .

I decide to stay put. Sometimes it's nice if academics don't get involved. Or former Boy Scouts. Indeed, I stand here instead, scribbling these notes, wondering whether they wonder why I haven't got anything better to do than stand here on the deck watching their fires go out. Poor fellows probably were not expecting to end up in a book when they left for work this morning.

I take my scope down to the lake before lunch. I'd seen white-winged scoters a few days ago, but they were distant and I only had my binoculars so I wanted to get a better look. I suspect that today might have to be the day because it's getting colder and there's precipitation in the forecast for the next seven days. I'm not certain how much longer waterfowl will be sticking around.

I am surprised to discover that a lot of the birds I was seeing when I first got here five days ago are no longer here. Gone are the bufflehead and common goldeneyes. I don't see any mergansers either, although my bird checklist shows them to be year-round residents. No common loons. I see a single pied-billed grebe and, finally, a single white-winged scoter. The scoter is in close to shore, and floating with its wings pushed down into the water so that its wing patches are completely visible. This bird appears to be either injured or too sick to have migrated.

I get an excellent look at it, and cannot help but feel a bit sad on its behalf. It's an adult male, with a distinctive white comma behind its eye, and its eyes appear closed, which makes the white comma stand out all the more.

I hike down to the apple tree by the dam hoping that the bear might still be foraging, but there's no sign of him. If he's smart, he'll be deep into his winter torpor[6] before this next storm comes along.

I pick up my wife at the Bellingham airport, here for Thanksgiving. We shop together for groceries, setting an all-time record for our grocery bill thanks to the purchase of a case of wine. Although I've been sipping box wines for the most part during my sojourn in the Pacific Northwest, Carol upholds traditional standards, especially during the holiday season.

We detour over to Anacortes to look at a boat. We have been thinking of purchasing a retirement cabin in the San Juan Islands, and the possibility we like best is on one of the smaller islands without ferry service. I drive while she birds, and we end up spotting a flock of at least one hundred snow geese in a field. Three bald eagles, all adults, seem intent on harassing them, but the geese are doing their best to ignore the eagles. We also spot perhaps a half-dozen red-tailed hawks during our drive. The hawks and eagles are the first diurnal raptors I've seen in weeks, but since they are down here on the coastal plains I can't include them on the field station list at the end of this chapter. A shame, my lists seem a bit anemic here in the Pacific Northwest, less than half as long as they were for Hastings.

It's dusk by the time we make it to the cabin, and the Park Service burn piles are alight. The crew must have just left, I tell my wife, since all the fires are still lit. She thinks it's wonderfully romantic to have bonfires scattered everywhere. We cook with the inside lights dimmed, enjoying the spectacle below, but we barely make it through dinner before she falls asleep, her head tucked against my ribs as we sit together on the couch, enjoying the fires. I let her lie there a while, watching as the rain begins again and the bonfires flicker out one by one. When she finally startles awake there is only one fire left burning. I coax her to bed, reminding the poor dear that her alarm went off at 4:00 this morning. She is beyond drowsy, and it's an effort to get her to brush her teeth before she crawls into bed. In the morning we cook up bacon and eggs; this is the first bacon either of us has had since before I started my rotation with

---

6. The literature suggests that bears don't truly hibernate because they can awaken at any moment should they be disturbed by something like a loud noise. While this may seem to be splitting a fine line to some, I use the word "torpor" here because it's the best way to describe the deep, prolonged winter sleep of both black and brown bears. I've heard the same term used to describe college students during lectures, but this usage seems largely hyperbolic.

Hawkwatch more than a month ago. While we eat, the Park Service crew shows up again, this time with double the amount of fuel for their driptorches.

After cleanup we decide to try to sneak in a hike before the showers commence, which the various forecasts seem to think will happen by noon at the latest. We head out in full rain gear, thermals underneath, and as we hike I point out many of the trees and shrubs I've learned in the last several weeks. Carol puts up with this by feigning a bit more interest in natural history than usual, perhaps because we're contemplating the purchase of a cabin in the Pacific Northwest.

A couple miles above the Environmental Learning Center our trail leads us over a ridge into another watershed, and this one is filled with smoke from the bonfires below the cabin, which are apparently relighting more quickly than they were originally lit. The smoke seems to have risen to this point and then stopped, apparently having met up with a temperature inversion. We hike no more than a hundred meters into the smoke, but it is thick enough to sting the eyes, so we retreat back over into our original watershed, heading back down. This turns out to be fortuitous, because the last fifteen minutes of our hike is in the rain, and we could have gotten a good soaking if we had not been turned back so early.

I can't help but think about Edward Abbey, how he never reports in *Desert Solitaire* that his wife, Rita, and their child had accompanied him to his ranger station during his second season in Arches. Should I not inform my readers how delighted I am to be reunited with my best friend and helpmate of thirty-nine years, how wonderful it is to get a break in the bachelorhood that has prevailed in my life since I started working on this book?

I've written about this in an academic paper,[7] how Abbey complains of his near-constant loneliness in his journal, later writing in the book, "I am twenty miles or more from the nearest fellow human but instead of loneliness I feel loveliness. Loveliness and quiet exultation." Well, I've felt plenty of exultation myself at these various field stations, whether it was discovering a new location where woodpeckers were nesting at Hastings, or watching a Santa Cruz Island scrub-jay retrieve cached acorns in a secluded meadow, or being the first hawk-watcher to spot a ferruginous hawk up in the Marin Headlands, or even during a long solo hike through old-growth in the Andrews. But there has always been the unexpected twinge of wishing Carol were here to share these experiences, a feeling of deep separation I've experienced at these various field stations. Even

---

7. Mentioned previously: "What Does the Desert Say? A Rhetorical Analysis of *Desert Solitaire*," published in the journal *Interdisciplinary Literary Studies*. A copy of that paper can be found at www.jsfarnsworth.net.

worse, the times when I put my field notes aside for the evening, settle in with a good book, and wish there was someone sharing the couch with me engrossed in her own book. Tonight, while I'm reading Scott Weidensaul's *Of a Feather: A Brief History of American Birding,* she will be reading Paulette Jiles's new novel, *News of the World,* and we will delight at being together in separate worlds.

I don't mind reporting that she is awhirl in the kitchen as I write this. The Environmental Learning Center is nearly abandoned; staff have taken leave, and most of the grad students have already headed home for Thanksgiving. "Let It Snow" is playing on my portable spotted-owl speaker while it drizzles outside. The fire guys from the Park Service are attempting to burn off the last of the logs from the bottom of the brush piles. In the last hour Carol has cooked two quiches and two lasagnas, all of which will be frozen so that I will have something more than hot dogs and soup to look forward to in the coming weeks.

Would Abbey approve? That hardly matters at this point.

A hike today up to Happy Creek Falls with Carol.

Although our trail guide insisted that our total route to the falls from the gate where they closed the highway would be less than two miles, Carol insists at one point that we've hiked more than two miles. I explain that a mile in the Cascade Mountains is different from a California mile, but her iPhone attests that we've already traveled 2.5 miles. We push on, of course, and within another ten minutes arrive at the falls.

Regardless of the mileage, these falls are well worth the effort. One of the trail guides I'd read while planning this trek had described the falls as "lackluster," and I was curious to know what lackluster falls might look like. Now that I've arrived, I wish I'd never read that description, for I may have allowed the falls' symbolic complex[8] to color my experience of this cascade. Of course, this starts with the name "Happy Creek Falls" itself. Would we view them as being less lackluster had they been named "Torrent Creek Cascades"?

Although I attempt to transcend the symbolic complex, I do not get a sense of power from the water itself. But before one concludes that these falls are truly lackluster, the observant hiker should notice the disarrayed collection of logs at the base of the falls. It took some power to move this detritus into place.

8. In "The Loss of the Creature," an essay I teach in one of my courses, Walker Percy argues how prepackaged ideas form a symbolic complex that prevent the casual observer from authentically discovering a site.

I try to imagine what it would be like to be here where I currently stand while what's left of a tree washes down the falls.

The understory here seems sparse, more like a garden than the wild space it is. There are fewer plants here with which I'm not familiar. I have been expanding beyond trees and shrubs at this point, not that I'm ready to take exams in either subject. The Environmental Learning Center has a tiny bookstore, and a week ago I picked up a thick field guide on Pacific Northwest coastal plants that has been tempting me since my arrival here. As a result of this extravagance, I'm starting to pay attention to true mosses, liverworts, and all that other green stuff—a whole new world for someone schooled in desert flora. As much as I love hiking with my true love, it will be nice in a few days to return to botanist pace so I can continue keying out plants. Today, however, is not the day for that.

We return to Little Dog just moments before combined rain and snow hit. We could not have timed things better. Sometimes the pace is just right.

Thanksgiving is tomorrow, but we decide to cook the turkey today. A looming forecast suggests that Thanksgiving might best be considered a moveable feast. Worst-case scenario: we can boil the bones tomorrow morning, weather permitting, to make Carol's famous turkey soup.

Although we've never considered ourselves fair-weather hikers, we surrender to the elements on Thanksgiving, the final full day of Carol's visit. Steady, here-to-stay rain awakens us at first light, and the forecast calls for the morning showers to turn into snow this afternoon. Overnight storm warnings have been issued. We make soup hurriedly in the morning, soup destined immediately for the fridge. Worried about the prospect of having to mush Little Dog through the snow tomorrow morning in time to get Carol to the airport, we opt to leave the field station now and spend the night in a hotel in Bellingham. A holiday date within a weeklong conjugal visit.

Once we descend far enough to get phone service, we discover that it's too late to make reservations for most of the Thanksgiving buffets in town, but we're able to squeeze into a second seating at an Italian seafood place. When we get there for our 6:30 reservation a thick line of folks with similar reservations has already formed. We try an old trick and ask whether we can order a drink at the bar, and get there just as two people from the first seating leave. We order a favorite chardonnay from far-away California, and ask the bartender whether it would be possible to order dinner at the bar.

"You bet."

It's a lovely, albeit untraditional, Thanksgiving dinner. I have ricotta and sweet potato ravioli with clams, Carol enjoys a seafood pesto, sneaking a few of my clams in the process, but leaving me the seasonal ravioli. We try to ignore the football game playing on the TV above us, which is hard to do when you haven't watched TV since before the baseball playoffs began. But we're madly in love so it works.

"Black Friday" takes on a new meaning when I drop her off at the airport in the morning. Nature works its wiles, however, during the drive back to the mountains. The skies clear, the sun comes out, and the high peaks dazzle with new-fallen snow.

Passing along an agricultural field, at first I think I'm seeing another gaggle of snow geese, but when two take to the air I quickly realize that the wingtips are not black. And the necks are too long. And they're huge! "Those are tundra swans!" I cry out to the empty passenger seat. Or maybe trumpeter swans. Little Dog comes to a quick stop, emergency flashers flashing, and I literally dump out the contents of my daypack, dirty socks and skivvies included, to get to the small backup binoculars that I keep at hand whenever I'm not carrying full-sized optics. I roll down the window but stay inside; tundra swans are sensitive to human intrusion, and Little Dog functions as a fairly good blind in these situations. I try to get a good look at a bill to confirm that these are not trumpeter swans, but there's too much vibration until I remember, belatedly, to turn off the engine. Once past that hurdle I'm able to confirm that the bill curves at the gape, and the eye is mostly visible, and the head is more rounded, all of which indicate tundra swans.

I listen a while—they sound like baying hounds, which in itself should have told me that these were tundra swans. Trumpeter swans trumpet, sounding something like an inexpertly played coronet, hence the name. While tundra swans migrate as far as Northern California, we never hear trumpeter swans that far south.

I continue on, realizing that I'm probably missing some great birds without my favorite bird spotter in the passenger seat. But I must focus on the road. I manage to glimpse a few bald eagles once again over the Skagit River— two adults in the air, a juvenile on a gravel bar—feeding. I pull over and once again attempt to switch on the emergency flashers only to discover that I never turned them off. Oops. Canvasback ducks on the wing, as I merge back onto the road, two drakes and a hen. I remember to switch off the hazard lights this time.

After coaching myself to pay a bit more attention to the actual process of driving, I proceed along a straight stretch of highway in the vicinity of Goodell Creek, where I notice that a work crew has conducted a thinning operation under the high-voltage lines near the highway, leaving several hundred freshly cut Douglas-fir saplings lying on the shoulder, waiting, it appears, to be dealt with mechanically. Driving past, I think to myself that it's a shame that these saplings couldn't have served as Christmas trees, and then I hit the brakes, realizing that I can save one of them from the ignominy of the wood chipper. Unable to pull onto the shoulders, I again employ the emergency flashers and hastily choose a tree that will just fit, diagonally, in Little Dog's bed. I manage to climb back into the truck before any cars come along. I would not have wanted to attempt such a tree rescue back home in Silicon Valley's traffic.

I've long been a minimalist when it comes to yuletide ornamentation. I maintain, druidically, that two strings of tiny LED lights, gold, and a single box of small glass bulbs, all one size, all one color, is all most trees can tolerate before their adornments obfuscate whatever coniferous gestalt is left after a tree is separated from its roots. But there's no need to insist on such austerity this year. This year, here in the evergreen state,[9] my tree will be nothing but green. I prop up my Christmas sapling with rocks in a five-gallon bucket. It's a tenuous affair, but it lends the apartment a solemn glory. John Rutter's "Birthday Madrigals, for Choir, Double Bass and Piano" plays in the background and more than makes up for any lack of visual sparkle.

I'm still writing about the tree when Carol texts that she made it home. We still share the same longitude, 121 degrees west, but we are now separated by eleven degrees of latitude, almost a thousand miles. What a world.

When I check the Lake Diablo forecast this morning I'm greeted with another winter storm warning, effective until 5:00 p.m. tomorrow, a small craft advisory, and a special warning from the National Weather Service about an increased threat of landslides throughout the mountainous region of western Washington. Today's hourly forecast moves from the current light rain to showers, then rain, then snow, then snow showers this evening. Between dawn's civil twilight and dusk's civil twilight we will have precisely nine and a half hours of theoretical daylight, although in deep forest in a valley floor on

9. According to the Washington State legislature's web page on state symbols, "the Evergreen State" is an unofficial nickname that has never been formally adopted. There is, however, an official state oyster, *Ostrea lurida*; a state endemic mammal, *Marmota olympus*; a state marine mammal, *Orcinus orca*; a state flower, *Rhododendron macrophyllum*; and of course a state tree, *Tsuga heterophylla*.

a rainy day hereabouts the darkness has a pervasive quality. It's the sort of day when you leave a few indoor lights on all day, and need to rely on a lantern if you want to find a scarf in an unlit closet.

I decide on a second mug of tea before I'm halfway through with the first.

I'm scheduled to join a local Audubon group next weekend on the Samish Flats, and have therefore been reading up on the winter birding there. Reports are that the best birding happens on the first sunny day after a storm, and when I wake up this morning to patchy blue skies, my first thought is what a shame we're not birding Samish Flats today. My second thought—*Why wait until Saturday?*—was no doubt influenced by the fact that the birding here at the ELC has been so dismal the past week. After a hasty bowl of cereal I summon Little Dog, and we're off.

Within a mile down the North Cascades Highway I notice a few droplets on the windshield, easily enough whisked away. Then a few more, until I finally have to concede that these sprinkles have become a shower. But there are bits of blue scattered above, so I continue on, forever optimistic. My optimism takes a bit of a hit when I reach the town of Sedro-Woolley, whereupon the shower is now a full-on rain event and there is no longer a trace of blue in the sky. But at this point I've already spotted an eagle eating a fish on a gravel bar, so I continue onward.

By noon the rain has turned into a solid downpour, but I hang in doggedly, having at this point identified snow geese, tundra swans, trumpeter swans, bald eagles, and a short-eared owl, mostly from within the pickup's cab. This can't possibly be considered a lousy birding day, right?

The question turns out not to be rhetorical, and is answered by a gyrfalcon, *Falco rusticolus*. It passes enormously overhead, almost as if it considered preying on Little Dog for a moment. I stop in the middle of the road, getting it in my binoculars to make certain it's not a huge female prairie falcon. It is not. Its wings are longer and broader than anything I've ever seen on a falcon, at least sixty centimeters long. Probably a female, judging from the size.

It vanishes all too soon.

Despite the morning chill I sit outside on a wooden deck to enjoy my tea. It's not raining at the moment, and goodness knows how long this will last. Out in the woods I overhear a conversation among red-breasted nuthatches; it sounds as if every nuthatch in the forest is clamoring at once. I haven't heard this before, but it may be that the rain has drowned out this conversation previously. Or perhaps this is how the nuthatch community proclaims its joy when there's a break in the weather. "It's not raining! It's not raining! It's not raining."

One can almost hear it that way, over tea.

One of the grad students overtakes me as I walk toward this morning's trailhead. "Going for a hike?" she asks without breaking stride.

"More of a stroll."

I have no idea where my response came from. I haven't consciously planned out my pace through the day, let alone throughout this stroll. There is, however, something slow about this morning; even now as I walk, I'm still sipping tea.

"Have a good hike," she calls back over her shoulder.

The second cup is never as good as the first, but it's sometimes vital.

The tea is gone by the time I arrive at a small shelter. The sun has just popped up over the eastern ridge, illuminating the canopy above me with shades of yellow I haven't yet seen in this forest.

These shelters are undoubtedly useful in the administration of the camp programs that NCI runs, providing a way to be outdoors and yet still sheltered from the rain long enough to have meaningful conversations with students. I take a seat on a hefty log, its bark removed and its top planed flat, and attempt to write.

In the morning's e-mails I was invited to a poetry reading down at a private residence in Marblemount tomorrow night. Tacos and poetry, two of my favorite things. The way the invite was worded I'm not certain whether I should offer to read something of my own or whether being present as a hungry listener will suffice. I decide to have my iPhone along, preloaded with a recent composition just in case.

Semirecent. I haven't written any verse since starting this project last June, and it seems a waste now that I can look back over six months and five field stations. I've been in a valley, on an island, up on the headlands of a coastal strait, and in two ancient forests—surely the muse might have experienced some inspiration in one of those venues.

It's cold—over my fleece sweater I'm only wearing a down vest this morning, and sitting here in the shelter I'm not active enough to maintain body heat thus attired. I put away the pen, break out the gloves and the hiking stick, and move along, all the while keeping an eye out for poetic inspiration.

As I wander, so does my mind. The Germans have a word for what I experience here, in this dark, wet woodland: *Waldeinsamkeit*, a noun combined from *Wald*, the word for "forest," and *Einsamkeit*, for "loneliness." It doesn't translate into English; the closest we could come would be "forest-aloneness," which doesn't fully capture the concept. *Waldeinsamkeit* connotes a feeling of being connected to nature while being alone in the woods. Emerson used the term as a poem's title without ever translating it. The poem's advice is worth the hearing:

> *See thou bring not to field or stone*
> *The fancies found in books;*
> *Leave authors' eyes, and fetch your own,*
> *To brave the landscape's looks.*

It's funny how Emerson continues to haunt me, even here in this lonely forest. In four years of grad school at Stanford, The Emerson Vortex was the only seminar in which I earned a lowly B. I did all the reading and wrote the requisite twenty-five-page paper, but was never quite caught up in the vortex. My failure was clearly transcendental.

Even though it's merely a stroll, the forest portion of the hike ends too soon. I decide to continue perambulating down to the dam, which from here should add a couple more miles to my morning. One last chance to see whether the bear is still out and about. I haven't seen him for at least a week at this point. I realize, as I saunter along the road, how silly it could seem to be strolling alone along a road where there's a chance of encountering a carnivore who outweighs me. But it's almost December and it's cold and it's a fat black bear, and the odds are that it has already entered torpor.

I make it to a covered float just short of the dam, and decide once again to take a seat and attempt some writing. But it's still too cold to sit there without moving about, so after a couple minutes I get up, dig the shell out of my daypack, and put it on while examining the posters laminated to the walls. The first one tells me that Diablo Dam is 389 feet high, and was the tallest dam in the world at the time of its completion, which was in 1930.

That's the year my dad was born. I'm suddenly feeling connected to this old dam in new ways. Nineteen thirty was quite a year: it's when the first Mickey Mouse comic strip came out. Some twenty-five years later, in the space in my baby book where the date of the child's first steps was supposed to be recorded, Dad wrote that I never learned to walk. According to Dad, all I could do was amble.

Now, eighty-six years after the dam was built, a son sits here, almost shivering in a down vest covered by a thin rain shell, hood up, wishing he could summon his father's spirit just long enough to amble together along the top of the dam, out and back.

Barring that, a bear in an apple tree would do nicely.

A dreary forecast this morning. It's Wednesday, and the nearest icon for scattered sunshine shows up next Tuesday. My cabin feels twice as dreary as it normally does. I'm told that in the wellness center at Western Washington University, down the hill in Bellingham, students can check out lights to help prevent seasonal affective disorder. And get free condoms. I head to the Environmental Learning Center library to soak up some decent light.

Reading an article in last summer's edition of the *Conservation Northwest Quarterly* on rewilding North Cascades National Park with grizzlies, I come across the factoid that this park contains 1,630 species of vascular plants. That's more than any other national park in the nation! No wonder I'm taking so long to become familiar with the local flora.

I've arranged to meet the park geologist for North Cascades National Park, Dr. Jon Riedel, in a coffee shop in the small town of Concrete, Washington. We arrive at the same instant, meeting just outside the front door, both easily identifiable: he is wearing a ball cap with an NPS shield on front, I am wearing a ball cap with the NCI logos on front.

Hi Jon, I'm John.

Two tea drinkers in a coffee shop, we are friends immediately. His youngest daughter is a high school senior and has applied to my university, hoping to study in my department, so he has as many questions for me as I have for him.

Jon studies the local glaciers, and I had originally hoped to accompany him up in the high country, but now that the pass is closed and the avalanches are flowing we're planning to spend the morning on the banks of the Skagit River, searching for "organics," pockets of organic materials that are deposited in the clay. We're going to get muddy, and it's going to be fun.

Jon suggests we take his car, which ends up not being the enormous Park Service pickup I'd expected and instead is an ancient VW diesel sedan that makes Little Dog actually seem sturdy.

Our first stop is at the base of an actively eroding cliff almost the height of a soccer field. Jon points out the various layers; some are gravel, some are sand, some are clay. All have been deposited by glaciation. It's mostly the clay that interests us, and I notice that swallows have previously taken an interest in this same sediment. There are at least a hundred nest cavities up there, all abandoned at this point. I'm guessing that these would have belonged to bank swallows, which would have left the neighborhood as early as four months ago. If I'm right, they should be deep into South America by now.

We have no need to climb. Large chunks of clay have broken off in the recent rains, and have gathered at the base of the cliff. Even though I worry that other chunks could be coming down any moment, Jon seems immune to such concerns, and we start breaking basketball-sized chunks apart. There is no need for a rock hammer here, only strong hands that don't mind a bit of clay under their fingernails. The clay has been deposited in thin annual layers called varves, much like the rings on a tree. Jon tells me that they once found an intact skeleton from a wooly mammoth in this cliff, which is something I wouldn't mind finding myself. But a geologist has to go through a lot of clay to get that lucky, and the best thing we'll find today are macrofossils, such as seeds, sticks, and cones.

Over the years I've noticed how fond geologists are of teaching nongeologists their secret language, and Jon is no exception. Once we're finished breaking apart the varves, we search through the rubble of fallen rock at the base of the cliff, most pieces of which are rounded by glaciation and run the gamut from apple-sized to grapefruit-sized. Jon points out the "erratics," which have come from west of our present location, moving opposite the direction in which the Skagit River currently flows. Noting my confusion, he explains that there are times when the glaciers have pushed westward over this spot, and other times when the glaciers have moved eastward. Both have contributed to the gravel on which we now tread.

We move to a second site, which involves a one-mile hop in the VW and then cutting across a riverside property for which Jon has permission to pass. We have an encounter with two large dogs who seem to like Jon, despite a ferocious bit of barking to begin with. The dogs pretty much ignore me, and I'm fine with that. Once past the dogs we bushwhack through a bramble of Himalayan blackberries, the same invasive species that blocked my access to the clear-cut back in Oregon. Jon warns, "If you walk through enough of this, you'll end up naked."

I'm thinking it would be really nice to be wearing leather chaps right about now. But when we make it to the riverbank we have other treacheries to navigate. Jon hustles over the moss-covered rocks as if he were still under fifty, and I do my best to keep up. Our destination is a vertical steep just above the riverbank. Water drips from everywhere, and Jon describes how it has permeated down to bedrock and flows horizontally through the various striations until emerging here. We look again for organics, and I find a finger-sized stick that's been flattened by geological pressure. Jon examines my stick, smiles broadly, and says, "Welcome, brother. You've just joined the Friends of the Pleistocene." It turns out my stick is twenty-nine thousand years old. Jon's team has been carbon-dating the organics from this seep, and they're pretty confident of the date within a millennium or two. After inquiring about the dues—there are none—I promise to include my membership in the Friends of the Pleistocene on my curriculum vitae. There are stranger things there.

I ask whether I can keep my stick and Jon replies, "Go ahead. It will probably fall apart when it dries out."[10]

We head to another site in a somewhat sketchy backwoods neighborhood. Most of the residents here are loggers who emigrated from North Carolina when the timber industry crashed there. The lots scattered here and there are mostly occupied by trailers, and there are few signs of affluence anywhere. Jon says, gently, that we have to be careful not to trespass in this neighborhood.

We stop in a vacant place near a cabin that's obviously been abandoned, and scramble through the thorns to a site some fifteen meters above the river. The bank here is a vertical cliff of clay, and there's a huge Douglas-fir log sticking horizontally out of the bark about halfway up, projecting at least twenty meters out over the river. Jon tells me that he wants to take a sample of that log for carbon dating. Guessing from the layers of clay where this log was buried, he thinks it's at least six thousand years old, even though it looks as if it died no more than a year or two ago. We don't have a rope, however, and can't find a safe way to get down to the log. Jon decides that he'll have to bring a raft down to get this sample. All in a day's work.

As we drive to our next site I ask Jon whether the park's glaciers are in decline. He tells me that over the past thirty years his measurements show a decline of three cubic kilometers of actual water content, which represents about 19 percent of the area of the glaciers. This translates into 800 billion gallons of water, enough to serve as the water supply for the entire Skagit Valley for a century. In essence, that much water, which should still be stored in the glaciers themselves, has all flowed out to sea.

Our third stop is along the highway and involves another treacherous bushwhack through invasive brambles. There's a face of clay here that Jon's been wanting to investigate a good while, but hasn't had the leisure to do

---

10. This prediction turned out to be prescient. Within a week, before it was even completely dry, my Pleistocene stick was reduced to sludge.

so until today. He takes along a trowel with which to scrape the surface, and I take my camera to document a scientist at work. He's cloaked in mud at this point, looking not at all like someone with the lofty title of park geologist.

He finds very little in the way of organics, complaining that most of it in this deposit seems to have oxidized. He collects a few samples of a darker layer anyway to take back to the lab, and then makes a cool discovery. He scrapes clean a lighter layer, tannish, that he identifies as volcanic ash. Jon explains that he found a similar layer less than a mile up the river and that it turned out to be from an eruption of Mount Saint Helens twenty-one thousand years ago. This is probably more of the same.

I try to share Jon's excitement, but I'm distracted, having a hard time getting my head around the fact that the glaciers up here have lost three cubic kilometers of water content on Jon's watch. I'm finally starting to realize how much water that actually is, and I can't help but wonder how this will show up in the sediment layers twenty thousand years from now.

Such questions will have to be asked another time. I must leave Jon to his explorations at this point because I'm scheduled to lecture the Western grad students later this afternoon regarding best practices for using a field journal as a teaching tool. This is a topic about which two colleagues and I conducted research and published a paper a couple years ago.[11] I've actually been looking forward to giving this lecture for some time, eager to engage with these students on an intellectual level because of how impressed I am with the group. They have a casual intimacy with each other that I don't see often, perhaps because they spent the summer backpacking together before actually hitting the books.

I've been assigned a slot from 3:30 to 5:00, which pretty much guarantees that the class will be exhausted by the time I begin. It doesn't help that the previous instructor, who was supposed to finish at 3:00, runs until 3:20. Nevertheless, the students return promptly after their ten-minute break, and not one of them seems to be in a snarly state of mind. One asks whether we can meet outdoors, but it's rainy and cold and will be dark before I'm half finished, so I explain that I've prepared slides, and that other than for the slides I don't have lecture notes. The class nods their collective understanding; they will soon be teachers themselves.

I ask them to partner up, and then I get them moving around with an exercise that tests their ability to describe simple figures, a basic natural history skill. They're forced to laugh at their own ineptitude accomplishing a task that

11. Farnsworth, Baldwin, and Bezanson 2014.

fifth graders should be able to perform. I ask them what it is in our education system that failed to equip them to perform this exercise, and we explore this question in light of their own educational histories. By the time we're ready to move to the next topic, learning outcomes, they're paying close attention, and when I introduce a ten-minute exercise for them to reconnect with the field notes they kept last summer, they're fully engaged.

The time swings by fast, especially for me, and the group seems surprised when, at the stroke of five, right as I finish sharing the high points from my research into best practices in the field, I dismiss the class. They glance from side to side before looking back at me: *Are we done?* With a wink I tell them something that grad students working on an MEd in environmental education need to know: *Humane teachers tend not to run late.*

I stick around to answer questions. One student hands me her field notes from the summer and asks whether I'd critique them. Another asks whether he can join me birding the Samish Flats on Saturday. Another invites me to join a group of them for dinner, where I will have my choice between lasagna and "mac cheese."

Gotta love grad students.

(Report from the Samish Flats, December 3, 2016)

I pick up my grad-student associate precisely at 6:00 a.m., a point when sunrise is still ninety-seven minutes away at this latitude. It's raining. Hard. He has arrived at our rendezvous point before I get there, and stands patiently under a tree with his hood up and his headlamp on, his face invisible other than for his bearded chin. This would be a better scene for the opening credits of a horror movie than for a day watching birds.

We hastily stow his gear in the back of Little Dog, and I proceed slowly in the dark and the rain, sharing that I'm worried about running into deer or elk. He mentions, patiently, that he rarely sees ungulates this high up the valley, and describes the point when I'll have to be cautious in that regard. Sure enough, when we arrive at that point, just around first light, there are a score of elk foraging close to the road's south shoulder. He spots them before I do.

He instructs me as to the best place to stop for a breakfast sandwich. I trust him implicitly about this—grad students develop considerable expertise in matters of culinary expediency.

Despite the breakfast stop we arrive at our destination a few minutes before eight, right on schedule, but no one else is there. My companion whips out his smartphone, and within seconds informs me that we don't have to be there until 8:30. Oops. We head down to the water to look for ducks, mostly finding scoters and buffleheads. But it's nice to stretch the legs, and the rain has stopped for now.

When we return to the parking lot at 8:25, a small covey of enthusiasts awaits. Judging from their optics, their garb, and the fact that they would come out on such a dreary morning, I judge them to be serious birders. They seem glad to have outsiders join them, even if one of the newcomers is a college professor. My grad-student compatriot is from Vermont, currently ranked as the safest state in the country, and the Skagit Audubon Society seems to appreciate the Vermont ethos.

The leader, Libby Mills, encourages us all to carpool, and since Little Dog won't accommodate additional passengers I ask whether anyone can accommodate two large academics. A retired couple with a luxurious SUV offers us the hospitality of their back seat. When we load our gear into their rear compartment, I am amazed at the variety of high-end optics already laid out in the back, including a super-telephoto lens the size of my leg. But there's still plenty of room for our gear.

By the time we arrive at our first observation site—a flat, fallow farm field fenced in by firs—my colleague and I are officially having a blast. It's fun to be with a group with equal or greater expertise, a group who enjoys birding so much that they barely notice how the wind cuts through our garments this time of morning, or how inevitable it is that rain will resume before we have had our fill of sightings.

Gotta love these Washingtonians. The one strange thing I notice about this group is that they tend not to be impressed by bald eagles. If there are three bald eagles to the right, and a tiny falcon—a kestrel—to the left, they're all watching the kestrel. But there's no lack of patriotism here. Familiarity, rather, is the operative factor. Bald eagles can be found everywhere on these flats. The couple chauffeuring us have an eagle nest in their backyard, for goodness sake! But an American kestrel, with its slender, pointed wings, subtle colors, and ability to hover midair—now that's something.

The group sticks together though a five-stop circuit. During our third stop, down on a narrow gravel beach, we spot more than a dozen species of waterfowl, including a rakish, fine-feathered raft of long-tailed ducks, *Clangula hyemalis*. The drakes of this compact, distinctive species appear to have spent the morning in the plumage shop, being preened to perfection. I announce quietly that this species is a "lifer" for me, a bird I've never before seen. This information is rebroadcast by Libby, and a cheer goes up from every corner of the beach. *Happy lifer!* Without exception, everyone in the group shares my joy; at this level of expertise, a new bird on anyone's life list is an occasion. The lifer experience is not merely mine; it is ours.

In bits and snatches I'm told some cool stuff about this lavish duck, which is apparently one of the deepest diving ducks around, sometimes reaching depths of two hundred feet. I'm told that it goes through four partial molts a year, an unusual number. I'm also told that long-tailed ducks will spend four times as long foraging underwater as they will spend floating on the surface. There's also some conversation about the name change. This duck used to be called "oldsquaw," and there was some concern about the name being offensive to Native Americans, but when the name was changed, the American Ornithological Union insisted that nomenclature updates are never made on the basis of political correctness.

The National Football League will probably claim the same thing when one of their teams finally becomes known as the Washington Redtails.

A group of eight long-tailed ducks, all drakes, takes off, together, almost in formation, flap-running on top of the water at first, then slowly gaining elevation, and then banking together like fighter jets. They streak away together in tight formation, only a meter or two above the water, a proper flight of Arctic birds. I feel blessed to have seen them fly; their high-contrast plumage is even more distinctive when they are airborne.

At the penultimate stop, a number of raptors glide directly overhead, providing photographic opportunities that even those of us wearing gloves can take advantage of. Most are bald eagles, but my grad-student buddy identifies one as a dark-morph red-tailed hawk. One of the locals corrects him, stating definitively that the bird is an immature bald eagle. I am looking directly at the bird through my telephoto lens, and despite its dark coloration I can clearly make out its patagial patches. It's a red-tail all right. I snap off a few quick photographs, but don't come to my grad-student comrade's defense. He needs to do this for himself.

He sticks with the bird, and calls out the field signs that he's observing: wing shape, size, silhouette. Our leader, Libby, having seen the patagial patches herself, corroborates—it's a dark-morph red-tail.

At the end of the day, back in Little Dog, I commend my grad-student friend for sticking to his guns. He smiles broadly, admits how difficult it was to do that, and then turns to his cell phone to look for a shop on the way home where I can purchase replacement boot laces.[12]

12. I've already busted one of the laces on my new boots, the ones that I purchased six months ago back at the Hastings Natural History Reservation. Fortunately, I've brought both sets of high-top boots up here to the Pacific Northwest, just in case one pair gets wet.

I end the day with fifty species on my personal list of observations, including the one lifer, as follows:

Northern harrier	Mew gull
Rough-legged hawk	Ring-billed gull
Red-tailed hawk	Glaucous-winged gull
Bald eagle	Pigeon guillemot
American kestrel	Marbled murrelet
Prairie falcon	Double-crested cormorant
Tundra swan	Great blue heron
Trumpeter swan	Black-bellied plover
Snow goose	Dunlin
Brant	Belted kingfisher
American widgeon	Northern flicker
Mallard	Common raven
Northern shoveler	Wild turkey
Northern pintail	Northern shrike
Surf scoter	Anna's hummingbird
White-winged scoter	Black-capped chickadee
Common goldeneye	Bewick's wren
Bufflehead	Pacific wren
Common merganser	Golden-crowned kinglet
Harlequin duck	Spotted towhee
Long-tailed duck	Meadowlark
Common loon	European starling
Red-throated loon	Brewer's blackbird
Horned grebe	Dark-eyed junco
Red-necked grebe	House finch

It's an auditory experience at first. The forest sounds different. I am still in bed, and when I check my watch, it's only 5:30. I instruct myself to go back to sleep, the rain has stopped, that's all. But my ears know that this is not all. The rain hasn't stopped, it has changed. Have I been too long in California to remember such a change?

I get up, finally. Might as well pee if I'm awake. And then, still not wearing my glasses, I cross over to the thermostat—I seem to have set the heat back too low last night. Crossing back in front of the deck, I look out. It's not yet first light, but something is different.

I switch on porch lights. Of course! It's snowing. Large, beautiful flakes that drift of their own accord, there being no breeze this morning.

My reverie is short-lived because I remember being warned not to leave my truck parked near the cabin if it snows—they are unable to plow the road this high, and it's possible for vehicles at the upper level of the Environmental Learning Center to become snowbound for the winter. I dress hurriedly, putting on my snow gloves rather than the driving gloves that I've been wearing up to this point. How long has it been since I've scraped snow off a windshield?

I have to chuckle at my first glance at Little Dog. The silver truck is all white, as if trying to pass for a Seattle City Light vehicle. I honestly can't remember if I've ever seen it this way. I can remember driving through snow in the little beast, but I can't remember ever seeing it shiver under half an inch of snow like this.

It's not snowing in the parking lot, just drizzling, and I realize that the snow line falls somewhere between my cabin and the level of the lake. I hasten back up to the cabin, hoping that it's still snowing there. It is, but just barely. I sit outside, listening to how snow works its way through Douglas-fir needles. What I'm hearing is not the silence one might expect; the snowfall sounds like the last swash of a wave that has reached its highest point on a beach. There's a bit of a sizzle to it, the sound of effervescence. As I sit and listen, sipping my tea slowly so that it will last, the sound changes, growing both in volume and intensity. Snowflakes turn to snow pellets, what we called "corn snow" growing up in Colorado, but which is more properly termed "graupel."

The graupel only lasts a couple of minutes, turning back into small flakes and then, five minutes later, stopping entirely. Is that it? I scurry inside to check the forecast. Scattered showers ahead, could be rain, could be snow. But clear skies on Tuesday, two days from now. I check the avalanche danger and it's listed as "considerable," even below tree line. The Northwest Avalanche Center has given us two exclamation points. I head back outside regardless, this time with camera in hand.

The sun breaks through, and just as this happens the graupel returns, a bit smaller this time. It bounces when it lands in moss, as if nature is playing tricks on itself. I feel like laughing at the cosmos, or sniggering along with it, and I recognize my manic state for what it is: I'm reacting to the fact that the quality of light has changed here in the forest. It has a warm, yellow glow that even the thickest canopy can't filter out. Even when graupel begins again to fall, lightly now, the grayness with which I've been living has vanished, at least for the moment.

I check my watch for the second time today. It's December fourth, and now that the snow has descended to my level it finally feels like December. And then it hits me that the ten-day forecast now extends through the expected end of my residency. I check it. Between now and then, the only day when it's not expected to rain or snow is next Tuesday.

I head back toward the cabin, no longer feeling quite so upbeat. I check the ten-day forecast once again, using a different weather app. Same thing—Tuesday is the only day out of the next ten when there will not be precipitation. And the forecast high for Tuesday is -6 degrees Celsius, or 21 degrees Fahrenheit, take your pick.

I check the forecast for Santa Clara, California. Out of the next ten days, rain is only forecast for two days, and even then the daily highs will be in the sixties.

I should not have looked. I've been away from home well over a month now, and I'm growing weary of being away. I read ten books during the month of November alone, and I've written thirty thousand words since I last shaved in my own basin. There have been lots of good hikes, but a lot of rain days. A whole lot of rain days. And the last time I got a haircut, the Cubs hadn't won the World Series for more than a century.

I call Carol. She likes the idea of me heading south on Tuesday, and reminds me that every leg of this trip so far has involved me driving through rain, including when I left in October, when it rained through the entirety of California. She'd prefer to think of me coming home on dry roads.

Another snow flurry arrives, this one turning our landscape back to its prevailing gray. It's a moment when I'd like to build a fire in a fireplace, any fireplace, adding some yellow to my world. Instead, I put one of the quiches Carol made over Thanksgiving in the oven for lunch, hoping to at least make up for a hasty bowl of raisin bran that never quite goes the distance.

There's a lot to be eaten if I want to get out of here by Tuesday.

I'm watching snow fall, something of a renewed pastime for me. A feathery blur lands just past the deck, and I get up and go to the window. From the size I suspect that it might be a varied thrush; the descending snow line has been pushing them down to our level because they forage on the ground, and this must be getting tough at the higher elevations where the snow is getting deep.

I spot the bird under a tree where not much snow has accumulated. In terms of shape and comportment, it looks much like a varied thrush, but instead of the varied thrush's orange-and-black head pattern, this bird's head is black and white. And instead of the varied thrush's single breast band, this thrush has two. And from the lower band black spots run down its flanks.

It seems obvious that it's a thrush, but not one I've ever seen before. I pull out a field guide, and am amazed to discover the bird to be an extremely rare visitor from the western Alaskan islands, perhaps having come down with this storm. I discover that they've been seen in Washington before, but not often and not recently. I suddenly realize that this is a bird I should document.

I rush into the bedroom to retrieve my camera from its case, but when I return the bird has vanished, as they so often do. I quickly don boots and a coat, and spend the next two hours wandering the forest around the cabin, stalking first, pishing later, attempting to call it in. But all I see that entire two hours are dark-eyed juncos.

I decide that for the rest of my time here the camera will remain on the dining room table, lens cap off, hood attached, always at the ready.

Feedback to Sally, not her real name:

Well, Sally, your field notes are gorgeous, as you probably already know. I found the biggest strength to be in the reflections, and I thoroughly enjoyed the sketches. A great start.

The mapping you did does not seem original, and you should credit your sources if ever you copy published materials. This can be a simple: "Based on USGS map 201065, 2004." It's also nice to indicate magnetic north and a scale.

You are mixing course notes and observations here, and while that works well for the present, think about what your field notes might look like when you transition from student to educator. Visualizing this may be instructive for the next time you're out in the field. What do you want to note if you're going to bring a class of your own out to a particular site five years from now? If you're serious about environmental education, field-based environmental education, your field notes become your lecture notes, so to speak. These current field notes don't quite get you there, because they're student notes. Figure out how to make them teacher notes.

Your sketches of flora are superior to your sketches of fauna. I'm convinced that this is a confidence thing. Anyone who can draw a great hemlock cone can draw a passable marmot. Get yourself a sketchbook and spend some time in a natural history museum over Christmas. I recommend you stop predrawing in pencil and then tracing over in pen. Start right out with pen in your sketchbook, if that's to be your medium. Be bold, knowing that you have talent. (The marmot drawing fails, by the way, because you don't adequately describe volume. When you figure out how to do that, send me a marmot. A fat, furry marmot ready for the coming winter.)

You might also want to experiment with speculation. Ask questions about behaviors, ecological relationships, et cetera. Let your ecological curiosity run wild—right now it seems a bit too controlled. You have been seeing things out in the field that no one fully understands, not even your professors. Question. Speculate. Inquire.

A minor quibble: you may remember, in my lecture, I mentioned that beginners tend to focus too much on species identification and too little on ecological relationships in terms of the larger landscape. This describes where you are at present. Move on toward the bigger picture. Don't just describe what the needles look like in various conifers, tell me where each tree thrives. Do some need more sunlight than others? More moisture? Start looking for these things. The needles will point you in that direction.

Okay, here's my biggest disappointment in your current field notes (and remind yourself that you encouraged me to be critical): VOICE. I don't hear voice here except in a few of the more brilliant reflections. Voice is where the author's personality comes through the text (including drawings.) I read through your entire journal without getting an idea of who you are as a person. Liberal? Feminist? Environmentalist? Activist? Funny? Sensate? Adventurous? You're holding your personality back here, withholding your Sallyness. This may be because you haven't yet developed your persona as an environmental educator, and if that's the case, it's time to get moving on that issue. So set this as a goal for the next block of field notes: suppose that you show those notes to some random professor—not your instructor— and ask for her/his feedback. *Will that professor have a better sense of who you are as a person after reading your field notes? I mean, something more than "Good Student Sally?" Bottom line: I just spent more than an hour reading through your field notes, and I still have no idea who you are. Don't let that happen again.*

Otherwise, wonderful. I have a much better sense of what your program is like having read through your field notes, and for that I thank you.

I've decided to head south on Tuesday. The last migrant to follow the Pacific flyway south. I've been in the field continuously since the second week of October, and I'm at the point where I need to head home and get a hair-cut. Please advise as to how I should get your journal back to you tomorrow.

Kind regards,
John

North Cascades Environmental Learning Center bird list

(Does not include birds from the Samish Flats. See above.)

Common merganser
Bufflehead
Common goldeneye
White-winged scoter
American dipper
Chestnut-backed chickadee
Black-capped chickadee
Pacific wren
Dark-eyed junco
Song sparrow
Red-breasted nuthatch
Bushtit
Ruby-crowned kinglet
Golden-crowned kinglet
Common raven
Pine siskin
Varied thrush
Dusky thrush

Afterword

Attention is the beginning of devotion.

MARY OLIVER, *Upstream*, 2016

It turned out to be harder to leave the Environmental Learning Center than I'd anticipated. Little Dog was frozen shut, both doors, and I didn't have access to a blow-dryer. One learns how to make do in a field station, however, especially if there's a Wi-Fi connection with which to consult the collective wisdom of humanity.[1]

My delayed departure gave the road crews enough time to sand the roads and clear away the slides that had come down overnight. Numerous large boulders had gouged into the roadway, and I tried not to concern myself about the fact that others were soon to follow. Nor did I stop to photograph the numerous cascades that had transformed into icefalls—that sort of gawking just wasn't safe in the current conditions.

The morning was cloudless and glorious. The North Cascades bedazzle when cloaked with new-fallen snow. But silver-gray clouds rolled in off the Pacific in the afternoon, and by dusk it was raining in the valleys and snowing

---

1. I'm happy to report that searching on the keywords "car door frozen" on YouTube resulted in over 2 million returns, including one for a video on how to open a car door with a Glock ammunition magazine.

on the passes. I stopped in Grant's Pass, unwilling to try my luck over Siskiyou Summit, the highest point on Interstate 5, where there was a conditional closure, meaning that motorists had to be carrying chains. I had the chains—they were purchased new in 2004, the year I bought Little Dog, and have never been used.

Over my solitary dinner in Grant's Pass, I became aware that I wasn't quite ready to be done with this adventure. While the greater part of me wanted to be back in the arms of my sweetheart, there was still a chunk of my psyche that wanted to tarry. I could only hope that spreading the sixteen-hour drive home over two days would be a good way to gain a perspective on where I'd been and what I'd done.

Projects of this nature rarely come off exactly as they were conceived, but this one came fairly close. I'd been to field stations before, and I knew that a fly-on-the-wall approach wouldn't work. I'd have to get involved—and I wanted to get involved—even when that meant spending a day or two in a blind.

The big question I had going into this was the sort of community I'd find in stations where long-term projects were under way. Frankly, I had not anticipated the warmth of the welcome I would receive almost everywhere.

Field stations don't come equipped with counseling departments, a human services division, a conflict resolution team, or much more than a well-stocked first aid kit. In most of these places you'd be unlikely to get a fire truck on the scene within an hour of dialing 911. Life in a field station is about making do with the resources at hand. When a fellow shows up with close-enough credentials and a smile on his face, he will soon find himself pressed into service in all sorts of ways beyond the skills listed on his résumé: tick remover, trail maintainer, career counselor, radio monitor, academic adviser, check-in buddy, lab partner, climbing safety assistant, field-notes recorder, program evaluator, bird bander, poetry reader, critic.

My ready acceptance into these field stations came as a surprise no matter how often it happened. Twice I was asked to provide a guest lecture shortly after meeting the person who would be hosting me. On reflection, this should not have been surprising: I never once saw a television set in any of the field stations I visited, a factor that no doubt adds to the appeal of lectures.

While each field station was unique in terms of how it conceived of its mission, there were patterns. The most notable of these seemed to be rooted in times past, in the collective history of field studies. Regardless of where I went, there always seemed to be an elder. Picture someone with facial hair, inevitably: a beneficent patriarch tainted by long years in the role of principal investigator. Like it or not, I understood myself to reinforce that history. As an academic in his sixties pursuing a book project while on sabbatical, and having a touch of gray in my own beard, I was often mistaken for someone who had acquired elderhood. It was an interesting dynamic to observe. I no doubt earned the confidence of research assistants earlier in the process than I would have in less-remote settings. A lot of these kids, after all, were kids.

Patriarchy will change over time. People who trained in male-dominated forestry, geology, and zoology departments in the sixties and seventies are slowly being replaced by people who never learned to associate the word "scientist" with a specific gender. I can report with confidence that females were a particularly vibrant force among the interns, research assistants, grad students, and postdocs with whom I've associated these past six months. In some cases, the males were overwhelmingly outnumbered, like the solitary male among the six GGRO interns. The four males within the cohort of fourteen WWU graduate students represented a ratio more typical of what I was seeing in the field except for postdocs, who seemed more evenly split between genders.

The above, of course, does not represent a scientific survey of North American field stations; it's just a report back from one fellow's sabbatical. I observed a world that in many ways felt like a man's world: all the directors of the stations I visited were men, as were the facility managers, otherwise known as "campus superintendent" or "reserve steward." As a whole these were a hearty bunch, equally adept running a chain saw, a backhoe, or a snowcat. But the research and educational functions are increasingly in the hands of women, and I am encouraged by what I saw. It would be lovely if someone, perhaps under the auspices of the Organization of Biological Field Stations, could study the feminization of fieldwork.

The reason I reflect on what I'm clumsily calling "feminization" is that the phenomenon seems to be affecting the experience of community at the sites I visited. How could it not? At a deeper level this transformation of fieldwork also affects how people within these communities experience nature.

I have been asked what it was like to compose an entire manuscript *in situ*. Was it a worthwhile experiment? Would I do it again? Advice for others?

One of many references that I consulted in preparation for this project was *Writing Ethnographic Field Notes* by Robert Emerson, Rachel Fretz, and Linda Shaw. The book offered a bit of advice for which I will always be grateful: that field time should be managed so that it doesn't exceed writing time. I realized, soon enough, that I couldn't put in eight hours shadowing and/or assisting a researcher in the field and then write it all up in an hour or two afterward, even if I took excellent notes during the time in the field. In practice, I needed almost a full hour of writing/transcribing time for every hour I spent working with someone else. This cut my effective daily field time to four or five hours whenever I was teaming up with a researcher. While at first I feared that I would not accomplish much by limiting my field time in this fashion, in reality I was quite productive, putting in long days once all the transcribing/writing/editing time was accounted for.[2] Add to that the time attending to logistics such as setting up the next day's activities, interviews, et cetera, and it ended up being an exhausting six months, with very little time for reading, reflecting, or relaxing. When I returned from the sabbatical and once again began to teach, I found my time in the classroom to be far less demanding than the time "off" had been.

On the plus side, the immersive nature of writing *in situ* added greatly to my experience of the natural world. Although a year of preparatory, pres-abbatical research had taught me a great deal about the natural histories of the organisms and ecosystems I'd be encountering, I learned far more than I'd anticipated from the researchers with whom I was spending time. Beyond that, I was considerably—and constantly—more attentive to my surroundings. Hiking outdoors with pen in hand transforms the hike, just as in my earlier experiences as a scuba diver I would find it existentially different to dive with empty hands than when I dove with a camera or a spear gun. In the underwater world, where each dive is limited in scope and duration, the exigence for the dive transformed the dive fundamentally. In a primal way, I was more the hunter, less the tourist. Similarly, my exigence for the writing transformed how I was paying attention to the natural world, causing me to become almost hyperaware of my surroundings. That was good, especially for a daydreamer like me who tends to space out as he walks.

Would I do it again? Yes and no. Looking back on things, covering five field stations in a six-month period ended up being a breakneck pace, and the *in-situ* process exacerbated how quickly time passed. In retrospect, I would have enjoyed spending a year in any of the three biological field stations I visited, just getting to know the lay of the land and having a more leisurely time figuring out what to write about. But my life as a working teacher has

2. "Prolific" might be a better term than "productive." During my time at the Hastings Natural History Reservation I composed 20,000 words in two weeks, and I wrote my agent to ask what she thought if the book ran 120,000 words, since at that time I was planning to visit six field stations. She wrote back, bless her heart, that a book that long was going to be expensive to publish, and that readers wouldn't pay that much for one of my books. I not only ended up tightening my approach, but also dropping one of the field stations. It's good to have an agent who can be frank with her authors.

never afforded such leisure, even with the generous sabbaticals that university faculty earn.

Some of the most memorable times—again, this is hindsight—were the times when I was able to drag my camp chair and writing table out to a site where I would plant myself for a day and just observe the flora and fauna with pen in hand and binoculars at the ready. Perhaps because of my introverted nature, these snatches of solitude were all the more precious after spending so much time tagging along with researchers, rangers, caretakers, and grad students. While I may seem critical of the early nature writers I wrote about in the preface to this book—Thoreau, Muir, and Abbey—I find that I have been so thoroughly schooled in their writings that I still romanticize and value the transcendental elements of their finished manuscripts. Despite my search for alternatives, I still resonate with Muir when he writes, "To sit in solitude, to think in solitude with only the music of the stream and the cedar to break the flow of silence, there lies the value of wilderness."

Sigh.

In the end, the sabbatical experience was so energizing, and the return to teaching was so abrupt, that I realized a latent desire finally to leave the classroom, at least as a full-time teacher, in order to devote more time to writing. This led me to pursue "early" retirement—a bit shy of sixty-five—having concluded that twenty-one years in the classroom was sufficient, as much as I've loved it all. I doubt I would have come to that decision at that time had not the *in-situ* writing experience been as intense as it was. As such, the *in-situ* project was transformational for me, both as a writer and an educator.

I honestly suspect that we're only just now entering the golden age of natural history. The kids these days are heading out into the woods with ecological insights shaped by evolutionary biology, biogeography, biogeochemistry, and environmental geography, disciplines that must still be regarded as in their infancy. The researchers I was working alongside have tools for collecting data and doing spatial analysis that Thoreau could never have dreamed of and that didn't even exist back when I was an undergraduate. To the better, collecting specimens is no longer the preoccupation it once was: collect a blood sample, or better yet a tiny breast feather, and the DNA will tell us all we need to know.

Natural history will be redefined by this new generation of researchers. It will lose its staid, parson-naturalist image, replaced by new combinations of rigor and vigor. For my part, I can only hope that natural history retains its observational emphasis. While it incorporates scientific research, it is certainly not limited to it. Based on my own observations at these five field stations, I feel that the millennials I worked with appreciate this. Their quantitative research was never so all-encompassing that it precluded the visceral experience of nature.

The old model insisted that the best way to experience nature was alone. If you want to connect with nature, go out into the woods, build yourself a ramshackle shack, simplify, and eschew companionship to the extent you possibly can.

Now we have a better way to experience nature. Forget the shack, find yourself a field station. Team up with an interdisciplinary cohort of investigators, many of whom will identify with a different gender than the one to which you subscribe. Become friends with each other, regardless, not merely working together but living together as well so that you are immersed in the ecosystem you're studying. Allow the inquiry to transform you, and understand that this is an intimate process, involving not just knowledge, but affection for your investigation.

Right now, as you read these final pages, there are thousands of researchers out there in field stations getting more deeply involved in the natural world than even the most devoted transcendentalists ever could. Many of them are affiliated with universities, others are affiliated with nature conservancies, bird observatories, parks, the Forest Service, and wildlife agencies.

I cut my hair today—there was a rumor going around that a wild man had returned to campus. Today was the first day in at least a month that I didn't wear thermal underwear, and my legs felt itchy in jeans. I'm planning to watch the news tonight on television. Maybe. Or maybe I'll tune my guitar and see whether I remember any fingerstyle Christmas carols. Little Dog spent the day foraging on his own out on the street—we've been seeing way too much of each other lately, and he's going to have to get used to a bit more solitude.

In 2014 the National Academy of Sciences published a monograph, *Enhancing the Value and Sustainability of Field Stations and Marine Laboratories in the 21st Century*. The committee that worked on this project, most of whom were eminent members of the academy, was concerned about the lack of objective criteria for assessing the value of existing field stations, something beyond the "look how much is getting published by our researchers" approach. They urged the development of "sound metrics for the development of program performance and progress including both quantitative and qualitative measures" (63).

Can you tell that was written by scientists?

While the development of such metrics would no doubt be helpful, I've been wondering whether it might be more effective simply to tell the story of what's going on in these field stations. There's some really cool stuff happening in field stations around the world, much of it science. At all levels, researchers are involved in inquiry that transforms not only how they view the world, but how they view themselves.

I was honored to spend six months engaged in other people's fieldwork, humbled by the genuine welcomes I received and the ready invitations to participate shoulder to shoulder. I asked people to let me enter into their projects, and they cheerfully led me through patches of poison oak, windswept expanses of pickleweed marsh, and impenetrable brambles of invasive thorns. We slogged up talus slopes, through alpine meadows, across beaches, through tide pools, and beneath old-growth canopies. We clambered across logs and up trees. Hot, windy, foggy, muddy, wet, and finally snowy, the research kept going until avalanche danger kept us out of the high country, at which point we explored a bit lower. I got to see a fox and a bear eating apples in trees—separate trees, two states apart. The birds were always the best part, whether it was nestling woodpeckers, an endemic scrub-jay, an endangered shrike, a fierce gyrfalcon, a long-tailed duck, or, coolest of all, an accidental dusky thrush foraging in new-fallen snow.

The study of nature takes place in a social context. It always has. Nature study becomes transformative as our collective practices of observation are sharpened over time. We can help each other get good at this. I would never go out into the woods and report back that "today I saw nature." However, if we are willing to become immersed, and willing to learn from each other, at some point we will be able to claim to have gotten a pretty good glimpse of our subject matter.

In his journal entry of August 5, 1851, Thoreau wrote, "The question is not what you look at, but what you see." He was right, of course, and I enjoy looking at nature through Thoreau's eyes, especially when I read from his journals. As I mentioned in the beginning of this book, when he writes that we can never have enough of nature, I agree wholeheartedly. However, when I get to the part where writes that he never found "a companion so companionable as solitude," I find myself wanting to issue a corrective. Solitude can be a fabulous way to experience nature, but in terms of natural history, it is not an end in itself. When we move beyond solitude, we discover, in companionship, nature itself.

Acknowledgments

I thank the many researchers and educators who welcomed me into their work and blessed me with their expertise, including Steven Ackers, Tim Coonan, Adam Dillon, Allen Fish, Natasha Hagemeyer, Ryan Harmon, Martha Henderson, Peter Impara, Walter Koenig, Lyndal Laughlan, Lindsey MacDonald, Katherine McEachern, Libby Mills, Gene Myers, Ida Naughton, Mickey Pardo, Jackie Randall, Jon Reidel, Nicholas Stranger, Frederick Swanson, Vincent Voegeli, Chris Walter, Erik Walters, and Step Wilson. I also thank the following Golden Gate Raptor Observatory (GGRO) Hawkwatch dayleaders, not only for including me in their counts, but also for their long-term contributions to citizen science: Jon Altemus, Tim Behr, Christine Carino, Lewis Cooper, Dennis Davison, Joshua Haiman, Mary Kenney, Horacio Mena, Kim Meyer, Brian O'Laughlin, Bob Power, James Raives, Laury Rosenthal, and Step Wilson. Regrettably, beyond the GGRO dayleaders, I did not record names of more than a hundred research assistants, interns, citizen scientists, graduate students, and administrative staff with whom I rubbed elbows during my time in the field. It was a privilege to share in their enthusiasm for their projects and their love of natural history, and I apologize that I'm unable to list them all here.

Thanks to the following field stations I visited and the residencies they extended me, and to the foundations, conservancies, and/or universities that support them: Hastings Natural History Reservation; Santa Cruise Island Reserve; Golden Gate Raptor Observatory; H.J. Andrews Experimental Forest; Spring Creek Project for Ideas, Nature and the Written Word; and the Environmental Learning Center of the North Cascades Institute. Thanks also to Santa Clara University for granting me sabbatical time to research this book. And thanks to the Whitely Center of Friday Harbor Marine Laboratories of the University of Washington for affording me time as a Whitely Scholar to attend to revisions after the peer review process.

Thanks to the anonymous peer reviewers who contributed their time to making this a better book. Enormous thanks to Kitty Liu, the editor of Comstock Publishing Associates, for whom a more appropriate title would be "guardian angel." Thanks also to Regina Ryan, my agent, who helped keep this molehill from transmogrifying into a mountain. Thanks as well to the dream team at Cornell University Press who once again helped make a book of my scribbled field notes, especially senior production editor Susan P. Specter, copy editor Marie Flaherty-Jones, and acquisitions assistant Meagan Dermody. And, of course, a heartfelt thanks to my friend Tom Fleischner, the executive director of the Natural History Institute, for the kindness of providing a foreword to this book.

Finally, I am forever grateful to Carol, the love of my life, for continuing to endure my wifeless wanderings through the wilderness in search of a book. Thank you, again, for the many ways in which you inspire and support my writing.

References and Further Reading

Abbey, Edward. 1968. *Desert Solitaire: A Season in the Wilderness*. New York: McGraw Hill.

Billick, I., I. Babb, B. Kloeppel, J. C. Leong, J. Hodder, J. Sanders, and H. Swain. 2013. *Field Stations and Marine Laboratories of the Future: A Strategic Vision*. National Association of Marine Laboratories and Organization of Biological Field Stations. http://www.obfs.org/fsml-future.

Brodie, Nathaniel, Charles Goodrich, and Frederick J. Swanson, eds. 2016. *Forest under Story: Creative Inquiry in an Old-Growth Forest*. Seattle: University of Washington Press.

Coonan, Timothy J., Catherin A. Schwemm, and David K. Garcelon. 2010. *Decline and Recovery of the Island Fox: A Case Study for Population Recovery*. Cambridge: Cambridge University Press.

Coues, Elliott. 1874. *Field Ornithology: Comprising a Manual of Instruction for Procuring, Preparing and Preserving Birds and a Check List of North American Birds*. Salem, MA: Naturalists' Agency.

Deakin, Roger. 2009. *Notes from Walnut Tree Farm*. London: Penguin UK.

De Voto, Bernard, ed. 1953. *The Journals of Lewis and Clark*. Boston: Houghton, Mifflin.

Ely, Theresa E., Christopher W. Briggs, Shawn E. Hawks, Gregory S. Kaltenecker, David L. Evans, Frank J. Nicoletti, Jean-François Therrien, Olin Allen, and John P. De-Long. 2018. "Morphological Changes in American Kestrels (*Falco sparverius*) at Continental Migration Sites." *Global Ecology and Conservation* 15 (July). https://doi.org/10.1016/j.gecco.2018.e00400.

Emerson, Ralph Waldo. 1858. "Waldeinsamkeit." *Atlantic Monthly*, October 1858.

Emerson, Robert M., Rachel I. Fretz, and Linda L. Shaw. 2011 *Writing Ethnographic Field Notes*. 2nd ed. Chicago: University of Chicago Press.

Farnsworth, John S. 2010. "What Does the Desert Say? A Rhetorical Analysis of *Desert Solitaire*." *Interdisciplinary Literary Studies* 12 (1): 105–21.

Farnsworth, John S. 2018. *Coves of Departure: Field Notes from the Sea of Cortez.* Ithaca, NY: Cornell University Press.

Farnsworth, J. S., L. Baldwin, and M. Bezanson. 2014. "An Invitation for Engagement: Assigning and Assessing Field Notes to Promote Deeper Levels of Observation." *Journal of Natural History Education and Experience* 8:12–20.

Fleischner, T. L., ed. 2017. *Nature, Love, Medicine: Essays on Wildness and Wellness.* Salt Lake City: Torrey House Press.

Fleischner, Thomas L., Robert E. Espinoza, Gretchen A. Gerrish, Harry W. Greene, Robin Wall Kimmerer, Eileen A. Lacey, Steven Pace, Julia K. Parrish, Hilary M. Swain, Stephen C. Trombulak, Saul Weisberg, David W. Winkler, and Lisa Zander. 2017. "Teaching Biology in the Field: Importance, Challenges, and Solutions." *BioScience* 67, no. 6 (June): 558–67.

Hannibal, Mary Ellen. 2016. *Citizen Scientist: Searching for Heroes and Hope in an Age of Extinction.* New York: The Experiment.

Holder, Charles Frederick. 1910. *The Channel Islands of California: A Book for the Angler, Sportsman, and Tourist.* Norwood, MA: Plimpton Press.

Koenig, Walter D., and Eric L. Walters. 2014. "What We Don't Know, and What Needs to Be Known, about the Cooperatively Breeding Acorn Woodpecker *Melanerpes formicivorus.*" *Acta Ornithologica* 49, no. 2 (December): 221–32.

Krutch, Joseph Wood. 1948. *Henry David Thoreau.* New York: Dell.

Lannoo, Michael. 2010. *Leopold's Shack and Ricketts's Lab: The Emergence of Environmentalism.* Berkeley: University of California Press.

Leopold, Aldo. 1949. *A Sand County Almanac: And Sketches Here and There.* Oxford: Oxford University Press.

Luoma, Jon R. 2006. *The Hidden Forest: The Biography of an Ecosystem.* Corvallis: Oregon State University Press.

MacKaye, Benton. 1946. "A Wilderness Philosophy." *Living Wilderness,* March 1946, 1–4.

Maloof, Joan. 2016. *Nature's Temples: The Complex World of Old-Growth Forests.* Portland, OR: Timber Press.

Marvier, Michelle, and Hazel Wong. 2015. "Move Over Grizzly Adams: Conservation for the Rest of Us." In *After Preservation: Saving American Nature in the Age of Humans,* edited by Ben A. Minteer and Stephen J. Pine, 170–77. Chicago: University of Chicago Press.

McEachern, Katherine, and Dieter H. Wilken. 2009. "Nine Endangered Taxa, One Recovering Ecosystem: Identifying Common Ground for Recovery on Santa Cruz Island, California." *Proceedings of the California Native Plant Society Conservation Conference* (January): 162–67.

Muir, John. 1911. *My First Summer in the Sierra.* Boston: Houghton Mifflin.

National Research Council of the National Academies. 2014. *Enhancing the Value and Sustainability of Field Stations and Marine Laboratories in the 21st Century.* Washington, DC: National Academies Press.

Naughton, Ida, Michael S. Caterino, Cause Hanna, and David Holway. 2014. "Contributions to an Arthropod Inventory of Santa Cruz Island, California." *Monographs of the Western North American Naturalist* 7, no. 1. (December): 297–305.

Oliver, Mary. 2016. *Upstream: Selected Essays.* New York: Penguin.

Pardo, M. A., E. A. Sparks, T. S. Kuray, N. D. Hagermeyer, E. L. Walters, and W. D. Koenig. 2018. "Wild Acorn Woodpeckers Recognize Associations between Individuals in Other Groups." *Proceedings of the Royal Society of London, Series B, Biological Sciences* 285, no. 1882 (July 11). https://doi.org/10.1098/rspb.2018.1017.

Reidel, Jon L., and Michael A. Larrabee. 2016. "Impact of Recent Glacial Recession on Summer Streamflow in the Skagit River." *Northwest Science* 90, no. 1 (January): 5–22.

Russell, Sharman Apt. 2014. *Diary of a Citizen Scientist: Chasing Tiger Beetles and Other New Ways of Engaging the World.* Corvallis: Oregon State University Press.

Shellenberger, Michael, and Ted Nordhaus. 2004. "The Death of Environmentalism: Global Warming Politics in a Post-Environmental World." https://s3.us-east-2.amazonaws.com/uploads.thebreakthrough.org/legacy/images/Death_of_Environmentalism.pdf.

Sibley, David. 2011. "The Proper Use of Playback in Birding." Sibley Guides. https://www.sibleyguides.com/2011/04/the-proper-use-of-playback-in-birding/.

Thoreau, Henry D. 1854. *Walden; or, Life in the Woods.* Boston: Ticknor & Fields.

Thoreau, Henry D. 1862. "Walking." *Atlantic Monthly: A Magazine of Literature, Art, and Politics.* June 1862, 657–74. https://www.walden.org/wp-content/uploads/2016/03/Walking-1.pdf.

Tomalty, Katherine M., Angus C. Hull, Allen M. Fish, Christopher W. Briggs, and Joshua M. Hull. 2016. "Differential Migration and Phenology of Adult Red-Tailed Hawks in California." *Journal of Raptor Research* 50, no. 1 (March): 45–53.

Torben, C. Rick, et al. (including Lyndal Laughrin and Kathryn McEachern). 2014. "Ecological Change on California's Channel Islands from the Pleistocene to the Anthropocene." *BioScience* 64, no. 8 (August): 680–92.

Tydecks, Laura, Vanessa Bremerich, Ilona Jentschke, Gene E. Likens, and Klement Tockner. 2016. "Biological Field Stations: A Global Infrastructure for Research, Education, and Public Engagement." *BioScience* 66, no. 2 (February): 164–71.

Weidensaul, Scott. 2007. *Of a Feather: A Brief History of American Birding.* Boston: Houghton Mifflin Harcourt.

Williams, Terry Tempest. 2016. *The Hour of Land: A Personal Topography of America's National Parks.* New York: Farrar, Straus and Giroux.

Willig, Michael R., and Lawrence R. Walker, eds. 2016. *Long-Term Ecological Research: Changing the Nature of Scientists.* Oxford: Oxford University Press.

CPSIA information can be obtained
at www.ICGtesting.com
Printed in the USA
LVHW092240250220
648235LV00002B/423